WHAT OTHERS AR
SEDUCED BY CC

Jack Pransky's new book, *Seduced by C* personal memoir, it reveals his life and experiences and those of his friends, relatives and clients in such a revealing, raw and honest manner, it brought me to tears! Although I worked with Sydney Banks for many years in the early '70's, I have never heard or read of anyone who understands the Three Principles in a more clear, direct and helpful manner. What I loved most about *Seduced by Consciousness* is that in the different aspects of consciousness the author always connects these events to the ultimate reality of our inner selves, making it, in a way, a book on the spiritual life. The book made me think about the events of my own life in all kinds of crazy and new ways, after reading Jack's insights and experiences. I learned more about myself from this book than anything I've read in years. Jack's writing 'seduces' us into wandering down a trail beside him until we realize, "It's ME he's talking about!" I know I will be reading this powerful book again and again.

-Linda Quiring, author
Island of Knowledge and *Beyond Beliefs*

What struck me most when reading Jack's book was what a gifted storyteller he is. I got lost in it at times. I loved it! Jack brings us along with him as he goes through his own life challenges and adventures as well as those of his clients. He gives us a window into what it means to have the backdrop of living life with an increased humility and understanding, which Jack has spent numerous years exploring and sharing with others. I came away grateful that Jack stumbled into this learning. Not just for himself but for all those he has impacted along the way.

-Terry Rubenstein, author
Exquisite Mind

As difficult as it is to put form around the formless, Dr. Jack Pransky has done this masterfully once again in Seduced by Consciousness. I have used his books in my classes for over 20 years because his writing engages students on a deep and authentic level, touching their hearts and heads. In this book, Jack is willing to reveal himself in a very personal manner. Speaking straight from his heart, and using his personal experiences, he makes himself vulnerable to all as he shares intimate details of his own struggles in life. He articulates a deep understanding of the Three Principles in common, understandable language that feels like a friend talking to us, using words that awaken something inside us that we recognize as truth. Reading it I came away feeling the freedom that we are, truly radiant, resilient beings, blessed by the gift of the Three Principles.

-Diane P. McMillen, Ph.D., co-author
"Exploring the Nature of True Resilience"
in *The Strengths Perspective in Social Work Practice*

Jack Pransky owes me! I missed my stop because of his new book, not once, but twice! I was so engrossed in the stories that I totally lost a track of time and ended up with a fine as a result. Was it worth it? Hell yes. Jack's book totally blew me away as he took me on a journey as a human being… being human, of how easy it is to forget the illusion we're creating and what lies on the other side when we remember. I absolutely adored it!

-Damian Mark Smyth, author
Do Nothing! and *The Entrepreneur Success Formula*

Seduced by Consciousness is a tour de force. Easing the way for others facing their own seductive pitfalls, Jack bares his soul through intimate stories and personal insights. We can each be hoodwinked by life's illusions, and now we have a logical explanation of why and how it occurs, thanks to the Principles Jack explains. We'll have a different world—a more peaceful, understanding, and compassionate one—if enough people grasp what is contained in this book. I recommend it to everyone who will read it to the end.

-Lori Carpenos, author
It's an Inside-Out World

In *Seduced by Consciousness*, Jack Pransky makes himself an open book, sharing private moments and personal stories that demand from the reader an open mind and an open heart — and fortunately, the author is the perfect role model. Be prepared to be inspired by Jack's vulnerability and self-awareness, which make his insights into the Principles even more beautiful.

-Mary Schiller, author
The Joy Formula; Mind Yoga; and
A-*ha! How to Solve Any Problem in Record Time*

Jack is masterful at drawing out the wisdom inside each person—no Mr. FixIt lurking in these sessions! I felt as if I was in the room hearing these encounters between Jack and his clients. Jack understands that listening deeply is key, both to his client's inner guidance and his own, and this leads him to ask the "just right" questions: no script necessary, no "correct" 3P vocabulary, just incredible trust that Mind will provide the way. It is easy to see that Jack is in the moment with his clients and he models how change can happen in the very ordinariness of everyday situations. Jack follows exactly what Sydney Banks taught: "Begin the process of nourishing the soul by living in the now."

-Barb Aust, author
The Essential Curriculum

Jack has a unique and powerful way of taking a life changing understanding and making it accessible to the reader. He is a master of using real life examples, beautiful metaphors and the clarity of his own embodiment to create a literary masterpiece that can stir the heart and enliven the soul of the readers.

-Rudi Kennard, Three Principles Movies

Seduced by Consciousness

A Life with The Three Principles

Jack Pransky, Ph.D.

CCB Publishing
British Columbia, Canada

Seduced by Consciousness: A Life with The Three Principles

ISBN-13 978-1-77143-320-4
First Edition

Library and Archives Canada Cataloguing in Publication
Pransky, Jack, 1946-, author
Seduced by consciousness : a life with the three principles
/ by Jack Pransky. -- First edition.
Issued in print and electronic formats.
ISBN 978-1-77143-320-4 (pbk.).--ISBN 978-1-77143-321-1 (pdf)
Additional cataloguing data available from Library and Archives Canada

Book production and design by CCB Publishing.
Editing by Katja Symons and Joel Drazner.
Cover artwork by Jonas Gerard www.jonasgerard.com

Back cover photo by Holly Mitchell, HAMM Photography.

For permission or information address
Jack Pransky, Center for Inside-Out Understanding,
www.insideoutunderstanding.com

Publisher: CCB Publishing
British Columbia, Canada
www.ccbpublishing.com

DEDICATION

To the ever-growing number of *Three Principles* practitioners quietly out there in service to humanity changing lives—one person, one organization, one community at a time—with great courage as they pioneer an entirely new inside-out paradigm that seems to work far better than the norm while running counter to the prevailing view.

And of course and always to Sydney Banks, our inspiration, without whom none of this would be possible.

ACKNOWLEDGMENTS

Thank you Amy, from the bottom of my heart.

Thank you to my editors, Katja Symons and Joel Drazner, and to Nancy Lopin for her early editing.

A special thank you to John Wood, Tom Kelley, Richard Rolf, Rob Somers, Mette Louise Holland, Sally Wyse and Dorota Juszkiewicz Martin, for your inspiring contributions.

Thank you to George Pransky and Dicken Bettinger for helping to pull me beyond myself when I needed steering, as reflected in the final chapter.

Thank you to Amanda Gachot, Amanda O'Shea, Anni Campbell, Chantal Burns, Christie Binzen, Diane McMillen, Gabriela Maldonado-Montano, Holly Mitchell, Janet Rhynie, Jean-Jacques Guyot, Karen Raimbault, Kay Evans, Katja Symons, Ken Matzner, Lise Dandanelle, Lori Carpenos, Marien Perez, Yoga Mark Jones, Mick Tomlinson, Nicole Beasley, Paula Francis, Richard Rolf, Robin Johnson, Rudi Kennard, Serena Fox, Sheela Masand, Sue Pankiewicz, Susan Costa, Susanne Lanng and Sylvie Walls, for your friendship and inspiration while writing this book.

And to all my trainees and learners too numerous to mention, from whom I have gained so much.

Finally, thank you to everyone who had to put up with me and my one-track mind while I wrote and completed this book.

All we are is peace, love and wisdom,
and the power to create the illusion that we're not.

—Jack Pransky

A mind searching for itself can never find itself.

—Sydney Banks

INVOCATION

Life Unbridled

Beyond frozen fears and unmet needs
Lies a realm;
A realm unrivalled.

Beyond beliefs and judgements
Is a place;
A place called compassion or kindness.
Beyond acceptance and tolerance
Is a space;
A space of innocence.
An all-embracing warmth
Melting the edges of division;
Evaporating the illusion of you and me.
This internal universe is home,
Is love,

Is life unbridled.

John A. Wood
Midland, Australia

FOREWORD

PART I

Nobody had to tell me that Jack Pransky's new book, *Seduced by Consciousness*, would be another gem. This book is beautiful, inspiring, generous, hilarious—full of love and compassion. Painfully honest to the bone, to the quick. Profoundly human. Written with child-like innocence, spontaneity, vulnerability and wisdom. An exquisite painting using every color on the palate of Thought. What an exhilarating experience to squeeze through the eye of a needle with Jack Pransky and come to light on the other side with life-changing insights.

In *Seduced by Consciousness* Jack bares his soul—discloses his own struggles—exposes his humanness. Jack takes us with him as he and his students encounter life's unexpected twists and turns, squeeze through life's narrow crevices and crannies and confront obstacles that at times appear insurmountable. Jack shines a bright light on the fact that mental health is more than merely experiencing positive feelings such as joy, peace of mind, gratitude and love. He makes it crystal clear that where the rubber meets the mental health road is resilience—the well-being that flows from "knowing" that mental health is innate and can't be damaged; that we are always safe even when life show up as hard, unkind, merciless; that what appears "real" is really an temporary illusion—a house of cards—constructed by Thought and Consciousness.

So buckle up, my friends, strap yourself in, lighten up—relax. Jack Pransky, a student of Sydney Banks, is one of the best insight guides available. Jack's personal stories and those of his students will nudge your inner wisdom—resonate with your spiritual essence. So get ready to "see" at a deeper level how three Universal Principles coalesce to form everyone's psychological life; to realize that you (and everyone else) have all the mental health you need already within you; to understand that we all are in the same boat—continually vulnerable to being seduced by consciousness—the "ultimate illusionist."

Thomas M. Kelley, Ph.D.
Wayne State University
February, 2017

PART II

To go from what we know to what we don't know can be a confusing journey.

I had been brilliant in seeing the effects of life and all the reasons why. I had painfully experienced the consequences of entering the door of "because" only to fall deeper into the rabbit hole of what I know.

But instead of allowing me to swallow my own conclusion of my "reality," I noticed how Jack Pransky kindly and inexplicitly suggested that I turn my head in another direction to have another kind of experience. Jack went behind the stream of my thinking and showed my soul that it might not be as real as I think it is. I then recognized the relieving feeling of getting my nose above the sea of thoughts to breathe the breeze of life.

No one sees that breeze, only the effects of it.

Instead of *telling* me how the nature of things works, Jack listened deeply, responded to every nuance and underlying meaning like a percipient musician and guided me to my own clarity of mind and natural ability to see beyond what seemed like reality. This was lifechanging.

The flood of insights that washed through my consciousness during my time with Jack had as a consequence that I forgot to be depressed, entangled, worried, to seek problems to solve, and I sort of wondered where it all went and how. Instead, new possibilities began to present themselves without my really seeking it; or rather, I began to recognise possibilities that might have been there all the time but since I was only seeking solutions for problems, I didn't see them.

A solution is bound to a problem; a real possibility is free and creative. You could say it's a journey from solutions to "Soul-utions."

That is what this beautiful book offers.

Richard Rolf
Stockholm, Sweden
March 2017

TABLE OF CONTENTS

PREFACE/AUTHOR'S NOTE

Wouldn't it be something if our entire life experience boils down to three Principles,[1] Principles that exist in the universe and act upon us whether we know about them or not?

And wouldn't it be something if how we "use" these Principles (most often without knowing we are using them) determines every possible feeling we can have, every possible perception, everything we call reality?

And wouldn't it really be something if simply *understanding* the nature of these Principles and how they work within us—truly grasping them—is all it takes for us to live more in well-being, with less stress, better relationships and more effectiveness in life and work; that this understanding can actually determine whether we live a life of joy, peace of mind, love, wisdom, or a life of misery, anxiety, worry, frustration, anger, depression, being troubled?

This book suggests this understanding is, in fact, all one needs.

Unfathomable though it may sound, not only has this been true for me but I have seen repeatedly that when people gain insights into how this understanding plays out in their lives moment to moment it changes those lives for the better—sometimes such massive changes it is difficult to believe. Yet it happens.

There is one catch: These Principles cannot be understood by the intellect. The Three Principles are spiritual; they must be grasped from within.

* * *

---

[1] I capitalize the word "Principle" throughout this book when referring to a fundamental, universal truth, and I capitalize the names of each of the Three Principles and sometimes the words "Truth" and "Reality," etc. when attempting to distinguish their Universal nature from the personal. I capitalize "Three Principles" when it refers to the name of this understanding.

I never thought I would write something akin to a second self-help book—even my first took me by surprise. When I finished *Somebody Should Have Told Us!* I firmly believed I had said everything I had to say. True then.

When I wrote *Somebody...* only a handful of Three Principles books existed. Now a glut of them have been written—some deep, some not. In fact, so many Principles-based books have appeared in the last few years I almost considered not writing this one. Who needs another?

Yet something wouldn't let me stop. Thirteen or so years after writing *Somebody Should Have Told Us!* I see it much more simply and deeply than I did then. *Somebody...* unquestionably helped many lives change for the better, which simultaneously thrills and humbles me—and I still stand behind every word in it. But now I have something more to say; something deeper, potentially even more helpful to humanity.

However, *Seduced by Consciousness* is not *Somebody Should Have Told Us II* (or, Somebody Should Have Told Us, Too). While it still attempts to convey this understanding simply in a way people can understand and still contains many real stories of how lives have been helped and changed, parts of this book are also autobiographical, depicting my own personal experience of living and working with my understanding of the Three Principles. The closer I come to retirement—I honestly thought I'd be retired already but that doesn't appear to be happening—the more I find myself reflecting back upon my life, mostly to gain new perspective. For most of my life I did not understand these Three Principles. Even when I did, where I did not see the Three Principles in action in certain areas of my life I bumped against many blind spots and found myself in difficulty, as this book makes quite evident. As I look back through the eyes of Three Principles understanding I now see everything that happened makes perfect sense, the perfect unfolding—always more to grow through, always more to learn. Always new hope. And as I discovered humbly while writing this, as readers will see by the end, the growth continues. I am a work in progress; it is never-ending.

However, despite the semi-autobiographical nature of this book, my own life is not important here. While I think I've had a fairly interesting life—more interesting than some, less interesting than others—it's been nothing out of the ordinary. What *is* important here is *your* life. If looking through the eyes of the Three Principles at some of the difficulties I ran into—what I did not see at the time and the insights I had along the way—helps others to gain new perspective and to improve their lives, this book's mission will have been accomplished. Hopefully this is bolstered by the other stories herein, including quasi-transcripts of counseling and coaching sessions.

Regarding the other stories I often change people's names to protect their privacy.[2] It is also important to note that the counseling and coaching sessions included are not meant to be examples of how Three Principles coaching, counseling and therapy is or should be conducted; they merely depict how I conducted those particular sessions at those times.

I fully realize some of what I say in this book may be controversial. I don't mean for it to be. All I am doing is expressing the way I, personally, see it.

Especially for readers new to the Three Principles, to receive most from what this book offers it may be wise to read a chapter or two at a time, then allow time for absorption. As with *Somebody Should Have Told Us!* its chapters are meant to build upon each other, culminating as a whole. Reiteration of points in different ways occurs on purpose. As many readers of *Somebody...* have reported, they got even more out of reading it a second or third time.

I would like to be able to guarantee that all you have to do is read this book and all your problems will be solved, but I can't. This book is in the outside world. Only your own personal insights can create change. Only when the mind clears does it allow us to grasp what we all already know deep within our souls. The intent of this book is to allow what is *known within* to be realized, unleashed. What I can safely say is, if you have your own insights about how these Three Principles work within you (and everyone) to create your own experience of life, you will have a better life experience, no matter what problems you think you have.

Mostly, this book is testament to the power of understanding the Three Principles—Universal Mind, Consciousness and Thought—as

---

[2] Sometimes I don't. I decided it would not be necessary to always specify when I do and don't because readers won't know anyway.

uncovered by Sydney Banks. If readers of this book have not experienced Syd, I highly recommend reading, listening to and watching him directly. It is best to go is to the source.

Jack Pransky
Boca Raton, FL
October, 2016

INTRODUCTION

Suppose we grew up in an area always engulfed in extremely thick fog. We could see only fifty meters in front of us. Now suppose that fog *never* let up. We would never know what our surrounding area truly looks like. We would only know an approximation of it, and not a very clear one.

Then one day, for the very first time, suppose a miracle occurs: The fog lifts. We would be shocked, stunned, astonished, in awe.

For the first time we would see a crystal clear world. Bright colors. Clear shapes. We wouldn't know what to make of it, but we would think it beautiful.

It is not that this new, sunshiny, sparkly world didn't exist before the fog lifted; we just couldn't see it. We were unaware of its existence. Suddenly a whole new world of possibilities opens up—a world we never imagined, though it always existed.

Forgive my lack of scientific knowledge but I suspect fog is water molecules filling the air, causing condensation when warm meets cold. Now imagine these foggy water molecules as thoughts. We all are born thinking thoughts, even before language. With those thoughts we create a way to make sense of this new world. In a fairly short time we accumulate more and more thoughts about "what is." These thought-beliefs fill our mind-space, much like growing up in our own personal fog. We look out at the world through this thought-fog and lose sight of *what truly is*—until that moment of miracle when the fog clears, our typical thinking departs and we are left with clarity.

This possibility exists for everyone. It can happen at any moment. Understanding how it all works within us is a pathway to clarity.

Even knowing this, sometimes we still find ourselves caught in the fog. We get lost. This can happen quickly, without notice. It is the human condition. But at least now when we get lost, way deep inside we understand what truth looks like, so the fog cannot pull us so far into the depths and it becomes a lot easier to find our way home. We become more resilient. "The truth shall set you free."

To get the most out of this book and have the best chance of seeing something new it is wise to let go of the old, to not read through filters of the already known, to allow the mind to quiet, to be completely open, empty, to not pay attention to the words so much as the feeling and direction to which the words attempt to point. An unencumbered, clear mind allows a better opportunity for new insights to pop up from within and, as I said, one's own insights are the only thing that counts. I don't want anyone to take my word for how this understanding works and for its power to create change.

Trying to grasp the Three Principles is like trying to catch a bar of soap that falls into a bathtub of water. Go after it too hard and fast and it actually pushes the soap away. Success is more likely if we allow our hand to relax, to open, to soften, to move toward the soap gently, allowing our hand to "give" a little; thus affording the best opportunity for the soap to fall into it. Same with understanding these Principles. A relaxed and open mind allows new ideas to be grasped.

Finally, it is extremely important that people do not get the wrong idea about the meaning of "Seduced by Consciousness." What I mean is simply this: *Consciousness makes our thinking look and feel real, which is why we get seduced into believing the truth of whatever we think.* I do not mean Consciousness has a life of its own and makes us do anything. It does not! It can't. Consciousness is a neutral force. Consciousness, by itself, cannot seduce us into anything. It is our thinking—our beliefs, our ego, our fears, our blind spots—which our consciousness sends right through our senses to give us an experience of "reality" or the "truth" of it. This is what seduces us! What we believe is reality tricks us and sucks us in, and Consciousness is simply the force that makes whatever we think look and feel like reality. My own personal stories in this book illustrate how I got tricked and seduced into believing the reality of my own thinking. Why? Because I did not see it deeply enough at the time—until I did, and then consciousness made my new, more evolved thinking look real. [More on this in Chapters 3, 10, 13, 19 and throughout the rest of this book.]

Welcome to the best kept secret in well-being—

1. TSUNAMI

What's thought got to do with it?

Middle of the night. Loud voices awake Amy out of a sound sleep.

She crawls over me out of bed. I remain in my stupor. She grabs her bathrobe and steps out into the jungle night toward the voices.

The Jungalo in Hanalei, Kauai looks exactly as its name suggests, set on the outskirts of a jungle near the end of the road before the Kalalau Trail on the Napali Coast, probably the most beautiful hike I've ever been on. Head up the cliffs far above the gorgeous turquoise Pacific, take a left midway up and end at an extremely high waterfall splashing hard into a blue-green pool. Paradise. Except for the night jungle noises this night had been quite quiet—until Amy heard serious voices in the distance uttering words like "tsunami," "evacuation," "tourists." It got her attention.

In the dark Amy walked toward the commotion. The fire department emergency service had sped into the Jungalo, alerting the proprietor to mandatory evacuation. A tsunami was heading our way to hit later that morning. Everyone needed to get to higher ground.

Amy made a bee-line back to the hut, waking me.

"Huh? What? Really? A tsunami is no joke," I gulped. "This could be bad." I had visions of Japan. "We've got to get out of here!"

I decided the best thing would be to quickly get off the island. We needed to be ahead of the game. But the airport had already closed! No flights in or out. Uh oh.

Tiny Hanalei is nestled in the lowest part of the island about one foot above sea level. Yesterday we'd walked across the road to the ocean. Great then; most unnerving now. Next move: Pack up everything quickly and drive to higher ground.

Already traffic lined the road. How did they know so quickly? Cars meandered much too slowly, crawling across the one-way bridges out of Hanalei up the hill to Princeville high atop a cliff out of danger. Seemed a good place to be. Everyone had the same idea.

They also had the same idea to head to the "supermarket"—more like a big grocery store—to pick up water, granola and other foodstuff that didn't need cooking or refrigerating in case the island lost power. A swarming mass of people packed the market, long lines everywhere. The entire island kicked into high gear. The hardware store hadn't yet opened, but a queue already formed outside with people waiting to buy flashlights, batteries, propane and whatever else. This line wasn't as long as the supermarket so we chose this. As soon as the doors opened we raced in among the throngs.

Flashlights in hand, just in case, we waited in the checkout line, striking up a conversation with a family from Minnesota buying a barbeque grill to feed their entire visiting family vacationing in a Princeville condo. When we told them we had just evacuated our Jungalo they invited us to join them; they had plenty of food and welcomed us to even stay over if we needed to. They were so nice! We thanked them profusely and said if we needed to we would take them up on it.

On to the supermarket—tough to get through the scared, rushed masses. Crazy scene! We thought it wise to divide shopping tasks, so Amy and I set off in different directions, walking the aisles perusing what it made sense to buy, dodging humanity—the fear in the air palpable.

As Amy leaned in to pluck an item off a shelf she encountered an older woman having a meltdown. Anxiety attack.

"Are you okay?" Amy asked.

The woman burst into tears. "We just arrived. I've never been through anything like this in my life. I'm not ready to die in a tsunami. I can't believe this is happening!" she wailed.

Amy placed her hand gently on the woman's quaking back, talking calmly. "We're really all safe way up here on the cliff. Just be prepared in case there's an electrical outage, like when a hurricane is about to strike. That's all we can do—just get what we need for that."

The poor woman was a wreck. Amy hugged her. The husband stood off to the side trying to ignore her, watching. He shot Amy a tiny, embarrassed look.

Amy watched many others panic too. This was truly a wild scene!

Ready to pay, she saw a huge line stretching from the cashier at the front of the store all the way to the back wall. This could take hours! Amy is not fond of long lines.

Groceries in hand I strode up to her, surveying the situation. "Hold this place," I said, "I'll scope things out."

I walked the store perimeter. Another long line stretched from the register on the other side of the store along the wall to the back. The end of both lines almost met in the middle. No hope there. I walked quickly down the middle to the front.

I couldn't believe my eyes. Two more cash registers, complete with cashiers, sat in the middle front of the store. Not a soul stood in front of either of these registers! I must be in the wrong place. I walked up to the cashier. "Are you open?" "Yes." I paid for my groceries. Couldn't believe it!

I hurried back to find Amy, who had scarcely moved an inch.

"Come with me," I said, grabbing her hand. I led her to the still-empty middle register. Amy laughed as we sailed right through. The other line hadn't budged.

Moral to the story: Most everyone was in a state of panic. Panic equals fear. Fear equals people not having their wits about them. Not having one's wits equals obscured wisdom. Obscured wisdom means common sense departs.

We drive ourselves crazy believing something is truth when it is not truth. All those people standing in the two lines stretching all the way to the back of the store believed in the truth of those lines. In their panic it looked as if standing in the long queue was the only possibility.

This means our "truth" is a lie. It is a truth we make up with our creative power of Thought. Therefore, it is not really True. This is what we innocently do, and we do it far more than we realize.

This would have been about all I needed to say of import about our tsunami experience, but readers would never let me get away with it. So what happened?

Grabbing what we needed and assuming our gas tank full enough not to wait in the long car lines stretching from the pumps all the way down the road, we figured it would be an excellent time to find a bathroom. On our way up the hill I remembered passing the Wyndham Hotel, a fine resort at which I had once stayed for a Syd Banks seminar. Luxury bathrooms—perfect! So we walked halfway down the hill to the Wyndham.

Amy emerged from her bathroom first. A concierge approached her. "The first four floors of the hotel are being evacuated. Would you like a pass for our sister hotel up the road at the top of the cliff?"

"Yes. Thank you. I'll need two."

Amy met me outside the men's room with a huge grin and two passes. I laughed. What better place to be! But wait, the Wyndham had only evacuated their bottom four floors; what if one were on the fifth floor when the tsunami hit? Shaking our heads we walked back up the hill.

By this time the scene had turned into a be-in from the 60s. All kinds of happy craziness lined the side of the road. We stopped to listen to a group of native Hawaiians hanging out playing ukes and bongos, having a grand old time singing of storms and tsunamis, welcoming it to their island. Hippies came out of the woodwork smoking pakalolo. Other enterprising groups sold crafts. It reminded Amy of a Grateful Dead concert tour. All this while others still visibly panicked.

Loving this scene we walked up to the sister hotel. A security guard stopped us at the gate, asking who we were and for our room key. Oops. Amy fumbled around in her bag, feigning looking for her key.

"We have these passes," she said, handing them to the guard

The guard squinted at them, looked at us skeptically but let us through.

Out of guard earshot we laughed again. Amy and I were having such a good time we almost forgot what we were there for. Oh, a tsunami is coming! Its arrival time had been delayed again, so for most of the afternoon we stayed at that beautiful resort hotel, swimming in their everlasting pool, which looked as if it dropped off the edge right into the ocean—except we were about 200 feet up a cliff. Gorgeous!

With tsunami time finally approaching we wanted to secure a ringside seat. We walked along the top of the cliff until we bumped into deserted condos. We commandeered lawn chairs, pulling them to cliff edge overlooking the ocean and beach far below. We laid towels on the ground and waited in the warm sun for the tsunami. We had the most beautiful, pleasant, relaxing afternoon.

The so-called tsunami proved vastly anti-climactic—not even much of a wave. From our very high perch we watched it roll in—we think—but it looked almost as if the waves were rolling out. Tough to describe. Eerie. A wave would break, then seemed to pull back into itself and go out farther and farther. Neither of us had ever seen waves roll out as they rolled in. Freaky! But the waves themselves were not so big. We were almost disappointed—aw, we didn't get our show—until we remembered the devastation that could have been caused. Then we felt relieved—a very happy day all around.

Then we remembered all the people panicking. For what? For nothing.

Thought rules. Consciousness takes our thinking and seduces us into believing in the "truth" of it. Yet it is a "truth" we create! Wisdom gets obscured. The perfect system. And it always works the exact same way, tsunami or not.

But then I think of a real tsunami, which causes so much devastation, despair and tragedy for so many. I had sat mesmerized watching the astonishing tsunami scene of the movie, *The Impossible,* feeling in the middle of that tidal wave. But I wasn't. I watched its ferocity from the safety of my theater seat. Still, it gave me a sense of the power—that nothing could be done to save oneself, except seemingly by luck or if able to get to high ground before too late. And for too many it was too late.

So, by talking about the Three Principles in light of a true tsunami, are we negating this exceptionally real, horrific tragedy?

Not at all.

First, my heart goes out to those people, many of whom lost family, loved ones, their possessions—everything. Truly tragic!

Secondly, for what the Three Principles have to say about this and everything else, the rest of this book beckons—

2. RICHARD AND THE CAVES

Richard is a supremely gifted, creative musical instrument maker and a fine guitarist and poet who lives on a small island off the coast of Sweden. A handsome chap, he is a wonderful man, delightful to be around—at least I think so. He also lived with a lot of demons, plucked from thoughts of childhood.

I had met him briefly on my European Tour at a training I conducted in Stockholm. Touched by it, he then attended my Three Principles Extended Professional Training (EPT) in Spain, where he had life-changing insights. I figured he must be totally filled, but here we were together again hiking in the mountains around Albir, Spain on the final day of a three-day Three Principles trek with a group led by one of my favorite blokes, Yoga Mark Jones.

Probably from all the gluten I'd eaten, lack of sleep the night before and not drinking enough water I woke up with a terrible headache. I guzzled water but it didn't help. Finally I had to break down and borrow some painkillers from Mick. But we were on the third day of this work-trek and I was supposed to be the main draw. The day before, I'd spent many hours giving informal, individual coaching sessions to various members of the trek group as we hiked along, each session impactful and gratifying, but I had exhausted myself. Now I had to be "on" again, and sharp. People were counting on me.

We drove two hours past Alicante to the beautiful old medieval Spanish mountain town of Bocairent. Luckily, as we pulled into town the painkillers began to work. Good timing. Good stuff! Mark's original idea had us roaming leisurely around this town; instead we found ourselves hiking down a ravine then up toward high cliffs. One person in our group who didn't think she could make it wisely turned back. A steep cliff loomed in front of us. On the wall of this cliff, way up high, appeared many round holes.

What were they? They looked like ancient Navajo cave dwellings, but these openings were much smaller—holes that led directly into the cliffs. How could anyone get up there? The brochure says these are "artificial caves with holes like windows, situated in the middle of the vertical rock wall, at 300 meters…It has got approximately 50 windows that enter to another 50 rooms. The windows are lined up in three levels but without forming regular 'floors.'" That about sums it up.

We could only go in with a guide. In very broken English he told us to leave our backpacks and gear outside at the base of the cliff. We could bring cameras only if they weren't too big. We climbed a narrow fire escape-type ladder somehow bolted onto the side of the cliff. Already we had climbed about twenty or thirty feet when we turned right into a cliff hole and squished into a first little room. It would be the biggest room we would see.

We sat while our guide, who glided through these caves like Spiderman—a marvel to watch—explained that these cliff rooms were actually used for storage. People didn't live in them except to hide from enemies, which they had to do from time to time.

Once in, we couldn't simply walk from room to room because no rooms were on the same level. Only narrow tunnels connected them. It immediately became clear why we had to leave our gear outside; we wouldn't have fit through the holes! The only way to get from one room to another was to crawl in and out of these holes, some of which were barely wide enough for a medium-sized body to slink through.

As Spiderman explained all this, he pointed to a narrow round hole in the ceiling where our journey would begin. I noticed Richard's face become white as a sheet.

Richard: Due to some logistics I had to choose between two different events which brought me to a trekking event in the mountains. Of all places on this earth I was standing with Jack and the rest of the group in front of a big mountain with small caves inside. As long as I can remember I've had nightmares where I get stuck in a cavelike hole in a mountain. Before I get stuck in the hole (most often with my head) I am always being chased by three or four violent men out to kill me. I flee and run but finally get stuck in the narrow hole in the rocks. I had this dream for over twenty years. Here I was about to enter small caves through narrow passages in a big mountain and I asked myself, "How on earth did I land here?"

"Are you going?" Richard asked me, his voice betraying panic.

"Yes," I said.

With great trepidation he said, "Okay, if you're going, I guess I'll do it."

I was the first one up the seven-inch-wide, rickety iron ladder, with its one-centimeter-thick round bars for rungs, which disappeared into a hole in the ceiling. Holy cow! The hole was so narrow I couldn't bend my knees enough to ascend to the next rung; my knees kept bumping into the sidewalls of the hole.

I had an "uh oh" thought. My legs began trembling.

After a few failed attempts, somehow by twisting my leg around I managed to get up to the next rung, then the next, until I climbed through the hole enough to pull myself up onto the rock floor of the room. I admit to thoughts of trepidation but set those aside to help everyone climb off the ladder up into the room. If shades of white are possible Richard came up whiter than before.

That's when he told me he was claustrophobic. He hated tight, confined spaces. He didn't know if he could make it.

But again, if I (the old man) was doing it he would steel himself and somehow try to make it through.

After helping everyone out of the first hole I found myself at the back of the line. I couldn't hear what the graceful, slithering Spiderman guide told everyone up front. I do know we sometimes crawled, sometimes pulled ourselves down and up thick, very frayed ropes to get from one room to the next, and most rooms were too low to stand up in. I had a blast. This was fun! Richard was not amused.

R: We climbed in and dragged ourselves through openings between the caves inside the mountain with ropes and small holes for our toes. I was not comfortable at all but was ok due to the high spirit of the group.

Toward the end of the cave journey everyone stopped at the front of the line. By the time I caught up only four of our group remained. Where did everyone go? Apparently Mr. Spiderman informed them we were about to enter the most difficult part of the cave system, so anyone who wanted to could escape out the window onto a ladder and head outside down the cliff wall where the rest of the group had bailed. All but Karen, Susanne, Tanya, and now Richard and I, who brought up the rear, remained. I had no idea Spiderman had said all this to them. The caves had not been so easy up to now. Would I continue? Okay, I'd had so much fun to this point I had to try it, but not without trepidation thoughts again creeping in.

Meanwhile, Richard's face turned a new shade of ashen. He wanted out.

R: After having passed through many different small caves through narrow tunnels the guide said, "This is where you need to decide if you want to continue or not, since the passages gets narrower and harder to get through. Now I really got uncomfortable and instinctivly headed for the exit, but my eyes landed on Jack, who had just appeared in the room, and the trust I had grown to him made me ask, "Are you gonna go?"

"Yes," he said, totally relaxed and self-evident, as if it was the most natural thing in the world to do.

"Oh shit. Then I also have to go," I heard myself answer.

I struggled with the decision: Richard to go or not, and felt fear build up, when Jack looked at me and gently said...

"Fear is only thought."

It stopped Richard in his tracks. He said, "Tell me that again."

"Richard," I said, "It can only be thought making you feel claustrophobic."

R: My mind heard what he said, but my system didn't get it at all. So I asked him to say that again. He did. And I asked him to say it again, and again, since my intellect went crazy. I asked Jack to say it three times in a row. He refined it each time. It started to sink in and I finally asked him to whisper it in my ear.

"Tell me once more," he said. "Whisper it in my ear." He cupped his hand over his ear and leaned toward my mouth.

"Are you kidding?" I asked. "You really want me to say this again into your ear?"

R: Jack asked if I was joking. I told him in a voice of someone in a plane about to crash. "I'm not joking. Seriously, please just say it another time."

He accepted and with emphasis said, "Fear is thought. Fear is *thought! Fear is* only *thought!"*

I don't remember exactly what I said, but I was thinking something like, "Fear would not even exist if not for our own creation. We have this amazing gift of the power of Thought to create anything, and sometimes we use it to create fear. Then we get seduced by consciousness so it really makes us feel in every way as if it's the truth, that it's absolute reality. But it can't be! If these caves were causing the fear, everyone would be equally fearful. We believe it because our senses trick us into believing our thinking is true reality. But that's all it is. It can't be anything else!"

R: And he whispered right in to my soul, Fear is only thought. Because I was in a space of my intellect taking over, it went crazy, because there is where the fear is created. It is dependent on thinking about it—wherever it came from, whatever the thoughts I used to make up the fear, which is unconscious. So the fear is just running all over the place. You can't grasp it. So that's why I asked to repeat that, because intellect could say, "Yeah, I understand, I understand. Fear is just thought. Yes, I know"—but my system didn't get it. I still felt the fear. So it didn't sink in. It didn't integrate. So when it whispered in my ear I could feel my system hearing it beyond my thinking, beyond my intellect.

Richard jumped up, figuratively of course—had he literally jumped he would have smashed his head on the cave ceiling. Something he heard gave him the strength to push through his fear.

He said, "Okay I'm going!"

R: The sound of Jack's voice resonated and supplied my inner system with the reassuring awareness that there is nothing out there to be afraid of; it's all *created in my personal mind, just doing its job of thinking. I was sort of sinking down into another level of myself. It was more from the heart, where I knew there was only one thing to do, and that was go in through the remaining holes: Do that which I was afraid of. Or do it even though I was afraid. And that conviction came from heart level, and I had only one option, and I was totally free because I knew in my whole system what to do. There were not options, like, should I take this or this or this?—reasoning which one is best. When you have a lot of options in your mind you think you're free because you have more options than one, but all those options are in the personal thinking mind. It could be just bondage because you're stuck in your intellect. But here, now, there were no options! And in that oneness of knowing what to do was freedom, because all energy I had went to that, not thinking about it because it went beyond thinking. And then there was just energy. The energy needed to do it! I felt this raw life-force just wanting to act and get through these narrow (bloody) holes and get out of the illusion of them causing the fear. Life isn't afraid of tunnels; the "I" that thinks it is afraid is. I sensed my personal "I" like a living thought-entity that believes it "is" by constantly thinking in order to maintain the experience of "I/me" separated from everything else, defending itself to survive. And then the fear almost turned into excitement, because my system sort of got that it's a creation of my mind. There is nothing out there to be afraid of! It's just created in my thinking about it—in my experience-machinery: thinking and consciousness.*

Again I was the first one up. Because we had all been sitting on the cave floor and couldn't stand in this room, from my crouch I had to stand up into that little ceiling hole. Now my head was sixty percent to my destination. How in the world would I get up the rest of the way? The guide instructed me to lean back hard against the wall of the hole, place my right foot onto a tiny toe-hole in front of me, and somehow push up with my leg and shimmy my back up the hole until I could get my arms high enough to pull myself up until my butt got high enough to slide onto the floor of the room above us.

My legs now dangled high above the floor, with only my arms to support me. I had another uh-oh thought. Where did my arm strength go? I couldn't believe it! Even a couple of years ago I would have had no trouble at all pushing myself up there, but I could barely do it! It took every ounce of strength I had. In one year and a little over a month I would be 70 years old! What is this now; suddenly I'm weak? I decided right then with my now extremely aching arms that I had to start lifting weights or doing something with my arms or I would lose the rest of my strength. Use it or lose it, and I was losing it! I felt incredulous. I used every ounce of strength I had and even some I didn't to push my body up onto that floor level.

I barely made it, but I did! Then Richard came up. Then Susanne, Karen and Tanya. I offered each my hand. The five of us sat in that very tiny cave room, so happy and satisfied at what we had done. We all formed a strong bond having accomplished it together.

Except then we had to get back down through the same hole—not so easy either. Luckily, Spiderman sat on the level below grabbing our legs to help us down.

R: The righteous wrath of life itself forced me through the tunnels. [J: I told you he was a poet.] *Getting through the last hole, Jack reached for my hand and I finally got out in the sun with a lion's roar, and a relief I can't remember I ever experienced before. I could so clearly see how I've avoided life in order not to feel and stare that basic existential fear in its eyes. Filled with this feeling of freedom and the right to live, I was excited beyond thought.*

Richard had conquered his fear.

In the book *Island of Knowledge,* Syd Banks says, "Everyone must face their fictitious fears." Why fictitious? Because we inadvertently make up the fear! Then our consciousness comes along, grabs hold of that thought and seduces us by making it look and feel *absolutely real* through our five senses. We feel it in our bones. But it's only an illusion of our own creation made to look real and feel like truth via consciousness. And it *is* totally real—but only at that level! And, as Richard proved, there are always more levels—always higher levels of consciousness from which to see it. Then our new level seduces us and now that level looks real. But it's on a higher level this time so it feels better. And there are even higher levels, and of course lower levels, too.

"Reality," it seems, is not real!

To me this is automatic hope. Every time we're stuck and it looks and feels as if there really is no way out, there is! Because there are always higher levels from which to see it.

R: Sometimes I see consciousness as a spotlight. What you direct it towards becomes real. If I direct it towards thoughts which create fear, I get fear. And now we were directing my awareness on that it is only thought created in my mind. Then the other aspect of my being that would really constitute my existence, which is life itself—that there's another reality underneath my thinking going on, despite what I'm thinking. It's always there. And as long as I think the only thing that is real is what I am thinking—I mean, my heart beats, everything in my body is working, and I think. It's like the waves coming in. It doesn't matter what we think about that; they are still coming in. It's sort of life itself doing its thing.

Richard practically bounded down the stairs that led down from the cliff caves, Karen on one arm, Susanne on the other. Everyone looked so happy!

R: Coming down the stairs having come out of those caves, having come through all those tunnels, coming out into the open into the sun was such a relief! Because that fear of the caves, of the claustrophobic—was sort of a representation of all kinds of fear in life, which is created in my mind. It's such a relief coming out having done that, which I thought was real—the reality of fear—and I did it anyway. Like I said, I had that dream of being chased and getting stuck in caves for over twenty years and I haven't had the dream since that day. You reached out your hand and I grabbed it and got out of the damned black cave.

Later, I asked Richard what it said about himself that he was able to accomplish this?

R: I sort of got rooted in something else than I thought I was that was there all the time. Sort of discovering what makes me alive, that something is going on that keeps me living, that I am not really aware of all the time, but it works anyway. Getting in touch with that is a totally different quality of energy than my thinking about it. It is so much more alive and zestful.

The day ended perfectly. We walked the enchanting "Magic Path" back up to the village. We sat in a wonderful old square. We ate tapas together, everyone with a beautiful feeling. Richard was almost giddy. He had entered a new world, and it didn't only have to do with crawling through caves. This put all past fears in perspective. It had implications for every fear he would face in the future.

And that is the story of Richard and the caves. But far more than that, it is about the conquering of fear, the fictitious fear of fear itself. A lesson for us all.

3. THE FACTS OF LIFE

When I first began writing this book I thought the audience primarily would be people already somewhat familiar with the Three Principles or who had read Somebody Should Have Told Us! *I then realized this would not necessarily be true, and that would be fine—even encouraged. So I figure I'd better take some time explaining how I see the Three Principles. Mercifully, this is the only chapter like this in the book. But as the foundation for everything that follows, it is essential.*

Something was bugging me. I couldn't quite put my finger on it.

I seemed to be losing my enthusiasm for teaching the Three Principles—not my enthusiasm for living through this understanding because I would never lose that, but losing enthusiasm for helping others understand it. Me? Tired of teaching the Three Principles? I couldn't believe it. This was about eight years ago as I write this. My book *Somebody Should Have Told Us!* had been published about five years previous and continues to inspire changes in many lives. But now I found my teaching getting stale. I had run out of new things to say.

LOOKING BACK

In retrospect, every time I've felt stale teaching anything, it's because I get to the point where I think I know something. Always dangerous. Each time it happened I didn't see the signal: Time for me to rise to a new level of understanding, and I didn't pay attention soon enough. In its midst it is not so easy to see. Each time felt unnerving. Without fail a new level of understanding eventually appeared but not before getting me into trouble.

Since the early 1970s I'd been happily and successfully conducting prevention trainings—that is, preventing problem behaviors such as delinquency, alcohol and drug abuse, child abuse, teen pregnancy, teen suicide, violence, etc. before they start in the first place—and loving it. I had become fairly well known in that field after creating a "Prevention Framework" based on research, a "Prevention Wheel" showing the intersection of all problem behaviors we try to prevent, a "Prevention Pyramid" showing effective prevention program types communities needed to put in place at all levels. I traveled around the country running trainings and giving speeches. I was in reasonable demand. I went over well. The State of New Jersey adopted my model as its state approach to prevention. My first book, *Prevention: The Critical Need*, was about to be published. Suddenly I began to fail.

It culminated in Aspen, Colorado at a conference at which I was keynote speaker. I found myself on stage completely flopping. I couldn't seem to recover. My heart wasn't in it. Bad timing! I wanted to do so well there. The mountains were beautiful, the Aspen prevention folks wonderful; I didn't want to let them down. I wanted to be asked back. I knew more about prevention than ninety-five percent of people in the field, and I was failing! I couldn't find the spark. The day before I had hiked in the gorgeous Maroon Bells (where a big elk or worse discouraged me from proceeding further, making loud rustling noises in the underbrush, so I gingerly turned back). I even showed up late for a presentation—my worst work nightmare, about which I actually did have bad dreams. But standing in front of that roomful of people giving my keynote speech I found myself staring at a wide aisle directly in front of me, chairs filled with many people to the right, chairs filled with many people to the left, but no one in the middle! I found this unnerving. I talked about the importance of building relationships and pretty quickly ran out of things to say. I couldn't get behind it. Also, I was letting down the prevention practitioner who had gone out of his way to get me hired in Aspen after hearing and loving my presentation at a regional conference. Worse, I was failing myself. I'd become ineffective. I felt embarrassed, horrible. Unbeknownst to me it was a harbinger that I could no longer teach prevention from the outside-in. A new light was about to dawn on prevention from the inside-out via teaching the Three Principles.

Fast-forward another almost twenty years. Again the same thing began to happen. How could this be? I loved teaching the Three Principles. I knew no one could ever truly get to the bottom of this understanding, so it was always fresh for me. It didn't make sense that teaching this no longer worked for me. My heart was thoroughly behind living the spirit of the Principles. Yet something did not feel right.

For one thing I'd gotten a call from Dr. Roger Mills strongly encouraging me to stop using the name, "Health Realization." What? Roger himself had invented the name. I loved the name. To me it meant we all have a state of natural *health* deep within us and all we have to do is realize it. I'd named my business the Northeast Health Realization Institute. "Health Realization" was the official name used by the Santa Clara County, California, Division of Drug and Alcohol Services. Those of us involved in prevention from the inside-out had just begun to make a bit of an inroad into the prevention field and into psychological journals; for the first time "Health Realization" was gaining a bit of name recognition. It didn't make sense to pull the rug out from under it now. For what reason? I asked Roger. His answer could be summed up in one word: Syd.

That notwithstanding, I felt something missing in my teaching. I was saying the same things over and over again, running out of things to say. I became less effective. Maybe I should retire.

FRESH SIGHT

One day in the middle of conducting a long-term professional training I heard something that shocked me. My trainees had the wrong idea about what Three Principles understanding is all about. Some people said it's a great theory. Others said it's a wonderful philosophy of life. Others said the Principles are the means to live a healthy life. Others saw them as tools. People were all over the map. None were correct!

I was stunned, appalled. This wasn't the fault of the students; I placed the blame directly on the teacher, and the teacher was me!

Returning from the training I queried other learners taught by other Three Principles teachers. I heard the same answers! It wasn't only my own teaching; it seemed to be almost everyone.

Suddenly a new breath of life whooshed into me. I had to straighten out the misconceptions! I recharged. I now felt a challenge to help people see the right idea. So I had to ask myself, "What is the right idea?" The inquiry felt exhilarating. I felt rejuvenated. My enthusiasm returned. My teaching became even more effective. I found my own voice for perhaps the first time. Suddenly I had lots to say. I no longer desired to expose new people to the Principles; I now only wanted to help people go deeper who had already been studying the Principles. I called together an advanced, informal group in Vermont for those who had been through my long-term professional trainings to explore the Principles in greater depth. I've never looked back.

WHAT IS "THE THREE PRINCIPLES?"

If the Three Principles is not a theory, a philosophy, the means to live a healthy life or tools, what is it?

Facts!

The Three Principles are simply spiritual facts[3]—simply the way things really are; the way things work. They tell us how everyone's psychological/spiritual experience is created moment by moment in the same way—nothing more, nothing less. That's what Syd Banks had been trying to tell us from day one.

Years back I had looked up the word "principle" in the dictionary. The root of the word read, "fundamental law or truth"—something that exists in the universe whether we know about it or not. For example, whether we know it or not, a particular note on a stringed instrument is always determined by three laws: 1) the thickness of the string, 2) the tightness of the string; 3) the length of the string. Those are the *principles* behind getting a particular note. A string the same length, same thickness, same tightness will produce the same note every time. No exceptions! We get a different note depending on our use of those principles; for instance, once the guitar strings (thickness) are tuned

[3] An early reader of this chapter commented, "I can see how you were influenced by what Syd said in *Beyond Beliefs* [by Linda Quiring] by emphasizing that the Principles are facts." Actually, my insight about this occurred years before I knew *Beyond Beliefs* existed. I love that *Beyond...* corroborated what I say here, though, and I highly recommend that book, as well as *Island of Knowledge*, and all books, audios and videos by Sydney Banks.

(tightness), the length of the string is changed with a finger on a fret—sort of like how thought changes our experience.

I had been calling the Three Principles "fundamental truths," but even when calling them that I had not grasped the enormity of what it means to realize Mind, Consciousness and Thought as actual *facts.*[4]

Many people, however, get nervous when they hear the word, "facts." I don't blame them. Facts imply absolute, and many don't believe in absolutes. They absolutely don't believe in absolutes! They rebel. Do we expect them to just take our word for it? No! We can't. How do we know they're facts? People have to realize these facts for themselves, look within themselves and see if it rings true within their hearts. Each of the Three Principles must be seen as a fact so obvious it is irrefutable. I don't want anyone to take my word for it.

THE FACTS OF OTHER HUMAN SYSTEMS

First, a detour. Seeing facts is not such a stretch. Are there not facts behind how our circulatory system works? Are there not facts about how our digestive system functions? Our respiratory system? Our nervous system, including the brain? Why would our psychological system be an exception—just because we can't see it?

At one time in history no one could see the circulatory system. They didn't have x-ray machines. They hadn't yet cut open a cadaver. Did that mean the facts of how the human body functions didn't exist? Facts simply exist whether anyone can see them or not. I'm no scientist (a fact that will become quite obvious by the end of this sentence), but it would be hard to refute that the facts behind the circulatory system must be something like 1) a pumping mechanism—the heart pumps fresh blood into arteries; 2) a transportation mechanism—arteries carry fresh blood throughout the body, into capillaries, then into veins that carry the old blood back; 3) a purification and nourishment mechanism—the transportation mechanism loops through the lungs

[4] In the last few years an increasing number of Three Principles learners have caught onto this, so writing this now sounds almost like old news. Five years before writing this it was not so obvious. To me, it would be wise for everyone learning Three Principles understanding to realize the Principles are merely a description of the facts of how our experience of life gets created.

where the blood gets purified by oxygen so it can nourish the body's cells. Even if my high school biology teacher would cringe at my explanation, those or something like them are the basic, simple facts or principles of how the circulatory system operates.

Within the simplicity of those facts there is tremendous variation. Not every circulatory system works optimally. Some get clogged and don't function well. Some become damaged. Others work flawlessly. Regardless of how each individual's circulatory system functions, all make use of those same facts; the principles of that system always remain. Take any system of the body—digestive, reproductive, nervous, etc.—and it is possible to see the basic facts behind how it operates.

THE FACTS OF EACH PRINCIPLE

Facts need to be irrefutable or they are not facts. So what are the facts of the Three Principles?

Fact # 1: ***We are alive (via some life force energy)***

Try to refute that we are alive! What makes us be alive? Some *life force energy* within us. What exactly this force is remains a mystery, but it is the same force that propels a sperm toward an egg, the same force that makes all systems of the body function in the first place, the same force that makes the heart beat, the same force that powers up the brain and allows it to function. This life force energy is part of the *formless energy* that exists behind all life, which physicists insist exists. Even Einstein, a fairly smart fellow, said all matter is simply energy in another form. Human form is matter; therefore, we, too, are this energy in another form. If formless energy is behind All things it must be our *essence*. We must be part of the All; therefore, we must be One with the All. Syd Banks refers to this "principle" as Universal Mind or **MIND**, because this energy also appears to have an Intelligence. All we have to do is open our eyes. Bees in a hive. The intelligence behind life—All life. We are not talking about our own little minds here. We're talking about the energy-intelligence our minds make use of to function in the first place.

God only knows (probably literally) where this force comes from or how it becomes manifest within us. But it would be tough to refute that some life force energy exists within, through and around us, causing us to be alive and holding all life together. This is a fact. And with this first fact we enter a fascinating, incomprehensible realm. It is behind everything. It *is* everything. It is us.

Fact # 2: ***We have consciousness***.

We are conscious beings. Anyone who denies this fact would have to be conscious to deny it. There must be some power within people that gives us the ability to be conscious. Consciousness can be quite complex and extremely deep. Here we stick with the simplicity of the fact and deal with the complexity and depth later, in Chapter 19. Consciousness is our ability to have experience of life and to be aware of that experience, to be aware of existence. Without Consciousness we would have no experience we could ever know. We call this second fact or principle, **CONSCIOUSNESS.**

Our consciousness comes into us as pure universal energy manifesting in our soul. Its pure state is pure peace, pure love. It is the pure nothingness out of which wisdom springs. We can only drop from pure consciousness—rather, have the illusion that we're dropping from it—to varying degrees or levels through our use of the third fact.

Fact # 3: ***We think***.

There must be some power within people that gives us the ability to have or generate or create thoughts. Anyone who denies this fact would have to be using the power of Thought to deny it. It must be a fact! Thought allows us to connect with the pure consciousness within—that pure state of peace and love within ourselves—and Thought allows us to contaminate our pure consciousness to varying degrees. It is the only thing that can. We create either state for ourselves to varying degrees. This is our creative gift: the principle of **THOUGHT.**

These Three Principles are the essential facts of human psychological/spiritual functioning. They are formless. We have given them names—Universal Mind, Consciousness and Thought—but names are words and words are form and can't possibly capture the true meaning of the formless. If you don't like these terms, call them something else—your names won't come any closer than these to capturing their essence. All words are inadequate. In human form we are incapable of grasping the full magnitude of their meaning.

SO WHAT?

The obvious question is, "So what?" So what if Mind, Consciousness and Thought exist within us? What's so important about that?

The big answer: We can have no experience without them. We would have *no perceptions* without them. We would have *no feelings* without them. Without them we would have *no experience of "reality."*

Pretty big.

How we make use of these facts is the *sole determinant* of every experience we can have in this life: from peace, love, joy and wisdom to worry, anxiety, depression, anger and violence. In other words, our (usually inadvertent) use of these facts brings us to one emotional place or another and many levels in between. It is the *only* way we can ever experience any feelings or emotions.

HOW IT WORKS

Let's say we get blamed for something that happened at work. Universal Mind offers us all possibilities. Using our incredible gift of the creative power of Thought, we create a thought, land on one possibility.

Let's say we land on worry: "Uh oh, am I in trouble here?" We don't go out of our way to create this worry-thought; it appears in our head. This thought gets picked up by our consciousness, sends it through our senses and gives us a "real" experience of worry. We really feel it! But worry is only "real" at the level we're seeing it. With our power of Thought it is possible to see the same situation from innumerable levels of consciousness—many different perspectives—and whatever level we're on gives us the particular "real" feeling we experience.

Let's say we come up with a thought such as, "How dare they blame me for something I didn't do!" That produces a feeling of anger, a very different feeling-experience than worry, but it feels just as real.

Let's say we come up with, "Oh well, that's his problem. Nothing I can do about it. I can't let it bother me." Then we would feel neutral, which would feel just as real as the others.

Or, we might come up with, "The poor fellow must be so lost to blame me when he doesn't know what he's talking about," and actually feel compassion.

Or, "It's a blessing. I wanted to get out of here anyway," and get a feeling of gratefulness—or a million other possibilities, all of which look and feel equally "real" within our consciousness.

In other words, worry cannot be caused by the external situation—in this example, getting blamed. Worry must be *created* by our *own thinking*. Realizing this can be very humbling. We make up our own misery.

In essence, what we see is what we get.

We all get into states of stress or distress or anger or worry or bother or depression or jealousy or misery and more. Each time it's because we are "using" the Three Principles in a way that brings a particular emotion to us. That emotion cannot exist in any other way; the *only* way emotions can ever exist within us is by our own creation, by our own thinking. So when we're caught in the "reality" of any emotion we have the opportunity to realize (with another thought), "I'm the one making it up." Then we get a different feeling. Our feelings and emotions change with each different thought. All look and feel equally real, and all are illusions of our own creation.

The more deeply we understand this the more our lives improve.

Even more important, because pure consciousness is built into us already as pure spiritual essence—some would call it our soul—and, as I keep saying, the qualities of pure consciousness include pure peace of mind, pure love and pure wisdom and other beautiful feelings, there is nothing we have to do to get there because we already *are* there. Look within to see if when your minds clear of personal or habitual thinking you feel closer to that state. We can only *not* experience pure peace, love and wisdom by using our power of Thought to obscure what *is*.

Even if Sydney Banks had not had his extraordinary, spiritually enlightening moment in 1973 on Salt Spring Island, British Columbia where he *saw* how it all worked, even if he had not chosen to be helpful to humanity by sharing it with the world, these facts or principles would still be operating in us and through us automatically. Lucky us, Syd *saw* clearly how everyone's experience of life gets created in the exact same way in every moment.[5] And from our use of these facts, we then think, feel and act.

POINTING IN THE DIRECTION OF THE FORMLESS

As I said, words are form and none are adequate. To find truth we can only point in its direction. Each of the Principles is far more huge than we can possibly conceive.

For example, what we think of as Thought is only a tiny part of the magnitude of its meaning. When most people hear "thought" they very often conceive of it far narrower than we mean it. One set of people hears "thoughts," which is not at all what we mean by Thought. "Thoughts" are the product of *Thought*, the forms created by the formless power of Thought. We can create anything in our minds using the power of Thought.

---

[5] Way back in the 1800s William James, the father of American psychology, believed there were psychological "principles" that, once discovered, would turn psychology into a science. James never found them, though he came fairly close. Sydney Banks was fortunate to *see* them. He tried to tell the world of psychology of this discovery. Extremely few heard. It went against everything they were taught because, by then, James's vision for psychology had been largely forgotten or ignored. The world of traditional psychology rejected, ridiculed or ignored what Banks said. Regardless, Syd took it upon himself to share what he had *seen*. Those who heard experienced greatly improved lives. They were less stressed, experienced more peace of mind, more well-being, improved relationships and more effectiveness in life and with others. A few mental health professionals caught on—George Pransky, Roger Mills, Keith Blevens—who then began to teach others what they had found for themselves. As a result they began to achieve better outcomes with their clients than they had in all their years of traditional study and practice. In time, other psychotherapists and practitioners also caught on, and they experienced similar results. I am one of those people. Some wonderful teachers of the Three Principles are out there quietly changing lives, one person at a time. For the history of how it all began and spread, see Pransky, J (2015). *Paradigm Shift: A History of the Three Principles as Uncovered by Sydney Banks*. British Columbia, Canada: CCB Publishing.

Another set of people recognize that their thinking has something to do with what they experience as "reality." Many do not realize that most thoughts creating our feelings are invisible to us, hidden, working behind the scenes, yet creating our experience just the same. All this invisible thinking—about things such as how worthwhile I feel, how well I am doing, comparing, judging, worry thoughts, little anxieties, all that stuff—works its magic, and combines with consciousness to create those feelings in us. Feelings look as if they are independent of thought, but they are not.

Thought includes everything we take in through any of our senses.

But Thought is even bigger than that. We are talking about actual *creation* here. Thought is our creative gift. With it we get to create our very lives! How huge is that?! I am not talking about creating what happens to us; I am talking about creating the meaning we give to everything that happens in our lives.

Still, Thought is even huger than that. Thought exists even before we come into existence. This is extremely difficult to grasp; it was for me. Yet Thought is what brought us into being. Some would say God's Thought created life, including human beings; others would say that God's Thought set evolution in motion that led to human beings. For those who believe in God, either way it is God's creation. And we use thought to either believe or not believe in God.

Not long ago as I write this I was feeling sorry for myself, licking my wounds over a personal little tragedy that had befallen me—you'll have to wait until later in the book to read my saga—and suddenly, out of nowhere, a series of thoughts jumped into my head. The sequence went something like this:

Oh wow! I am the creator!

I have the power!

As God creates All life, I create *my* life.

I create every experience I can possibly have!

No one else creates it for me. No one and no thing—nothing—can ever make me feel any way. It's all me, doing it to myself, most often inadvertently, and I'm not often aware of it.

This means no matter what happens to me, I make up the control over me that I give to this person or situation. I decide how much power to give anyone or anything in my life.

No one else can cause *any* emotion to be unearthed within me and take me over.

It's all *Me.* It can't be any other way.

More important, beneath it all, behind it all, no matter what tragedy ever befalls me, something lies within me that cannot be touched, that cannot be harmed, that cannot be damaged: my spiritual essence at the core of my being. And what comes with it? Pure peace, pure love, and the pure incubator from which wisdom springs from out of nowhere. My innate health.

What is sadness, or so-called emotional wounds, really, in the face of all that?

EXPERIENCE ITSELF: THE SENSES, PERCEPTIONS AND FEELINGS

Contrary to popular belief, what we perceive does not come directly from our senses—seeing, smelling, hearing, tasting or touching. The outside world is always filtered through our own thinking. If we see something with our eyes, such as a leaf blowing in the wind, we must have a thought of its existence. If we didn't have the thought of the leaf we would not "see" it, even though it exists. The leaf does not exist *for us* if we do not have a thought about it—even an unconscious thought. Same with hearing, smelling and tasting. If we brush against someone in a crowded subway car we may not even notice. If the same brush happens while passing someone in the woods we might notice it so much it would freak us out. Thought calls the shots of our senses.

Same with feelings. If I get a feeling of insecurity it's because a thought of insecurity enters my consciousness and makes me feel it. Insecurity is impossible without such a thought. My insecurity would not exist without my creation of it. Humbling! Consciousness seduces me into feeling the insecure thought as "reality."

That, in a nutshell, is how it works. It always works that way—no exceptions! When people truly see "no exceptions," they have seen something huge.

To completely grasp this is to be free.

Lucky us, we have the *free will* to use these facts or principles in whatever way we want for ourselves in any moment—to our benefit or to our detriment. And we do.

SUMMING IT UP

In sum, then, the Three Principles are not a way of seeing the world; they are the way the world works, no matter how one sees the world.

The Three Principles are not a way of being; they are the way we are, the way we function as human beings, no matter how we are being.

We can't get away from these Principles. They are always acting within us perfectly and precisely. They are all we need to know to live a happy, peaceful life of well-being. Understanding them is our ticket out of leading a miserable, fearful or angry life. But the purpose of understanding them is not to live a happy, peaceful life; it is simply to see how it all really works within us. It just so happens when we understand how every experience we have is our own creation from within ourselves, we tend to lead a happier, more peaceful life. It is not the goal; it is the byproduct. It happens naturally, with deep enough understanding.

The Three Principles are not a prescription; they are a description, plain and simple.

The description means we can no longer blame the outside world for how we feel. Humbling!

4. SYD & ME

My ex-wife Judy answered the phone.

"It's Syd Banks," she said.

I gulped. Syd would call me from time to time, just to chat. I never really knew why. But I always got a little nervous. For some reason I didn't want to get too close. But I liked Syd very much, and he seemed to like me.

This time he began telling me that someone (I learned later it was Linda Quiring) had just found and given him some of his original writings from soon after his enlightenment experience. As Syd read them the memories flooded into him. He said it brought him right back there; reading it felt so beautiful, he cried. At that moment, he said, he knew he had to write his autobiography.

"But," he said, "I want to include other people's stories of how their lives had changed. So I'm asking a few people if they would write something to include in my book. And remember that story you told me about what happened to you when we first met?"

"How could I ever forget that?"

"I just love that story. Would you mind writing that up so I can include it in my book?"

"Syd, I would be honored!"

So I wrote it up, not without emotion myself, and sent it to him.

He called me again. He loved my write-up and would include it happily.

That's why I originally wrote what you're about to read here.

Long ago I decided not to put this story in any of my other books because it was for Syd's autobiography. Twelve years later as I write this I'm still waiting. Syd did in fact write his autobiography. He did include my and many other stories. He told me he was holding out for a big publisher because this book deserved to be spread far and wide. Then, unfortunately for us all, Syd passed away—may he rest in peace, and I'm sure he is. Someone took it on and decided it needed to be written differently. Thankfully that didn't work out. It got into someone else's hands and, as of this writing, still has not seen the light of day. I hope it does, because it will be a blessing and gift to the world, but I'm not sure it will in my lifetime. I also don't know whether it will end up in the format Syd wanted.

I decided the time has come for my part to be told.

For years and years I had been very reluctant to tell this story. It is very personal to me. After my experience with Syd my life was never the same; something shifted fundamentally deep within my soul. For many years I couldn't even tell the story without getting emotional, so I rarely told it. Besides, what happened was weird. A lot of people wouldn't know what to make of it. I'm not sure I know. Nor did I think it held any real value. But it happened and now it no longer makes sense to keep it hidden.

So here it is—I took what I had sent to Syd and improved the writing.

On February 3, 1993 my life changed forever over a personal encounter with Sydney Banks.

Because I have been asked countless times over the years to share how I became exposed to the Three Principles prior to my encounter with Syd, and because I included that story in my book, *Modello* [see next chapter] I approach the story here from a different angle. Despite my work in the field of prevention and sometimes as part of it, for the previous five or six years I had been on an undefined, personal, spiritual search. The search itself had been fun—I read spiritual books, attended spiritual groups, practiced meditation. I enjoyed it all and loved meeting periodically with good friends going through the same type of search, but I wasn't getting very far. It seems funny to me now: I was searching for my higher self outside myself, searching for spirituality outside my own self. No wonder I couldn't find it!

That's where I was at when on March 22, 1991 I showed up at the conference at which Roger Mills spoke with Elaine Burns and Cynthia Stennis, from the housing projects in which he worked. After his talk I asked Dr. Mills if I could squeeze something about his project into a book I'd just completed, *Prevention: The Critical Need*—the first book written for the field of prevention that combined research with practical application. I asked him for a couple of his articles. He made me pay for them!

Somewhere in the conversation he asked me if I was related to George Pransky. I didn't know. Probably. I had to ask my mother. She told me George and I were second cousins, I knew his brother, Jimmy, pretty well. She said George had gotten into some offbeat pop psychology that the family looked down upon.

I placed my brief write up of the Modello project into the chapter called, "Spirituality and Prevention," though Roger never referred to the project as spiritual. Ironically, independently around the same time, a good friend of mine, Katie Kelley, a school guidance counselor, had begun to study this understanding, went to a Florida training for a week and came back raving about it. She invited me to sit in at her elementary school for a training she'd arranged with the people who trained her in Florida: Jeff Timm, Ann Thomas and Susan Gardner. I then attended a class taught by Janice Solek-Tefft and Barbara Jordan of the Vermont Center for Human Understanding. Janice had a few tapes by George Pransky. I liked the tapes a lot, but I still didn't get it. I pressed Janice for more. Finally she relented and leant me a tape by a person she called the source of it: Syd Banks.

I couldn't fathom a word of it. This tape was only a year or two old, the first tape Syd made calling it "three principles"—he called them Divine Mind, Divine Consciousness and Divine Thought—and said they had everything to do with our reality. The tape had a slight warble, so it sounded to me like he was from outer space. Really!

Nonetheless within a year and a half I felt driven to write the story of how the Modello project unfolded from beginning to end. With Roger's blessing I spent a few weeks in Dade County, Florida in and around the Modello and Homestead Gardens housing projects, interviewing the residents whose lives had been most affected. Since I was now writing about it I had no choice but to try to understand it. I knew this was great stuff, but how could I write about something I didn't completely get? I had to get to the source. The source was Syd Banks. But how could I talk with him?

I learned that George and Syd were giving a talk in Vancouver. I had to go! But I didn't have the money. Out of the question. Bummed!

Then I remembered I was scheduled to do a prevention consulting job in Atlanta close to that time. I had an idea! They were already flying me from Vermont to Georgia and back, and I discovered, oddly, that it would cost even a little less if they flew me from Burlington to Atlanta to Vancouver to Burlington with a Saturday night stay-over than if they simply flew me to Atlanta and back in the middle of the week. So I asked the hiring agency, and to my surprise they said yes! I was thrilled—I could go!

Until I realized I'd miscalculated the dates by a week. Damn! That would mean I'd have to stay in Vancouver for an extra week awaiting this seminar. I didn't know anyone there, so my airline savings would be eaten up by hotel costs. Bummed again!

As I moaned this to my friend, Peggy Sax, she said, "My best friends live right near Vancouver. I'll bet you could stay with them."

"Wow. Really?!" It was set.

So after my Atlanta job I flew to Vancouver, met Peggy's friends and settled into their house. I decided to call Syd to see if I could interview him before the seminar. When dialing I had the thought, "I wonder if I should be doing this." I didn't know Syd.

"Hello?" I recognized his Scottish accent from his tape.

"Hello, my name is Jack Pransky. I'm a cousin of George's and I'm in the process of writing a book about what Roger Mills accomplished in the Modello housing project, and I'd love to talk with you about it."

"Oh, that's got nothing to do with me."

"I know you weren't directly involved with it, but you were the original inspiration behind it, and—"

"No, that's got nothing to do with me," he cut me off, "and besides, I'm getting ready to do this seminar and I've got a lot of people coming in from all over the world, so I'm sorry but I really can't talk with you now."

That was the end of that. Bummed again! So I called Roger at the hotel where the seminar would be held. The faculty of Psychology of Mind (which they called themselves then) were meeting there around Syd's talk. Roger invited me up.

The next day I took a bus into the city and met Roger in the lobby. A bunch of people milled about, chit-chatting. Roger introduced me to everyone. One was Syd Banks.

Oh!

Syd was friendly, unassuming, and seemed almost shy. Before I knew it I was in a restaurant eating lunch, not just with Roger but with eight or ten others, Syd among them. We sat at a big round table with Roger and his wife, Clytee to my right, and Christine Heath, then someone else, then Syd to my left, but because of the round table I had a good view of him. I watched him with interest as he and everyone engaged in small talk. I saw nothing special about Syd at all.

Somewhere in the middle of the meal, out of nowhere, he turned to me and said, "I can see you're here looking for help. Ask me anything you want."

Who me? What? Gulp. Everything I'd ever wanted to ask the guy went flying out of my head. My mind went completely blank.

And then Syd began to talk. He talked like he talked on his tapes. I couldn't understand a word. All other conversation ceased. I felt all eyes at the table upon me. I began to feel embarrassed.

Then I started to feel irritated.

"Oh God," I thought, "Syd's going into his rap. These people around the table must have heard this a million times. They must be bored out of their minds. This is so embarrassing. Oh God."

I wanted to slide under the table. My irritation increased. I felt extremely agitated, off-kilter.

Somewhere in the middle of what he was saying, through increasing irritation I remember managing to ask, "Why didn't you decide to become a guru, with a huge following and all that?"

He said, "Because that would go against everything I'm talking about. I'm saying the answer lies within everyone. The last thing I want is for people to look to me for the answers. That's the wrong direction."

Okay. Impressive. Then back to hearing more I couldn't comprehend.

Somewhere further on I heard him say, "The secret is to understand that all life is nothing but one Divine Thought."

Completely over the top of unfathomability.

I heard myself ask, "Do you mean, thought of God?"

"No," he said. "Thought *is* God."

At about that point the strangest thing happened. The most peculiar feeling came over me. To this day I could never describe it. There are no words. There cannot be words. I felt something akin to being transported into another realm. I began to *hear* what he was saying way beyond my intellect. Way, way, way beyond the intellect, as if deep within my soul—or something.

I only knew one thing, and I *knew* this beyond a shadow of a doubt. I knew that Syd *knew* that he was talking Truth. I knew that he Knew! That's all I knew. And it was the most powerful thing I'd ever known in my life.

At that moment, everything became completely weird—I've run out of words. I felt unbalanced. It was almost like dizziness, but I wasn't dizzy. My brain went foggy, almost buzzing. I no longer knew anything I thought I knew about life.

I wanted to run, but there was nowhere to run. I wanted to hide, but there was nowhere to hide. I was left only with myself, whom I no longer knew. My irritation completely disappeared, and I felt a strange yet uneasy peace overcome me—a contradiction in terms—as if I'd come to Know something beyond knowledge, something huge, only I didn't know what. I only knew life was far more than what I had been seeing in this form.

Meanwhile Syd talked on, zeroing in on me. Everyone else disappeared.

Suddenly without warning Syd stood up, excused himself, did a 180-degree turn and left. Everyone's mouths hung open.

I felt discombobulated, out of tune with the self I'd known, disoriented—so out of it I had no idea what was going on. I no longer had any idea about anything. The world I knew had completely blown apart with my mind—what mind?—and I stood at the precipice of I didn't know what.

Clytee Mills came up to me, put her hand on my arm and thanked me.

"Huh?"

She said, "Syd never talks like this, except when he's giving a talk." Others thanked me. It seemed they considered it an honor to have been in the presence of whatever had happened.

Michael Bailey walked over to me and said, "I know exactly what you're feeling now. The same thing happened to Joe [her husband]."

"What?" I thought, through my haze.

All I remember next is Clytee, Michael and Valda (Keith Blevens' wife) leading me, literally, through the streets of Vancouver, looking in store windows, going into different shops, while the faculty went back into their meeting. All the while I felt in a daze, so out of it I could barely function. If it hadn't been for the three of them I would have sat down in a gutter. They were so nice, so wonderful. I still felt so strange, discombobulated.

Years later Clytee told me, "I remember that day. You were stunned—with the vulnerability of a child—and it was so touching to be around you."

I don't know how I managed it but somehow I got myself on the bus back to where I was staying. As soon as I sat down I felt like crying.

I knew I would never be the same. But I had no idea what that meant.

By the time the 45-minute bus ride ended I'd begun to recover and feel more like myself, so when I got to the house I blurted out the whole story to these near-strangers who must have thought I was nuts. I'll never forget the bewildered look on Claude's face. He had no idea what I was talking about. He probably thought I'd gone off the deep end.

The next day I caught the bus back to the hotel. The seminar would start that evening. Tomorrow I was scheduled to meet George for breakfast. In a cavernous ballroom I waited for the faculty to come out of their meeting. I looked up from reading George's book and saw George, arm around Roger's shoulder, talking to him as they walked out of the meeting. At this point we had not yet met—except when we were kids because an old home movie shows the two of us at the same Purim party. George had moved to the west coast and I stayed east. But I knew what George looked like from the back cover of the book. Besides, he looked more like a Pransky than I did. I stood up and waived. George waived back. We started toward each other. As I went to give my long-lost cousin a big hug he suddenly recoiled. He had no idea who I was! I found out later that from across the room he thought I was someone else he knew. Before I could say anything he brushed me off and was gone. I didn't know what just happened but didn't think much about it. I'd find out tomorrow when we were scheduled for breakfast.

I began wandering the hallways. I turned a corner and bumped into Syd.

"Syd, what did you do to me yesterday?"

"I didn't do anything. That's just the way I talk." He said it so sincerely.

So I started to tell him what had happened to me, including my initial irritation, and he started to protest, as in that's not what he'd meant to do at all.

I said, "No, wait!" and went on and finished. Syd gave me a knowing smile, nodded subtly, turned, and that was it. I'm not sure whether it was then or shortly thereafter that he said to me with a wry smile, "Now I've got two Pranskys to contend with."

The next morning George found me and apologized profusely. He didn't realize it was me! He was *so* sorry! I laughed. At breakfast we really connected. We got along great. I told him what had happened to me with Syd.

He said, "Syd does that to me all the time."

In the middle of the seminar's second day, after the audience had asked a bunch of intellectual questions, Syd announced the seminar was over. He said we had started to go backwards and it didn't make sense to talk anymore; it was a beautiful day and everyone should go outside and have a good time—that would be much more productive. George, on stage with him, looked shocked—one of the few times in his life George didn't know what to say. He wanted to continue because people paid good money to be there, but Syd would have none of it. Syd walked off stage, leaving George to apologize to the aufience. I was amused by the whole thing, respected it, got up and walked out of the seminar while most everyone else sat stunned, some angry. Selfishly, I had already gotten what I came for before the seminar even started. I felt more than satisfied—filled completely.

I was even invited into a faculty meeting while Syd consulted with them, even though I had no business being there.

I returned home to a phone call from an old friend, Carol Sauceda, from my old VISTA days (Volunteers In Service to America—sort of like a domestic Peace Corps) in Southern Illinois. I hadn't seen Carol in about fifteen years. She lived in California but had to be in New Hampshire for work. We met in a large indoor courtyard of a Holiday Inn in White River Junction, Vermont. All kinds of people milled about, standing outside their rooms on the second floor balcony, leaning on the railings overlooking the courtyard. As I told Carol what had happened to me, she didn't know what to make of it and shot me funny looks. I think she, too, thought I'd gone loopy.

All of a sudden—I don't know how to describe this—as I gazed up at all the people on their balconies, something bizarre happened inside me. Suddenly I *saw* everyone in their separate realities. I *saw* them all in the separate worlds they had constructed for themselves unwittingly with their own thinking. I don't know how else to describe it, but it was so obvious to me. Like, "Oh wow! Of course! This is the way it *is*!" It was a very powerful experience. I decided not to tell Carol. She was already thinking I had flipped out.

A week or so later a friend, Sas Carey, came over to the house. Sas is a psychic whom I interviewed while in a tranced-out state about "spirituality in prevention" for my first (pre-Principles) book, *Prevention: The Critical Need*. I now asked her to connect with her spirits and clue into "Syd Banks on Salt Spring Island." She went into a trance for what seemed a long time. Finally she spoke slowly, eyes still half-closed.

"He's as solid as it gets."

Okay.

And that's my story. My life has never been the same. After my experience with Syd my entire exploration into spirituality screeched to a halt. I stopped meditating—no longer felt the need. I stopped attending spiritual groups; I stopped reading spiritual books—no longer necessary. From the tiny glimpse of truth I had seen I simply knew beyond a shadow of a doubt that whatever Syd was talking about was my truth as well as his, and everyone else's. I knew this is what life is really all about. I knew if I could just see this truth play out in my own life it would be the secret to life.

Interestingly, intellectually I didn't feel I understood anything more than I did before meeting Syd. It took a while for my intellect to catch up with what had happened to me. Mostly I thank George for that; he took me under his wing. But I now knew something deep within my soul. I knew what "wisdom beyond the intellect" meant. I knew it did not come from me, yet I knew it was of me. I knew it flowed through me, that it was always present, whether I realized it in the moment or not. I knew this was what "innate health" really meant—a part of our being so pure and deep within our consciousness, our true connection with our spiritual essence and connected to the Oneness of life. At the time the Psychology of Mind faculty came up with an explanation to define "innate health" as a concept. I didn't buy it. What I knew about it was unshakable; no one could talk me out of it. I didn't know much about anything else then, but I knew this.

It was enough to improve my life, though I was not looking for that. I'd thought I was doing fine. Yet what I realized beyond my intellect that day with Syd, complemented by George's and Syd's tapes, allowed me over the next few months to feel more solid and at peace than I ever experienced in my life. My relationships improved. My relationship with my teenage kids improved; I felt a lot closer to them. I had been living my life with a fair amount of stress, always running, running, running; I now felt much more peace. Before, I'd needed others around me to feel whole; now I relished being by myself. Everything felt great!

My euphoria lasted nearly three months, when I was brought down to earth—

5. WRITING *MODELLO*

—It happened over a run-in over my book *Modello*. I have almost never told this story.

First, some background. For those who haven't read *Modello* I highly recommend it, self-serving as that may sound. Had someone else written it I would equally recommend it. It won the Martin Luther King Storyteller's Award for the book best exemplifying Dr. King's vision of "the beloved community." The Modello project saw the first application of the Three Principles for prevention, intervention and community work. It became the inspiration for all inside-out community and institutional work to follow. Roger Mills ignited the spark. Roger was the pioneer, and we all owe him a huge debt of gratitude. May his name never die.

Modello is the name of an inner-city public housing project in Dade County, Florida, isolated down U.S.1 south of Miami. In 1987 the project was replete with poverty, despair, abuse and violence. Can we imagine what it is like to live with drug-dealing gangs at each of six entrances, cars driving in and out day and night buying drugs like cheeseburgers at Burger King? Can we picture what it feels like to live with the rival gangs battling each other, resulting in shootings every night? To live in fear of catching a stray bullet merely by going out to the clothesline? To live without taxi service or pizza delivery because drivers fear to enter? With police even fearing to come in unless part of a big drug raid where everyone is shaken down? With boyfriends hooked on crack beating their women unmercifully? With rampant child abuse and sexual abuse? With the widespread belief that the only means of escape is to lose oneself in alcohol and drugs? With toddlers playing with found used needles and syringes? With some mothers prostituting themselves or their daughters to get enough money to buy crack? With all manner of sex acts committed in the middle of the project for kids and everyone else to see? With teenage girls continually getting pregnant? With dropouts and truancy so rampant that school days looked like holidays with so many kids running around unattended? With neighbors fighting one another in the courtyards? With residents not having the thinking to support taking advantage of haphazard government services? Can we even imagine?

And into this mess walks Dr. Roger Mills, thinking, "This is the place for me!"

Most residents and service providers did not want him there. They wanted him out! Dr. Mills did the opposite of how everyone else thought prevention and community work should be done. They told him his approach would never work, especially in Modello. But Roger, who learned directly from Sydney Banks, knew a couple of things they didn't. Although he never actually expressed it this way (the following are my words), he knew beyond any doubt that *if people's thinking doesn't change, their behaviors will not change,* and he knew unshakably that *when people are connected to or aligned with their innate health and wisdom, problem behaviors are impossible*. Mills also knew from Syd that thinking cannot change from the level people currently think; new insight is needed that lifts people to higher levels of consciousness. So he and the staff he hired and trained—Lloyd Fields, Cynthia Stennis, Carol Murray—set out to help the residents understand how their entire experience comes from their own thinking, not from the horror show surrounding them. Dr. Mills accomplished this by 1) staying in his own health, despite people doing everything in their power to make him go away; 2) by seeing the residents as their innate health, not as their presenting problems, by building rapport and by helping their minds to relax so they could take in the new; 3) by deeply listening to them; d) by helping them understand, at whatever level they were ready to hear, how their feelings, moods and what they experienced as reality came from their own thinking, not from their circumstances, situations or others' behavior, and how underneath all that thinking they are perfectly whole and healthy. Only fifteen or so residents' lives changed beyond recognition, but that proved to be a critical mass that rippled out to change the entire 150-unit housing project, then spread into Homestead Gardens a few miles away with the same results.

To me, these results seemed a miracle. At the conference I attended

I saw with my own eyes how the lives of Elaine Burns and Cynthia Stennis had completely changed. My field of prevention working from the outside-in simply did not experience this magnitude of change. I became so intrigued I had to write the story of how it all unfolded from beginning to end. So, with Roger's blessing I headed to Modello.

Unfortunately, Hurricane Andrew beat me there, completely devastating the entire area, leaving war-zone-like rubble everywhere. What was left of Modello was deserted. With the help of Lloyd, Cynthia and Pam Gibson, however, I managed to track down the people whose lives had changed most. Clearly, these folks would never turn back to alcohol and crack addiction, never again be abused, never again abuse their kids, never go back to depression and attempted suicide, to drug dealing. They also seemed in higher spirits than the rest of the hurricane-ravaged population even after losing just about everything. If I hadn't experienced it firsthand I may not have even believed it.

While extensively interviewing the Modello ladies, as they liked to be called, we hit it off very well. We got along great! I recorded wonderful interviews.

Then I made a big mistake. Quite foolishly, in retrospect, I sent them my first draft of the first two chapters of *Modello.*

They hated what they saw! The two most vocal, Lisa and Virene, were absolutely furious with me.

I wasn't too worried. This was nothing that couldn't be straightened out with a face-to-face meeting. After all, I had never written a book like this before, and my entire purpose in sending the draft was I'd become concerned about how it was coming out and wanted their input.

I had felt uneasy about two things. First, as I sifted through the interviews I found many gaps in the story. Even though this was a true story I wanted this book to read like a novel. To maintain the flow I needed to fill the gaps, so I found myself making up the in-betweens. This felt uncomfortable. I wanted them to see it and tell me if I was off track.

Second, their language was so colorful, so expressive, so wonderful, I wanted their voices to sound the way they sounded to me. When I started writing the dialogue I didn't feel like I captured this. So I decided to write it in dialect—southern African American dialect.

This, too, felt uncomfortable. I wanted them to see it and tell me if they were okay with it.

Except they apparently didn't understand "draft." When they saw it in writing they assumed it cast in stone and that's what would appear in the book.

They felt violated that I had made up untruths to fill the story. They felt insulted that I'd written in dialect, believing it stereotypical. [Note: Later, I realized, "Of course! When they talk the way they naturally talk they see regular words on a page. They don't see dialect. To them it's just the way it is!" I could see how that might be insulting. If someone tried to write out the dialect of a Boston accent, I'd say, "What?" I learned something big.]

Plus, they had a third big complaint. I had told them I would change their names. I fully intended to, but at this stage in the writing I still needed to keep the characters straight in my own mind so I had not yet changed them—it was just a draft! They thought I disrespected them by keeping in their real names.

I drove two solid days from Vermont to Florida to meet with them. I had also sent the draft to Roger. I phoned him on my drive down and told him what was going on. Roger was very supportive. Clytee had read my draft and loved it.

So I didn't have much trepidation as I met the Modello ladies with Lloyd and Cynthia around a big rectangular table in a noisy restaurant.

They raked me over the coals—hot coals—up and down, back and forth, in and out and upside down. They told me how insulted they were. That wasn't the bad part; I could take that. But as much as I pointed back to the cover letter I had sent them stating in black and white that I was asking for their input and would change whatever they wanted, they would have no part of it. My confidence evaporated. Nothing I said could change their minds. Lloyd and Cynthia sat there without saying a word. Thanks, guys.

Then came the worst part. They announced it was over! There would be no book! Period.

Devastated! Shaken to my roots. I had already spent months on this. At my own expense I had traveled to Florida twice, now a third time, trying to get this story down. I had merely wanted their input on my draft so I could make changes. My intentions were pure.

Frantically I called Roger to tell him they said the book was off. I had to go see him. Roger was fine; he said he would call them, not to worry. Shaken, I drove from south of Miami to Sarasota on the opposite Florida coast where Roger and Clytee now lived.

In the almost three hours it took me to drive there Dr. Mills had called a couple of the ladies to get their take. By the time I arrived in Sarasota Roger had completely changed his tune.

I was not surprised that Roger backed them and not me. After all, Modello was Roger's pet project. He had carefully cultivated good relationships with the ladies—not an easy task. He was the one who had sparked the insights that completely changed their lives. Of course his allegiance would be with them! He hardly knew me. But something else made no sense to me. He was anything but easy on me. He now said I had overstepped my bounds. He agreed with them—the book was absolutely off!

"Hey," I said, "it may have been stupid of me, but my heart was in the right place. It was only a draft! I was enlisting their help to make it accurate, better and to their liking."

Roger was unmoved. One could cut the tension with a knife. I didn't deserve this treatment!

Fuming, I felt so horribly upset driving back in the car I was literally shaking. I drove all the way to North Carolina before I could even calm down. I let it completely throw me for a loop. I had thoughts of, "Forget this!" and a lot worse.

I said over and over again to myself, "They should have treated me differently, given what they're supposed to know! This is how supposedly-evolved beings treat each other? [Bleep] this! I'm out of here!" I couldn't let it go.

Only one thing kept me around: What I *knew* beyond a shadow of doubt from my encounter with Syd Banks. The truth I'd seen with Syd was absolutely unshakable, whether or not I believed anyone should have acted differently, given what they were supposed to know. Had my experience with Syd not occurred I would have been long gone from it all. That's the truth.

But I'd also learned some important lessons. It took me a while to get back on track. I figured once people calmed down at some point cooler heads would prevail. At some point I believed I would get back to writing because in spite of what anyone thought in the moment I knew this book had to be written.

Except I went into severe writer's block. I sat in front of my computer. Nothing came. I could no longer write.

A year or so later I read a completely unrelated book, *Loose Balls*, about the short-lived but crazy and exciting American Basketball Association. It was written only with quotes, one after another, from different players and coaches—and it worked. The thought came to me, "I wonder if I could write *Modello* the same way, using only their own quotes. I will write exactly what they said as they themselves said it—nothing else. Nobody could take issue with that!"

I worked long and hard on it. Finished it. It came out terribly. Didn't work at all. Again I plunged into writer's block.

Another year passed. Thoughts of the incident faded over time because thinking changed. My life became wonderful again. Could it be that only my distressing thoughts had kept me in a state of distress? Could it be that when those thoughts died away what I'd gained from Syd reappeared because it was part of me all along and had now simply been unleashed?

After almost another year the thought occurred to me, "Maybe I can do a combination of quotes along with writing the story. I wouldn't have to fill in any blanks or make anything up."

By that time everyone's feelings had calmed down, thanks mostly to Pam Gibson, Roger's colleague from Modello who continued to have a wonderful relationship with the ladies and who wanted very much to see this book come to fruition. I became far more careful about how I portrayed everything. I'd learned that much. Even Virine and Lisa stopped objecting. I can't say they were ever totally behind it, but they stopped trying to keep it from coming out. It took almost ten years from the time I conducted my first *Modello* interview for the book to actually hit the streets. I gave everyone I interviewed—plus Virine, who had never let me interview her—a free copy.

Meanwhile, I took it upon myself to try to turn on the prevention field to this new inside-out paradigm of "Health Realization," as Roger Mills then called it. I wanted to spread the word about its power. By this time I had begun to grasp it and nothing in the field looked right to me anymore. This was a bit unnerving. I'd been practicing prevention from the outside-in for about 25 years and had been so certain about it, while conducting trainings all over the U.S.

So I took the plunge. I started offering "Health Realization" workshops. At first I didn't know what I was doing, but my enthusiasm got me by. Working in prevention and in the state of Vermont I had no other Health Realization peers nearby. The Vermont Center for Human Understanding, with Dicken Bettinger, Janice Solek-Tefft and Barbara Jordan, did only therapy, counseling and treatment. Roger now lived across the continent in California. So, for better or worse, whatever I came up with I created on my own. I attended as many trainings as I could, mostly by George Pransky, to whom I could listen all day. I never went anywhere in my car without listening to either George's or Syd's tapes—being careful not to fall asleep to their hypnotic, soothing voices. I found I experienced most success and enjoyed it most when I worked with small groups and kept fresh with their questions and comments. As I found my own way, my workshops and trainings became more impactful. I taught Health Realization for many summers at the New England School of Addictions Studies.

But most prevention folks remained unenthusiastic. They didn't know what to make of it. It sounded too foreign to them. Most of my colleagues couldn't understand what I was talking about. My reputation in the prevention field began to wane. Still, a few were quite touched and had powerful insights, which kept me going.

I never let go—in fact, it's impossible for me to—because my experience with Syd touched me so deeply. Today what is known more accurately as the Three Principles is so much a part of my life it is difficult to separate work from pleasure. Work *is* pleasure. I have been blessed to touch the lives of so many people and organizations. I have seen people's lives turn around—some to an unfathomable extent. My books have touched people. Nothing could be more gratifying. I love my work and my life. I keep learning ever more, seeing it all more simply and more deeply, and it is reflected in my teaching and, I hope, my writing.

Yet I still feel like a babe in the woods when it comes to all that could be known about these three awesome gifts and powers.

6. WHAT HELPS US MOST?

I scheduled a training with my Vermont advanced Three Principles group. In preparation I asked myself, "What exactly is it about understanding the Three Principles that helps us most in our lives? What is most helpful for people to know?"

This question set my intention to see an answer. I then took it off my mind and went for a walk in the woods. This cleared my head and allowed my mind to drop into a state of deep reflection, a state of *not knowing*. Not knowing clears the decks. I hoped my head would clear enough to allow wisdom to send forth an answer.

It did. Four statements came to me. Thank you, wisdom.

Each is a simple statement. The depth of each is bottomless. Each is spiritual and, as I said, no words can describe the spiritual. Nor can the spiritual be analyzed, no matter how hard one tries. Each point deserves slow, deep reflection on its meaning for one's life. I believe the more deeply we *understand* the following the more we create a better experience of life for ourselves.

> 1. We can have *no* experience (within our consciousness) of *anything* in the outside world that is not our *own* thinking, and our thinking changes.
>
> 2. We can *only* have the *illusion* (through our thinking) that we are *separate* from the life force/formless energy/essence/Oneness/ Source of All things.
>
> 3. When our minds clear or calm down from personal thinking what remains as an experience feels more peaceful, more loving, more wise.

4. Our feelings always tell us whether our thinking is serving us well in any moment, and therefore whether it will serve us to believe, trust and follow that thinking.

In essence these are all we need to understand to live a peaceful, loving, happy, joyful life guided by wisdom. It is wonderful both to see the simplicity yet grasp the depth of how what these statements point to mean everything for our lives. Happy reflecting. Treasures await.

A few years later I had a far deeper insight. I realized that those four points, or whatever one calls them, can all be boiled down to *one.* One statement! It came to me out of nowhere one day in a flash of wisdom while walking Nantasket Beach. Left to the devices of my own everyday thinking I never would have come up with this in a hundred years. Left to wisdom via a clear mind it hit me like a rock. I loved it so much I put it on my website as the first thing people see. Alert readers may recognize this from the opening quote in this book.

All we are is peace, love and wisdom,
and the power to create the illusion that we're not.

I believe this one statement is all people need to know to live a mentally and spiritually healthy life—if they see it deeply enough.

7. OUTSIDE WORLD VS. INSIDE WORLD

Well before I moved in with Amy, yet fairly early in our relationship she bought a wooden storage shed. She wanted to stain it before Vermont weather pummeled it. Because she had to be away she could not do it quickly, so she planned to paint it as soon as she returned.

I had a great idea. I would stain the shed for her! I wanted to do this as a surprise to the woman I loved. The idea excited me. What could be better! My spirits soared.

The next morning I pulled up to her house, set up everything I needed, got my music ready and started. As I painted away to Bob Dylan and Neil Young, having a grand old time, it began to cloud up. The clouds became thicker and darker. I realized it would rain.

Suddenly I had to get it finished—fast! I started painting like a maniac.

Too late! Raindrops. Then hard rain. I knew I was in trouble when I saw beautiful tan water droplets splashing like tiny pebbles thrown into a pond, except the pond was inside my stain can. Not good. The drops became more intense. Worse, the soil near Vermont rivers often consists of clay, and shed construction had unearthed it. I now stood in it. I watched with horror as the shed bottom turned a splotchy red-brown as rain splashed clay all over what I had just stained. What a mess!

Ugh! I couldn't continue. I raced to put all the stuff away, leaving the shed half-naked. No way would I get this finished before Amy came home. My spirits dropped.

I called Amy and told her what happened. She thought what I did was so sweet.

"No problem," she said. "I'll just finish it. It's great that you did half. How will I know where you stopped?"

"It's obvious," I said. Clear tan stain on wood.

"Okay."

The weather cleared by morning. Amy wouldn't be home until noon. I could surprise her again by finishing the shed before she got back! I raced over there, finished the rest of it, cleaned everything up and left before she got home, thrilled with myself. My spirits soared.

That afternoon Amy went to stain the shed. She stared at it, unable to tell where I had stopped. It was not obvious at all. She stained the entire shed again.

When I found out what she did I got bummed! Not only had my surprise been dashed, but she went through all that work I was trying to save her from, and all my work went for naught. My spirits plunged.

Then, in appreciation for all the work I had done for her, she bought me a massage. That was so wonderful of her! My spirits soared.

I went to get my massage at the agreed-to time and sat in the waiting room. Fifteen minutes passed. A half-hour passed. I called the massage therapist and left a message. She stood me up! I had been looking forward to this so much! My spirits dropped.

The massage therapist called back. She was so sorry! For some reason she forgot to write it down and spaced out. To make it up to me she would give me a two-hour massage with hot stones. My spirits soared.

The massage was phenomenal! To cap it off I had free coupons for the Ben & Jerry's factory store, practically on my way home. I got all excited about getting a free ice cream cone as a perfect cap to the hot day. My spirits soared higher.

Happily, I handed my coupons to the ice cream scooper, ready for Heath Bar Crunch—I admit to being an ice cream freak. She told me my coupons had expired. My spirits dropped.

Driving home in my car, a realization struck: "Oh my God, I have been giving my happiness over to the outside world!"

If things were going well my spirits soared. If things went poorly, or what I perceived to be poorly, my spirits dropped. Therefore, I was at the mercy of the outside world for my own moment-to-moment happiness. It was the easiest thing in the world to slide into. Another humbling moment.

Here's how it looked:

- happy for opportunity to stain woodshed for the person I love ↑
- started raining hard before I could complete task ↓
- surprise her by finishing it the next day before she got home ↑
- she didn't notice I had finished it and stained over what I did ↓
- she bought me a massage for helping her ↑
- massage therapist didn't show ↓
- therapist made amends with 2-hour hot stone massage ↑
- discovered I had free coupons for Ben & Jerry's ↑
- at the scoop shop they told me they expired ↓

As soon as the whole picture lay before my very eyes and I recognized what I was doing to myself without knowing it I had to laugh. How easy to forget! What a cosmic joke! My spirits lifted. ↑

This time they lifted from within. In other words, I did not use the excuse of anything external to allow my feelings to lift.

Except here is something interesting: Before when my spirits lifted and fell it was also from within! It only looked like the outside world doing it to me. It was still me within, using the Three Principles of Mind, Consciousness and Thought perfectly, allowing myself to be brought up and brought down, giving me the illusion of the outside world doing it to me.

If we pin our happiness on what happens in the outside world we're at its mercy.

It's never the outside world!

In that little sentence the emphasis seems to be on "outside world." But the emphasis really is on the word "*never*." To grasp *never* is what separates the men from the boys and the women from the girls. *Never* is so important because something will always look and feel *as if it really is* the outside world. We would swear to it!

But it isn't. Once again it is only consciousness seducing us, doing its job perfectly, manufacturing our feelings from whatever we're thinking and making them seem so real.

8. THE CRUX

Just to be sure, I looked up the word "crux" in the *American Heritage Dictionary*. It defines "crux" as, "1. ...critical point; 2. The basic or essential thing."

I wondered what learners believed to be the crux of the Three Principles. I asked them to come up with two to five words that describe the crux of it all. Their answers were all over the map.

I, of course, had to ask myself the same question. I sank into reflection. I almost startled myself with the four words that came to me. The more I reflected on these the more I realized their truth, at least for me. No one I asked came up with any of these words.

The crux of what the Three Principles are all about, to me:

Creation
Illusion
Essence
Oneness

Might be wise to reflect on each. That is what we'll do in the next few chapters...

In Chapter 3 I state emphatically that the Principles are a description, not a prescription. That notwithstanding, I cannot emphasize enough that when we suffer in any way—such as my suffering I describe later in this book—it only means we are not seeing the Three Principles deeply enough. In other words, if in any moment we *truly see* creation, illusion, essence and Oneness at work within us, all our suffering and misery vanishes in that instant.[6] This is the hope for the Principles; therefore, the hope for us all; therefore, the hope for humanity.

---

[6] I am not talking, here, about cataclysmic events thrust upon people from the outside world, such as from a tsunami, an earthquake, a hurricane or tornado, a flood, a war, severe injury or illness or the like. Or am I? As horrible as those disastrous events can be, they occur in the external world. We still take them in through our own thinking and consciousness, and that becomes how we experience them, it is what we feel about them and is what our life becomes in relation to them.

9. CREATION

On my 2014 European tour I visited Amsterdam, one of the few places I did not have a scheduled seminar. Fine with me! I checked into my hotel, decided not to partake of Amsterdam's famous wild nightlife and went up to my room. A sign in the lobby announced breakfast the next morning.

After a decent night's sleep I spent a much-appreciated restful morning in my room reorganizing my belongings, then hopped downstairs to partake of their breakfast. Since I carried my own gluten-free cereal I ate very little of theirs, just a banana and a little orange juice.

At checkout I noticed a 15 euro breakfast charge on my bill, the equivalent of $20 U.S. I had assumed breakfast was free! I hardly ate anything. I spoke to the people at the desk. They were unmoved.

I found myself angry. They had not made it clear! It was outrageous. I stayed angry at them—for about four minutes—

—until I got angry at myself for not being more careful and checking first. I stayed angry at myself—for about one minute—

—until the thought came to me, "Wait a second! Do I want to waste my time being angry?" Here I am in beautiful Amsterdam, ready to visit the famous Rijksmuseum. Do I want to take my anger with me to the museum? It wouldn't make any sense. And just like that—snap of fingers—my anger disappeared.

Each different feeling I experienced—anger at them, anger at myself, realizing how it would not serve me well—came courtesy of my own thinking. Each was my very own creation.

The Rijksmuseum is perhaps the best art museum I have ever visited, and I have seen many. Besides being an artist herself, my mother had a special interest in art history, taught many classes and couldn't help teaching me, so she dragged me to many museums.

Though I can't exactly say I appreciated it as a kid I now had to admit I'd absorbed a lot more than I thought. Now I can truly appreciate great art. Thank you, Ma! Normally on my trips I shy away from visiting museums because with only a brief time in each city I would rather be outside—I'm an outdoors kind of guy. But this one was special. Here in the land of Rembrandt and Van Gogh, probably my two favorite artists, how could I not go?

Walking through the Rijksmuseum I could not believe how many gorgeous paintings hung on those walls, painted by some of the great masters of all time, including many great paintings from artists I'd never heard of. When I got to Rembrandt's brilliant self-portrait with golden turban I stopped and stared. How could he capture the light in his paintings the way he did? Awe-inspiring! Perhaps even more special if it's possible, Vermeer's "The Milkmaid," the one where a woman appears to be pouring milk out of a pitcher into a bowl, which has always been one of my favorite paintings. This painting's small size really surprised me. The photograph-like realism, the detail, is nothing short of miraculous. How did he do that? Four times I went back to stare at it. Seeing these and other masters' original works moved me.

I then walked across the park to the Van Gogh museum. No painter ever created greater expression in his paintings. Close up I could see his inch-long narrow brush or pallet knife strokes, one after another filling the space. Then one steps back to see raw emotion. Again I felt moved.

In that instant the thought came to me: Every one of all these awe-inspiring paintings began with a blank canvas.

A blank canvas! Along with some paints, a few paintbrushes and pallet knives.

Each blank canvas carries unlimited potential—built right within it. Anything could be painted on this canvas! All possibilities exist within each blank canvas.

Then creation begins. Each painting comes out differently. One canvas could turn into a masterwork. Another could be painted all black. Another could be painted like a kid's drawing. Another totally abstract. Every art-class student looks at the same life model and each painting comes out different. A trillion people can look at the same nude body and a trillion different paintings or drawings would be created—not one the same. Everyone sees differently. No way of seeing is the truth. None are really the object being painted. Yet each is that painter's truth, each painter's truth his or her own creation.

I then had the thought, "Whoa, this is our life!"

We are each given a blank canvas on which to paint our lives. Blank pure consciousness—then we imprint it with a thought. Different thoughts, using the same creative power; different lives created using the same power. Completely different paintings; completely different lives. The blank canvas/pure consciousness is the pure potential of each of our lives, the pure potential owned by every human being. Who would have ever imagined that Barack Obama, from his very humble beginnings and African American roots, could have ended up President of the United States of America? Who would have ever thought that young Sydney Banks, running around the streets of the Leith district of Edinburgh, Scotland would have had an enlightenment experience that helped hundreds of thousands of lives and will likely help millions and potentially change psychology as we know it? Pure potential! On the canvas of life anything can be painted via the power of Thought. Then our thinking appears on the canvas for the world to see. Like the canvas, Consciousness allows us to experience it—otherwise we'd be painting into the air, and it would mean nothing.

We can create anything, and whatever we create will be brought to life by consciousness. Then we get to experience our creations through our senses. Life, art—same thing!

As with oil paints, if we don't like what we see, in the next moment we can re-create it, paint over it, begin anew, when new thought comes. Each new day offers this for our lives; each new moment. We are never stuck with our own creations—unless we allow ourselves to be.

Same with a guitar sitting in a room unplayed. Total potential to be any kind of music: folk, heavy metal, jazz, country, classical, classic rock, soul, rap, Hawaiian, Spanish, Malian—anything! Thought makes it be played in any of those different ways. The plucking of the string creates a vibration within one's consciousness. This vibration hits our ear drums, which also begin vibrating. The sound we hear at the other end comes through our own thinking, picked up by our consciousness. Sometimes the music we hear is beautiful; sometimes it grates on the nerves. This can happen even with the same song at different times. Because we, as hearers or seers, have our own thoughts, our own creation, which makes us appreciate something—or not—in each different moment.

The public of his day couldn't handle Van Gogh's art. He went crazy and died a pauper. Now his artwork fetches millions. Different thinking.

The point, of course, is our own lives. Just like that blank canvas or unplayed instrument our lives could be—*will* be—anything we think them to be. Every time something happens to us or we find ourselves in some circumstance or situation we stand before that blank canvas about to be painted or the guitar about to be played. It's all up to the way we use our brushes or hands—all a result of our creative power of Thought brought to life by Consciousness.

Creation itself!

10. WHAT DO WE CREATE? ILLUSION

My sister, Joanne, was the last to leave our Nantasket Beach family cottage for the summer. Since I would be returning later to close the place for the winter she left me a handwritten note on the kitchen table.

I read the first line. "Bad is all made up."

"Wow," I thought, "that is a brilliant statement! I didn't know Jo understood the Three Principles!"

I scrutinized it again. This time it read, "Bed is all made up."

Oops.

Both are true.

* * *

I saw a review of the movie, *Saving Mr. Banks* (not Syd) in Vermont's *Seven Days* weekly. Could this reviewer possibly have seen the same movie I did? He proclaimed it a candidate for worst movie of the year. This movie had moved me so much it sent emotional shudders through me.

Seems to me this reviewer had watched the movie but hadn't really listened to it. He didn't understand what it was really about. This movie is about the creation of illusion.

First, there is the phenomenal creative process Walt Disney and his staff underwent to fashion *Mary Poppins* out of the book by P.L. Travers. Walt Disney inspired the project, then handed the story to his staff, who had to create an illusion that came alive on the screen, including creating a script, creating sets, creating animation alongside regular actors, creating a musical score, creating new songs, creating choreography and much more. *Saving Mr. Banks* did a wonderful job showing this creative process at work.

Before that, came the creation of the original book. Helen Lyndon Goff, writing under the pen name, P.L. Travers, had to create the story in the first place. Like that blank canvas or guitar, writing begins with a blank page, a pen or pencil or typewriter or computer, and all we have at our disposal is our imagination, words and the ability to type or write. Out of that white blankness can come a story that moves people to laugh and cry—one creation from all possibilities of a blank page.

Yet, neither of these is the most important creation of illusion portrayed in *Saving Mr. Banks*. What the movie reviewer missed most is the story of how Helen Lyndon Goff, beginning with the blank page of her own life, used her creative power of Thought to create her own life. At least according to the movie, what Goff created made her miserable and appeared to contribute to making the lives of other people around her miserable, too. This amazing woman, who with her own thinking created the incredible Mary Poppins, also with her own thinking created a miserable life for herself. Then she got to live with the "real" feeling of it. To be Helen Goff and to be around her did not look like a barrel of laughs. *Saving Mr. Banks* became the metaphor for saving herself. This reviewer missed all of that.

More important, this movie is about each one of us. With unlimited creation at our disposal we have the free will to come up with any life we want. We write our own script, we create the movie of our lives, and it comes out exactly the way we want it to look and sound. Oh, we may say we don't want our lives to look this way, but who created it?

Please, I am not at all saying if a kid grows up in an abusive household she or he is creating this. Rather, what that child is creating is her or his own personal experience of the beatings, the screaming, the put-downs.

Helen's father was apparently a nice, loving man but became an alcoholic, died from alcoholism and her mother didn't know how to cope. So little Helen took her gift of creation and, using her circumstances as a reason, made herself miserable. But here's the amazing thing: Largely as a result of the way Walt Disney dealt with Goff, she ended up creating a different life for herself than the miserable, obstreperous one she had created to that point. She created a different, nicer feeling, in which she then lived. Such power! New life! Not only did this movie reviewer miss all this and pan the movie, but most of the rest of us miss this truth about our own lives.

But here is the important point: If Goff first created a miserable life that felt real, then after dealing with Walt Disney created a happier life that felt real, which one is really real? Both realities, in truth, are illusions!

How important is this? It's one of the two most important things we can know about ourselves: We are the creators of our own life illusions, which we call reality, and then we get to live with the feeling of whatever illusions we've created. Yet, whatever illusions we've created can change with new thought so we're never stuck with our current illusions. Life is forever changing because thought is forever changing.

So who do we want to be? What do we want our lives to become? What will we accept for ourselves? Out of the creative potential to be anything, who writes our script and how will we write it? Do we want to be what we are experiencing right now? Do we want to create misery as Goff did, or do we want to be who we *really* are inside (which is the other most important thing we can know—as we will see in following chapters.)

I want to be very clear here. I am not saying we should go out of our way to think up what we would like our lives to materialize. I am saying that whatever happens to us in the outside world, with our power of Thought we (often inadvertently) create the meaning it has for our lives and call it reality when it is really only an illusion of our own creation.

We get to decide which illusions we accept for ourselves.

* * *

The primary difference between Three Principles therapy/counseling/coaching and all other therapies/counseling/coaching is Three Principles understanding explains that all our problems are illusions.

I do not make this statement lightly. Is it really true we can have no problem or misery that is not an illusion of our own creation? No anger or rage that is not an illusion of our own creation? No worry or anxiety that is not an illusion of our own creation? No depression that is not an illusion of our own creation? Are there no exceptions?

There are *no exceptions*! Why are these emotions all illusion? Because that feeling, that perception, that "reality" *would not exist* if we did not create the thought! I'm not saying we go out of our way to create the thought—it just seems to come, most times, but it is still created by us—no one else![7] And even though we create the thought, that illusion could still not exist if we did not create another thought that took the first thought seriously. In other words, none of these emotions would exist if we did not first make them up, then believe them. To truly realize this is life changing, and humbling. [Note: For another perspective on this, see Chapter 11.]

What about chemical imbalances? Faulty wiring? Trauma caused by severe abuse in childhood? Rape? Post-Traumatic Stress Disorder (PTSD)? Am I saying these are illusions?!

I don't deny these are terrible. I don't deny when things like this happen to human beings it is very easy to develop thinking that works against ourselves and creates problems. When the perpetrator created and committed the horrible action we certainly had no control over that.

Agreed, the trauma was horrible when it happened. But now it's over. Or even if it's ongoing we still have the power of creation to make meaning of it for our lives. What are we going to create: something to harbor and haunt ourselves with for the rest of our lives, or something that was horrible then but now can be left behind and no longer affect us? This very process is the creation of illusion. Yes, the event was horrific! But how far into the future will we allow it to rule us, take us over? This is where it becomes our own responsibility.

Sitting in a waiting room I picked up a *People* magazine and read an article about Jayce Dugard, the woman abducted at eleven years old in Antioch, California and kept prisoner for eighteen years, during which time she gave birth to two daughters, courtesy of her captor. Horrific! At the time of this article she was 36 and had an extremely impressive view of life. Of all the possibilities she could have come up with about her unimaginable trauma and losing eighteen years of her life, she said, "Something terrible happened to me, but I'm not going to let it ruin the rest of my life…" If after what she went through she can think at such a high level of consciousness, this possibility exists for us all.

---

[7] Some believe God sends certain thoughts to us and therefore they are not our creation. But even if true, once it gets into our own mind it becomes our creation, and we must own it.

Okay, that may be true about trauma, but what about chemical imbalances? Even here we must look closely. A chemical imbalance is real; it exists. It can be measured. But how does the chemical imbalance get there in the first place?

Often after a storm a little sand cliff appears on an ocean beach. At Nantasket Beach this cliff can sometimes be a foot high; in Florida I've seen it up to five feet. The waves then come in and bang against the cliff, akin to thoughts banging up against a chemical imbalance in the brain. The cliff affects the shape the waves then take; the chemical imbalance affects the shape one's thoughts then take. But stepping back further, how did the cliff get there in the first place? From the waves! The waves created the cliff! The cliff would not exist without them. Could it be the chemical imbalance comes from how we have used our thinking in the first place?

If we look closely we can see the imbalance does not always affect a person the same way at every moment. At different times people with chemical imbalances have better or worse moods. The trick is to see *Thought* way bigger than we have seen thought. Candace Pert discovered how movement of the molecules—peptides and receptors—produces emotions independent of and bypassing the brain; that the body has a *mind* of its own that has nothing to do with the brain. She also discovered that thought moves molecules. And the thoughts that move molecules most are most often not the thoughts we are aware of; it's those niggling thoughts behind the scenes, the ones so far beyond our recognition we would never even consider them thought. But if our mind is doing it, whether we know it or not, it's thought.

* * *

When the aptly-named Mad River in Vermont runs high it covers up most of its usually visible rocks. I'm pretty sure the rocks still exist under the high water, but I no longer have an experience of them. In spring, sometimes a huge ice-jam builds up from the melting ice, where big chunks of ice break off. The chunks can't pass between some of the biggest boulders sticking up through the water, so the ice jams upon them. The river keeps flowing, so more and more ice chunks jam against them, and it builds and builds until the Mad River Valley is in danger of flooding. This is not unlike a thought-jam in our minds. We think we have a problem, which we inadvertently created, which we experience via our consciousness, and our thought-jam builds and builds. On the ice-jammed Mad River it sometimes rains hard. The river rises. Suddenly, with a great burst and crunch, the ice-jam clears. This is what happens when a new insight arises from wisdom. Swoosh! All whisked away in an instant. New creation of new illusion. Some illusions feel healthier than others.

Once after a huge storm, part of a large roof frame floated down river and lodged atop one of the boulders near Amy's house. After the river died down some, we tried to dislodge it from the rock but it was way too heavy. For days it stayed. One day it rained ferociously, the river already fairly high. We walked down to the roaring river and saw the roof frame teetering on the brink. Gingerly we waded crotch-deep into the river and using only our fingers moved it off the rock with ease. Before, we had struggled in vain and could not budge it. New creation came along and lifted it easily. New thought comes along and raises our level of consciousness.

We could have struggled with all our might to get that roof frame off that rock from that same low level of consciousness. Or, we could wait for higher levels of water when it was no longer a heavy roof frame; it was a piece of cake.

This is what cures people of their illusory problems—seeing from a higher level of consciousness, from which they transcend those problems. From the higher levels we look back down at the problem, and it can no longer even look like a problem. New creation. The problem goes *poof*. Because to call it a problem is an illusion.

When people grasp the Three Principles intellectually they say, "Yeah, I know it's coming from my own thinking."

Oddly, although they say they know they're making it up, once it *is* made up it *is reality to them*. When people see "reality" they cannot see illusion—not at the same time. Remember, it is *all* illusion; no exceptions.

What we're experiencing is *only us doing it to ourselves*. It can *only* be that, with consciousness grabbing the thought and seducing us into believing it. The perfect system! Once we truly see *creation of illusion*, we are free.

Why free? Because if we don't see illusion we see its opposite: reality. Seeing "reality" gets to us, brings us down, lowers our spirits, infuriates us. To see it for what it is releases us from its chains.

It's like wandering through the desert without water, so thirsty we can barely stand it. Suddenly we see water in the distance. We get jazzed, go after it. We can almost taste it. But we get there and find no water. It's not reality at all. But it really, really looked like water! As soon as we realize no water exists there and it was only a real-looking mirage, from that moment thereafter, we are no longer fooled by how it looks. We might still see it but will not be taken in by it, because we no longer believe the so-called "truth" of it.

No matter how much anyone knows about the Three Principles everyone sometimes experiences their illusions as real. Everyone! I certainly do, as will become quite evident later in this book. Even Syd Banks did. We're in good company. No one is immune from the lure. What is our protection? To truly understand *creation of illusion.* In any moment we truly see this it is impossible at the same time to get sucked into "reality." If we don't see it in any moment we will be.

It's like wearing a bulletproof vest. The vest stands between a bullet and a potentially maimed body, protecting us. Seeing creation of illusion is our bulletproof vest.

And we have the free will to put on the vest—or not—with Thought.

Of course the biggest illusion of all is the illusion of the self. *Who we Really are is not who we think we are.* I don't want to say more about this here. It is a statement for quiet reflection. Hopefully, what it means will emerge over the next two chapters.

11. ESSENCE AND ONENESS

What exists, what remains, once we see illusion for what it is?

The essence of who we are as human beings, spiritual beings.

We *are* the essence of who we are. We are essence! Our true nature. We can only create the illusion that we are not.

Our essence contains pure peace, pure love and pure wisdom. How do we know? Because when our mind clears or shuts down or quiets from its personal thinking, this is what remains as our experience. We feel closer to it.

What is our essence connected to? The Oneness of All Things. We are one little teeny part of the Oneness. No real separation. A part, not apart. It only looks as if we're separate.

Within the realm of essence and Oneness no problems that appear within the world of form even exist. Within this realm all our form-problems are a joke.

* * *

On our first road trip together Amy and I and several educators from her school traveled to Richmond, British Columbia to hear Syd Banks. On the final day of the seminar as Syd finished speaking the audience rose for an ovation. I had been sitting behind Amy and saw her dart quickly through the applauding crowd and make a bee-line for the stage. The throngs seemed to part for her surreally like the Red Sea. Amy couldn't understand how she could get to Syd like that, but she hopped upon the stage to thank him before others surrounded him. From the audience I watched Amy and Syd give each other a big hug.

As Amy came off stage I tried to get to her through the packed crowd, but couldn't. Amy's face appeared strange, as if something huge had happened to her. I wanted to know. Finally, I broke through. Amy said she couldn't talk right now and scooted outside to a nearby park. I started to follow her. Another of her school staff appeared and asked to come along. Normally I would have been happy to be with Terri because I really liked her, but now I only wanted to be alone with Amy. If Amy wanted to talk about what had happened I wanted to be there; if Amy needed to be silent I wanted to be silent next to her, supporting her, holding the space.

We followed her into the park. Amy turned to us. "I really need to be off by myself right now," she said, and walked off alone.

Terri and I strolled around talking for some time, my mind often drifting to Amy and whatever had happened to her. Suddenly I looked up and saw Amy standing high atop a hill on a rock next to a waterfall. She spotted me and put her hand over her heart. I sent it back.

We climbed up to her. I asked Terri if Amy and I could be alone for a few minutes. Yes. Amy and I sat on a park bench. She tried to explain what she saw but had a hard time getting words out, the feeling emanating from her so powerful it felt as if I was basking in the light of her and her discovery. Amy's words—not that they can do justice to the experience—went something like this:

"Syd kind of ripped my mind open. What I heard from Syd is very present in me. I felt scared of losing it because of the way life can take over. Right after the seminar I felt it going away, so I left my thoughts as I entered the park and a serene feeling came over me as I melded with what was around me. The water, the trees, the ducks were not those things. I did not name them but felt them, their energy. I'd look at things like plants or the bridge or whatever, and everything was just all together, but it was too much almost—almost like I couldn't stick with it even though I wanted to. Of course as soon as I wanted to it was gone. But I had this moment without any thoughts at all, the feeling came over me of energy existing before time, space and matter, the life force that exists and is ever-present, regardless of life and death. Energy taking form, love taking form, truth taking form, purity taking form—call it anything, the words are irrelevant because IT does not change; only the form changes. The form is personal; life and death are personal. Through Consciousness, formless takes on an existence through Thought, formless takes on meaning, and whatever the form, the formless is forever—life and death are forever the same because it is through Mind that the formless exists always, always, always."

I was speechless. Amy had experienced something akin to what I had felt that time with Syd, for which I had no words. Amy articulated what she saw far better than I ever could.

For a moment in time, she *saw* Oneness.

Running on the beach at low tide I remembered I used to think Oneness was like little grains of sand on a beach, each grain a different size, shape and color, yet all one thing: sand on a beach. But even as part of the whole beach, in between those grains of sand separation still exists, so it is not an accurate metaphor.

Running along, I realized Oneness is more like drops of water in the ocean. There is no separation. It is all One. Who we are in relation to the Universe is not like a grain of sand on a beach but more a drop of water in the ocean. Any separation is illusion.

As I ran on in a state of deep reflection, feeling the wet sand under my feet with each step, a strange sensation suddenly overcame me. I could no longer tell where my feet ended and where the watery sand began. It became impossible to distinguish between foot and wet sand because there was no separation between the two. It was the oddest, most surreal feeling. [*Twilight Zone* music, please.]

* * *

To bring this full circle, it is important to note that we have the opportunity to see any of our creations of illusion through essence and Oneness, to see any of our thought-creations with love. We have the opportunity to allow any thought that arises—even thoughts that give us an uncomfortable feeling—to transform through grace. Either would be new creation. I do not want Chapters 3, 9 and 10 to be misinterpreted; I am not suggesting to exert will to create new thought. Thought arises from the formless, from Universal Mind. We don't have to do anything to get new thoughts; we simply open ourselves to hear them. If we allow ourselves to fall out of our thinking into the quiet we can hear healthier, wiser thoughts within. Such thoughts come with a beautiful feeling, a Knowing feeling. We have the opportunity to rest in the formless and wait for deeper insight from wisdom to arise. We might hear something like, "Oh, what I'm experiencing really is only an illusion of my own creation!" Such insight would make many aspects of life look different. Later we may get thoughts that still feel real, from which it seems we can't escape. This is because further underneath we have hidden, stickier thinking that still believes in the reality it created. But the opportunity always exists to bear this feeling gracefully, to trust that deeper wisdom in the form of new thought is around the corner. This would be creation aligned with essence and Oneness.

However—and this is important—sometimes when so caught up or in the depths of despair we don't have our wits about us enough to fall out of our thinking into the quiet to allow new, wise thought to arise. But with a deep enough understanding of how it all really works within, some Knowing remains in the back of our minds even in this low state that allows us to ride out the storm, wait it out, until we can fall back into the quiet. Meanwhile, we know it would be unwise to make any major life decisions from this state, or even communicate with loved ones on whom we might take it out. So we wait and know when our mind eventually calms once again we will be able to hear wisdom from the formless Intelligence.

Once we truly grasp the four cruxes (to me) of the Three Principles—creation, illusion, essence and Oneness—we are home free. When we see them in action in the moment we cannot go wrong. Even if we don't see them in a moment but see them after the fact, we still can't go too far wrong. If we lose a few precious moments of life caught in a troubling illusion, so what? It would be great if we didn't lose those moments, but we do. What are we going to do, waste more moments thinking about our wasted moments? It doesn't make sense. That's all part of the illusion.

The whole idea, the secret to life, is for us to go back to the Source, the Source from whence we came. The trick is to realize the Source never left us. It has only been obscured by thought of our own creation, made to look and feel real by consciousness. That is the illusion, and we fall for it all the time because it is so seductive; we feel it right through our senses. But when we can see it all for what it *really* is, the illusion disappears and we are left with realization of the Source. We are free. Simplicity itself!

12. THE FORM AND THE FORMLESS

This was a tough chapter to write, so please bear with me. The intellect is especially useless for reading this chapter.

If our problems exist only in the world of form, stepping into the formless leaves them behind.

Unfortunately, the world of form is extraordinarily compelling. Consciousness won't allow us to let go of the forms we see as "reality." Once we get stuck in a form, from that point on our subsequent thinking is based on that "reality."

Since we reside in the world of form, how do we step into the world of the formless?

To stretch the ocean/beach metaphor of the previous chapter further, let's say the ocean represents the world of the formless [Please, I know the ocean is really form—this is a metaphor!] As the metaphorically formless ocean allows the capacity to have waves, so formless energy allows the capacity or power to have Thought and thus create thought-forms. To be clear: thoughts are form; the power of Thought to form thoughts is formless.

What if a bridge exists between these two worlds, and this bridge holds the secret to life?

What do I mean by a bridge? When an ocean wave breaks upon the shore and travels to its furthermost point, if we look very, very closely we can see almost the exact spot it dissipates.[8] At this exact point of dissipation it is no longer an ocean wave and it is not yet the beach. Yet it is both. The wave comes in and becomes the moment of dissipation. At that exact moment we cannot tell whether it is wave or beach. This precise moment is the metaphoric bridge between the form and the formless.

---

[8] This can be seen most clearly at low tide with small waves. It cannot be seen well when big waves roar in with much foam.

As that moment of dissipation of wave onto beach is the bridge between those two worlds, so a bridge exists at the exact point where formless energy of Thought creates a thought-form. If we can grasp that precise moment, simultaneously we could see both the creation at work and the product of it—creation itself. The creator and the created as one. The form and the formless are One.

If we can see that moment of creation between formless and form, what we call a "problem" would cease to exist because we would see its creation in the process of becoming. *We would see us doing it to ourselves, creating our own problem.* We would see it take shape, take form, out of the nothingness. We would see how our problem would not even exist but for our own creation of it from the formless. We would see "reality" for what it really is; meaning, it isn't.

Beach sand is form. As solid, hard form, beach sand is real, of course. But sand is not exactly what it seems. Take white, tan, brown or black sand and place it under a microscope and we see a beautiful, colorful world of teensy crushed rocks, shells and crystals. The more powerful the microscope the more space we see between the solid grains. Put it under an electron microscope and we see even what looked like solid objects are mostly space. Molecules floating in space. Atoms gyrating within the space of the molecule itself. Electrons spinning around the space within the atom. When the Large Hadron Collider at the CERN Laboratories pulverizes atoms it sometimes allows the possibility of seeing a Higgs boson, which apparently sometimes appears as form and sometimes as a formless wave (a different kind of wave), depending on how one looks at it. Things can get mighty bizarre at the intersection of the form and the formless.

So as I walk along Nantasket Beach at low tide and keep my eyes open I see the different patterns in the sand. I look to my right and see windblown sand. I look to my left and see ripples of sand made from the rippled ocean. I look farther to the left and see muddy, watery sand. I look even farther and see a sandbar. Straight ahead of me are big potholes where waves have carved out parts of the beach. All different forms of form—all examples of possibilities of what can be created in the world of form, from (here, metaphorically) the formless creation of it all.

This is what *all* our problems are: Creations from the formless! Our very own creations from formless Thought, brought to us courtesy of formless Universal Mind. When we can see the very point of creation we are home free because we know our problems would not exist but for our own creation of them. These problems that feel so important to us *would not even exist!*

To me, that is really something! The implications are mind-blowing.

To truly see this is powerful in and of itself. It may be even more powerful to realize that whatever our little self-created problems, they mean nothing to the world of pure spirit energy. Do the crevices on the sand mean anything to the ocean that created them? The ocean doesn't care. The formless doesn't care about our problems; it only allows us the capacity to create them and therefore experience them however we want. Think about it: Could formless energy possibly care about our little form-problems? If we die in the next moment, what would our problems be? Some people believe when we die that's it, period; therefore, our problems are over, along with everything else. Others believe when we die our souls move on to the formless realm where no problems exist; thus, the problems are over. Still others believe our soul reincarnates into a new life in a different time, and we begin again with a new, fresh slate; therefore, no more old problems. Some may believe we take our unresolved problems with us into other lifetimes, but even if true, would we not begin anew in that lifetime with the power of Thought and Consciousness to re-create them or not?

And we think our problems are such a big deal! We let them drive us crazy, when in the world of the formless our problems are laughable. We've created something that is nothing but only looks like something, about which we get bent out of shape. A nothing that looks like something. Hilarious!

When we have a problem we can't seem to let go of—such as my own that I describe in detail later in this book—if we can truly see the spiritual realm, the realm of essence and Oneness, the realm of formless energy, the moment of creation, that problem would disappear. In my own example I could not see it—until I did. And there were still parts I didn't. So often we can't see beyond the form because we get so seduced by consciousness.

* * *

Richard [from Chapter 2] speaks again:

The day after the caves we had a class with Jack he called "Beyond the Known." We gathered in the morning and started with silence, he hit his chimes and started talking in the gentle and powerful way only he does. I listened to people's questions and comments, and after a while I drifted away sort of into and under the sound of all the voices. The meaning of the words melted into a soar as I sunk down under the surface of what was being said. I was sort of emerged into a sea of energy from which the whole phenomenon of language stemmed and what we were trying to grasp originated.

Tears floated up from being connected to this formless source behind it all. The main recognition of this formless undefined experience was a feeling of love. In this state of fulfillment I was turned inside-out and a clarity dawned upon me of how I, without this union, always try to seek it outside of myself, be it in a relationship, object, achievement or outer circumstance.

In the corner of his eye Jack noticed me. At the next break he asked, "What happened?"

As I slowly rose from the chair I dressed up into my body again as if it was my personal physical manifestation of my being to be able to navigate in this physical "reality." Trying to answer Jack's question I felt my thinking machinery reluctantly trying to explain, as it simultaneously realized its own futility. I could see in Jack's eyes that he saw my struggle... or lack of it, which ended up in a heart-filled laugh of understanding of what was going on.

New insight is always the way out, as we suddenly jump levels of consciousness and are able to see "reality" itself as merely thought. The "reality" in which we have been believing so fiercely then dissipates, and we are left with our formless essence.

13. LEVELS OF CONSCIOUSNESS

First, I need to clear up a couple of common misunderstandings about levels of consciousness. Higher and lower levels do not imply better and worse, good or bad. Better and worse are merely value judgments ascribed by people using their power of Thought. Nor does the existence of levels imply we should strive to be at higher levels. With the Three Principles there are no shoulds; there is no trying to get anywhere. Levels of consciousness is merely a description of what is[9] *(and if anyone disagrees with that statement, read on). When reading this section it is especially important to not read through what one already believes.*

Someone near and dear to me is a musician, a good-looking bloke with lots of sex appeal and stage presence who often has women falling at his feet. One day he met a woman who stuck. She was a knock-out—very exotic-looking. They hit it off and fell in love. He started thinking he could maybe settle down with her. They moved in together and got serious. She seemed a woman he could be with for the rest of his life, start a family.

He spent a lot of time away touring with his band. She didn't mind. She had her own life and interests in modeling and the fashion industry. One day he came home to find her with another man. This devastated him! She begged forgiveness. She didn't know what had gotten into her. It would never happen again, she said. He gave her another chance.

---

[9] As I note in *Prevention from the Inside-out*, some people say, "You shouldn't say 'higher and lower.'" But as Ken Wilber points out in *A Brief History of Everything*, people who say hierarchy is not as good as some other way are setting up their own hierarchy, one thing (no hierarchy) being better than another (hierarchy). We can't get away from hierarchy. What's important is, like it or not, at any given moment we have thoughts that either take us farther away from our spiritual essence/pure consciousness to varying degrees, or bring us closer it; hence, levels.

A month later he found her with still another man. Double devastated! Suddenly this confident musician felt lost, completely out of sorts. Depressed.

I wrote to him. After telling him how bad I felt for him and how I was there for him, I wrote this:

I know this is very hard. I also know from my own experience that the way we take it is even more important for our well-being. What I mean is this: Picture a ladder going from below the ground up to the heavens. Each rung represents a possible thought you could have about this situation. At the very bottom level are thoughts of murder. At the very top is total peace and love for everything and everybody. In between are uncountable other possible thoughts. It might look something like this [*read from the bottom up*]:

-	-Total peace and love
-	-Gratefulness for the time I had with her when it was really good
-	-I'm going to be okay, no matter what she did
-	-Hope, because lots of good women are out there waiting to meet me
-	-Humility for whatever my part may have been in it not working out
-	-Compassion, for she grew up in a screwed-up family with few morals
-	-Oh well, that's the way life goes sometimes; luckily I found out
-	-This really sucks
-	-Because of what she did, I can never trust another woman again
-	-Total devastation: she ruined my life
-	-Thoughts of murder

And many more possibilities.

Now here's the big question: Which one is reality? Which one is really the way to think in a situation like this? There is no real way! That means we make up whichever one we land on and then call it "my life." We have that power. The only problem is whichever level (rung) we think we are on produces the feeling we get to live with about it. So we make up which rung we're on, then we get that feeling!

I don't know how much of that he heard, but here is what's important: No matter what difficult or devastating situation we find ourselves in, similar levels of consciousness exist as above. All life is levels of consciousness. We make up the level we land on and get stuck at. It's the only way we can have that particular feeling or emotion.

Often I hear, "But I can't help feeling [or thinking] this way!

The secret to overcoming "I can't help thinking this way" is seeing the possibility of the existence of other levels. Truly seeing the simultaneous existence of all levels automatically raises our level of consciousness. Immediately this uncouples us from the particular "reality"-level on which we have been trapped.

Again, notice I did not say, "Try to think at a higher level." That would be a fool's mission because we would be "trying" from a lower level, from where we can't see very well.

* * *

A management consultant, Alex, asked if I would give him some coaching. I agreed. He had read my book, *Somebody Should Have Told Us!*, learned something of the Three Principles from me and several others, and we had a couple of sessions. I hadn't heard from him in a while, although over the years he referred a few people my way.

Out of the blue he emailed me and asked for another session. He requested that we cover two topics: 1) to go deeper into the Three Principles, now that he understood them better since we first talked; 2) to help him prepare for his upcoming holiday, which he was dreading.

Our conversation went something like this:

JP: Let me see if I understand this. You're dreading going on holiday to a beautiful island? What would make you do that?

A: It goes back to something that happened a few years back. Our consultancy had its most successful year ever, and then I took my family on holiday to celebrate.

JP: That's what made you depressed?

A: No. In order to reach that level of success I really had to bust my ass. I never worked harder in my life. It exhausted me. So when I arrived on this island with my family I was so spent I went into a deep depression. What made it worse was my wife reacted poorly. She's really attuned to pick up anything she thinks is even close to depression, and she gets on my case about it. Nothing makes me more depressed than her pointing out that I'm getting depressed. It just sends me into a tailspin, especially when I see it as just a prolonged, intense low mood. It's a huge trigger for me. It frustrates me and sends me deeper into despair. So we're about to go on another family holiday and I don't want it to happen again.

[*Note: I had to set aside for a moment Alex saying the cause of his exacerbated depression was his wife in the outside world, because wisdom guided me in a different direction.*]

JP: It sounds like your wife gets scared when you do anything that smacks of you going into depression.

A: That's true.

JP: It sounds to me like you do the same thing she does.

A: What do you mean?

JP: You get depressed (or show signs of it), then she gets scared and reacts out of her fear; then you get triggered by her reaction, then you get scared and react out of your fear. Same thing.

Alex became quiet.

JP: Infinite levels of consciousness exist from which it is possible to see anything. We pick one inadvertently and call it reality. Your wife allows the first sign of your depression to trigger her, she gets scared and says something out of fear, which triggers you, then you get frustrated and scared and go into despair. Instead of getting triggered it would be just as possible to see her with compassion.

A: What do you mean?

JP: Compassion toward her because she gets worried about what your depression is going to mean for her and your family. She can't help herself; she just goes there, gets scared and acts out of it. That's something to feel compassion about.

A: I'm trying to wrap my head around what it would take for me to see my wife with compassion at those times, but I'm having trouble coming up with it.

JP: That's not what I mean. I'm not talking about trying to see her that way. Compassion is only one example of a level of consciousness. There are many other equally possible levels.

A: Name some.

JP: Well, for example, humility. She can't help herself from going down that road, but neither can you.

A: Oh.

JP: Or gratefulness. You told me you had a really good relationship with her 95% of the time, except when this one thing happens. What if you had only a 5% good and 95% difficult relationship, which some couples do, and around many issues other than this? But you don't! That's something to be grateful for. Or—love. She cares so much about you she doesn't want to see you depressed. That is so sweet!

A: Oh, that frees me up. I was trying to find a way to feel compassion for her, but that's not what you're saying. You're just saying that there are all these equal possibilities. That's very freeing.

JP: Yes, levels of consciousness is often misunderstood. Many people conclude they have to think their way to a higher level, but that's not what I mean at all. It's also worth noting that other levels exist far below your current level, such as violent outrage or suicidal thoughts. All are equal possibilities. And at the very top level there's pure consciousness—consciousness uncontaminated by any thinking. I mean, what's left within our consciousness when there is no thought? Just pure peace, pure universal love, and pure wisdom when our mind is so clear we get new insights or epiphanies from out of nowhere.

A: Huh, I always thought that was a function of Mind. I never thought of that as pure consciousness.

JP: Well, in a sense we're talking about the same thing. Universal Mind is both All things—the energy behind All things—Allness—and if it's All, then All must also be One—Oneness. I have trouble wrapping my head around that one, myself, but I feel the truth of it. So it's both like the pure white light coming into a prism and also all the colors of the rainbow coming out the other side. The aspect of pure Oneness of Mind is what enters our consciousness as pure white light, so to speak. And that's who we really are—our essence, our soul—and it contains those aspects of pure Mind: peace, love and wisdom. So that's within us—who we are—the spiritual "stuff" we're made of. Mind also gives us the power to have Consciousness and to have Thought. And when we have a thought it creates a form that contaminates our pure consciousness to a certain degree, and the extent to which our thoughts contaminate it is where the different levels of consciousness stem from.

A: Huh. So Mind is the light going into the prism, and the prism is consciousness. [*Alex paused.*] Isn't the prism also thought?

JP: Careful not to try to intellectualize the metaphor too much. What I mean is the light coming into the prism is pure, but it also contains all possibilities of levels within it. So when we have a thought, that thought enters the prism and comes out a particular color of the rainbow. It's like a kaleidoscope into which light shines. The kaleidoscope would show nothing but the light if not for the colors and shapes in it. So it's like the pure white light of Mind is all that would appear in our consciousness if we did not think up thoughts of all colors and shapes. We turn it a notch and see a particular design. Then we turn the kaleidoscope another notch, as with another thought, and we see a different design. The pure white light of Mind would be all that existed in our consciousness if not for thoughts creating the illusion of different levels.

A: Yes! I see. The possibility of all the levels exists within the prism, within Consciousness.

JP: Yes, absolutely! I just saw something new, too. It's simplicity itself! All that's ever going on is we use our power of Thought to create a thought that brings us to a particular level, and that level *is* the feeling we live with, which we call "real." That's all that's ever going on. It's the only thing that can ever drop us out of pure consciousness; or more accurately give us the illusion that we drop from it. How simple is that!

I didn't hear from Alex for a while after that, but he recently reached out to me to tell me that year he and his family had their best holiday ever, and his depression has not returned.

More on levels of consciousness in Chapter 19.

14. HIDDEN THOUGHTS AND ROOT UNDERLYING BELIEFS[10]

I'm not a very good cook—my thinking doesn't support it—but I make a mean tuna casserole. I make the best tuna casserole I've ever eaten. So one night alone at our family's Nantasket Beach summer cottage that's exactly what I did. I loved every forkful.

Later that night when shutting off downstairs lights to go to bed, in pitch darkness in the kitchen I sensed I'd forgotten to put away the leftover casserole. It still set on the counter next to the refrigerator exactly where I left it to cool before burdening the refrigerator with its heat.

In the darkness I grabbed the casserole dish handles. Suddenly I felt something crawling on my hands, up my arms. I gingerly dropped the casserole dish back on the counter, jumped around like a maniac, ran to the light switch and turned on the light.

Oh no! The entire casserole was full of ants. Apparently the glass cover did not fit snugly on the dish.

I'm embarrassed to say this but the next few moments wreaked of ant carnage. Usually I'm not one for killing God's little creatures, but this was too much. Poor innocent little ants! I hope they thoroughly enjoyed their last supper. I went to bed feeling guilty.

The next morning while running on the beach a thought occurred to me. Those ants would not have appeared on my counter in my casserole dish if the left-out casserole had not attracted them.

Ah ha! Same with our thoughts! The ants are akin to little thoughts scurrying around in our heads. It's hard to get rid of them. But the little scurrying thoughts would not even exist if not for a deeper, hidden, more primary root thought attracting them. The leftover casserole is like a big root thought—the root from which the trunk and all branches

---

[10] I originally titled this "core beliefs," but I didn't want to confuse it with the "core" or essence of our being.

and leaves grow. This primary root thought attracts all the other little thoughts to it like a magnet. Without the hidden root thought the little annoying thoughts would not exist in our minds.

More often than not this central thought usually consists of one of two things: a deeply held hidden fear, or an underlying belief held dearly. For example, if one sees through the eyes of "I'm not worthy," imagine all the scurrying, niggling little thoughts that show up attracted by a root belief such as that. They could fill a head as easily as ants fill a casserole dish.

These root, underlying beliefs work behind the scenes, hidden from view. We're not usually aware of them.

What root belief might we carry unknowingly that drives our entire being?

Actually, it may be unwise to go looking for our hidden, root beliefs because the search itself often lowers our spirits. Yet, if we experience the same kinds of difficulties again and again we could open ourselves to seeing what root may have grown and be hidden in the recesses of our minds. We could set our intention to see it, then forget about it and go about our business. When our mind relaxes, if we're meant to see a particular underlying belief, at some point it may pop into our heads. If we can't come up with one, we might ask our partner or closest friends for what they see are our underlying root beliefs. Often we can see them in others, and they can see them in us, but we can't commonly see our own.

Last point on this subject for now: Remember what we talked about in Chapter 10. It does little good to see our underlying belief or deeply hidden fear and bring it out into the light if we do not ultimately *see it for the illusion it is.*

15. WORRY AND HIDDEN THINKING

I mentioned earlier that before I found Three Principles understanding I gave numerous speeches and conducted many workshops around the United States on various aspects of prevention. I spoke at conferences from Alaska to Florida, Maine to California. I used to have a recurring dream—not a true recurring dream because the dream always happened in different places under different circumstances with different stories, but they always had the same theme.

The dreams went something like this: I'm scheduled to speak at a conference but I either get lost and can't find my way, or I get the time wrong and will be late, or some random event derails me from getting there. As hard as I try—and I try with all my might—I can never quite get there. In real life this never happened (except that one time arriving late in Aspen, Colorado) but in my dreams it showed up often and vividly. Great anxiety accompanied each occurrence. I often woke up sweating, unsure at first whether it really happened.

It doesn't take a rocket scientist or a Freudian psychologist to uncover that I had fear of screwing up. It caused a great deal of worry—worry that my presentations would not be good enough, worry about letting people down. I cannot handle the thought of letting people down.

This had nothing to do with feeling competent. I had things to say that no one else in the prevention field talked about; many practitioners and organizations were interested. This had nothing to do with my performance; I went over well—my presentation ratings averaged "very good," with some excellent, and only a few fair. What did I have to worry about? But I did worry. The larger the anticipated crowd the more worried I became. I used to have to go to the bathroom like clockwork every time before I went on. Kept me regular.

At the time it never occurred to me to ask myself why I worried about my presentations, to ask why others didn't worry who weren't as competent as I, to ask why I worried sometimes more than other times. I had no clue then that worry was my own creation, that I made it all up. I truly believed the presentation or event caused my feeling; I never imagined my own thinking caused my worry. With my incredible gift of the power of Thought I created thoughts such as—

"How will I do?"

"Am I going to do it well enough?"

"Okay, last time was good, but this is a new event with new people. What will happen this time?"

I didn't even know such (mostly future) thoughts whizzed through my mind. They were hidden from me. I simply got a "real" feeling in my gut. Quicker than the blink of an eye, good ol' consciousness took what I didn't know I was thinking and converted it into a "real" gut-filled feeling of worry. Worked to perfection every time.

But out of all possible options, why did I come up with worry? Why worry, and not something else? Because I had a thinking habit! Somehow I picked up worry from my childhood, from the way I interpreted what my mother said to me—never her intention I'm sure. I picked up fear that I wouldn't be able to do it well enough. I picked up a belief that I had to be extra vigilant to do it well enough. Those kinds of thoughts equaled worry about myself, which equaled strain. The presentation became merely a convenient excuse to have my ingrained worry rear its head.

Consciousness doesn't care what I think; it gives me a real experience of any thought I come up with. Then it seduces me into believing the reality of it, making me forget completely it is my very own creation of illusion tricking me. Yet, it's all me. Me! If I were not creating worry it would not exist!

The perfect system. Simplicity itself. This cannot be repeated enough.

Unbeknownst to me, other equal possibilities of thought beckoned.

Suppose I had the thought, "Hey, I've got some great information most of them don't know, and they can either take it or leave it." No worry there. I would feel okay, no matter how they reacted.

Suppose I had the thought, "I don't care whether I do well or not; makes no difference to me." No worry there. I would feel haughty; the audience be damned.

Suppose I thought, "The only thing I can do is my best and if it's not good enough for them, sorry," No worry there. I would feel comfort within myself.

Suppose I thought, "Oh, the butterflies in my stomach are just a bubble of energy—adrenaline kicking in so I can rise to the occasion." No worry there. I would be exhilarated.

Suppose I simply wondered how I could turn them on to the importance of what I have to say. No worry. I would feel challenged.

Suppose I had complete faith I knew my material so well that whatever came out of my mouth would be simply tapping into the vast resource within me and would come out well. Instead of worry I would feel solid in my complete faith.

All equal possibilities, and many more.

As I have said repeatedly, simply knowing all other possibilities exist within the realm of creation would in and of itself take the pressure off the worry. I would know it can only be me making up one possibility. Do I really want to take seriously the worry of one of my own creations? All equal illusions!

Or, if I realize, in light of my spiritual essence/pure spirit/pure consciousness/the Oneness of all things, none of it matters anyway, I certainly would have nothing to worry about.

But I knew none of this then.

In the car one day listening to a sports-talk radio show I heard former NBA[11] player Eddie Johnson say he's never seen a U-Haul[12] behind a hearse. At first I didn't get what he meant. Then it hit me. When we die we can pull all our worries behind us, take them with us, and what will they mean then? How serious will they be then? So how seriously do we want to take them now? Wisdom.

Even after realizing this, can I stop worry-thoughts from entering my mind? No! Because they are such a habit! But now when worry

---

[11] National Basketball Association

[12] For nonAmericans reading this, U-Haul is a truck rental/hire company used for moving things.

arrives I can see it comes only as a result of my habit; it does not come from the presentation. Not only worry about the presentation; this is about all possible worries. Seeing this is my key to freedom.

So now if I start to feel a bit worried about an upcoming presentation, once I realize it I say to myself (mostly subconsciously because I don't know I'm thinking it), "Okay, this is just my habit talking." It takes the pressure off. I don't have to talk myself out of it. I just have to realize I am the creator. "Wait a minute, it's just me! Just my habit. It means nothing!" Or I realize what would be left if I wasn't thinking up worry: a feeling of peace.

If I am the creator of worry, am I not also the uncreator? What a gift!

"Jack, not so fast! What if you and your girlfriend have sex and then she misses a period or two? You're going to be really worried that she's pregnant! Are you saying this worry isn't real?"

I remember this actually being one of the biggest scares of my young life.

Well, does worry do any good? She's either pregnant or she isn't. What does worry have to do with it?

If I find out she isn't pregnant after all, then all that worry I did would have been for naught. I would have driven myself crazy for nothing!

If she is pregnant I want clear-headed wisdom to speak to me about what to do. Worry would simply get in the way.

Either way, worry is completely wasted energy and irrelevant. Worthless!

16. ASSUMPTIONS AND INNOCENCE

For years I wanted to visit Nancy Lopin in a Boston prison. No, she wasn't an inmate; she teaches the Three Principles to inmates. Her success speaks for itself. She began as a volunteer; the correctional system now pays her.

For those who have never visited a prison it is a surreal experience, at least to me. Heavy metal doors clank shut loudly echoing behind me, locking me away from the outside world, from life as I know it. For one brief moment I wonder what it would be like to actually be locked in, unable to leave. Then I remember many people are. "There but for fortune may go you or I."[13] It is sobering.

I have been in my fair share of prisons. As one of my many tasks as Juvenile Justice Specialist for the Vermont Governor's Commission on the Administration of Justice I visited many correctional centers to ensure compliance with the Federal Juvenile Justice and Delinquency Prevention Act. I never got used to it. Especially knowing in the good old U.S.A. we have the world's highest per capita prison population—far above the second highest, Russia, and third, South Africa—with an overabundance of African American males and other minorities. Not a lot of wealthy white males can be found in U.S. prisons; they can afford good defense lawyers and are often favored by the system. I have unsettling thinking about the entire thing.

But walking into this inner-city Boston prison with Nancy I had to put aside such thoughts. Nancy is wonderful. I liked her the first time I met her years ago. She *feels* life. For example, when she read Amy's and my children's picture book, *What is a Thought (A Thought is A Lot)* she cried. I hadn't thought of that book as a real tear-jerker, but her response was so beautiful. Mostly, though, something doesn't compute about her working here—very petite and gentle Nancy working in a

---

[13] Thank you, Phil Ochs. A reader asked me what this means. To me it means, "There but for the grace of God go I."

prison filled with big, tough, largely African American and Hispanic men. But armed with her grounding and understanding of the Three Principles she becomes larger than life. First lesson about thoughts of assumption.

Nancy had been teaching in this prison for twelve years. Before we entered to attend her class she told me the men wouldn't talk. Therefore, Nancy talked. Early on she made up her mind that she would talk and they would get whatever they got. In many different ways she explained how the Three Principles work within everyone. Though the inmates didn't talk they must have been listening because it had impact. The correctional center wanted Nancy back year after year.

I didn't want to take Nancy's word for it that these guys wouldn't talk. Getting everyone involved in the discussion is the way I, personally, teach the Three Principles best. I would have to find out for myself. So I sat down with the men and started asking questions.

Lo and behold, they talked! They talked a lot.

As wonderful as Nancy is and as effective as she is in helping them, Nancy had made an assumption. It became what she knew. What we know often limits new possibilities.

Once the men did start talking the first thing that struck me about them was their innocence—not whether they committed the crime that ended them up there, but that they ended up there because *they innocently believed in the reality of their thinking*. Innocently they didn't realize any other possible "realities" existed. They didn't know any other possible levels of consciousness existed through which they could see. They were stuck with the reality they saw and felt compelled to act on what they believed was the only thing they could do under the circumstances. Pure innocence!

It is no different from any of the innocent things we do that end up causing problems for others or for ourselves. We, too, see a certain reality we believe is all there is. The only difference between the inmates and us is when we caused our problems we either didn't break the law or didn't get caught. They are behind bars; we're not. Other than that, we are all doing the exact same thing, except in some cases their actions may have been more extreme. We, too, make the innocent assumption that there are no other possibilities. All innocence.

What if these men, when they first get the urge to do something that would be breaking the law or causing harm to others or to property, instead of assuming they have to follow that urge, what if they came to realize that what they call "reality" at those times isn't. What if they realize they are essentially making up the reality on which they feel so compelled to act? What if they realize what they feel they must do is only an illusion of their own creation? What if they do not have to follow their thinking at those times because they know the reality they see is only one possible "reality," and all other possibilities exist? What if they know the reason it looks and feels so real and so compelling is only because consciousness makes it look and feel real and they get seduced by that? In that moment of realization everything would change. No destructive urges would have to be followed, no crimes committed, no harm done. They wouldn't have to commit the act that landed them behind bars.

Same for all of us. Within our minds we inadvertently construct our own prisons.

Further, what if they come to realize that underneath their creation of these illusions they are beautiful, mentally healthy human beings at their core, filled with peace and love, with potential always to be guided by wisdom when their minds calm down? What if they saw the only way they can have the illusion that they're not their true nature is when they innocently use their power of Thought against themselves by thinking they're not? If they saw their own health and satisfaction within, would they still have to search for illusory satisfaction outside themselves?

One of the many wonderful men who spoke up in Nancy's prison group was a fellow I'll call Ray because he had a smile like Ray Allen, the all-time three-point scoring leader in NBA history. A delightful, charming man, Ray had an interesting point of view. The reason he is in prison, he said, is "because I don't like to work, I need to have a roof over my head and enough money to get by; therefore I steal." You can't fight logic like that!

The flaw in Ray's logic is he considers his first thought, "I don't like to work" as an absolute, as reality. In truth it is only something he made up about himself with his own creative power, which looks so like truth to him he believes it to the root of his being. Then he acts on this "reality" and it lands him in prison. The fact is, Ray does work; he works hard at his craft of robbing. Ray is a very deep guy, too, really nice—except he thinks he doesn't like to work, therefore has to steal, then ends up in prison.

"I don't like to work," is an assumption-thought, with power, from which all his other thought-dominoes fall. If Ray could call this self-created "reality"-assumption into question he would gain a second chance and would no longer have to be behind bars. I find that amazing.

As for Nancy and her own assumption, she wrote me afterwards. "I have actually thought about it a lot. It is certainly true that we bring our expectations to the moment. I think I have trusted more since that day you came in with me, trusted more that they will 'speak.'…Our day together really helped me see that assumption…Sometimes, like this morning, I just say, 'Talk to me,' and they do."

Pure innocence.

Bless you, Ray, and the rest of you. And of course, bless you, Nancy, for all you do and for who you are.

17. EGO and FEAR: CO-CONSPIRATORS

What do we make of people who embellish stories? I am not a story embellisher. But I found myself doing it once, and for probably forty years kept perpetuating the embellishment to where even I almost believed the truth of it, myself. If I embellished a story even once I should be able to relate to why people embellish stories.

I will begin with the whole truth and nothing but the truth. Then I will point out where I began to embellish and why.

My story is this: Fresh out of college in 1968 I decided to hitchhike around the beautiful U.S.A. I planned to go with a couple of friends but they chickened out. I refused to let that stop me, so I went myself. I got a ride with a friend from New York City to Minnesota, then set off across Canada into Vancouver and down the West Coast. In every city I landed I would head to where the hippies hung out and ask if they knew of a place to crash. The good ol' Sixties!

Just outside Portland, Oregon I lucked out catching a long ride all the way to San Francisco with a very nice couple. They seemed to get along beautifully, but each time one of them took a break and left the car the other would tell me what a difficult a time they'd been having together and were on their way to San Francisco to get a divorce. Very puzzling. Anyway, they dropped me in San Francisco in the early evening with the sun about to set. My goal was to get to Haight-Ashbury because I knew that's where the hippies lived, but I'd been dropped off on the other side of the city and it was too late to make the trek. What to do?

I spotted a hippy-looking couple standing on a corner. I walked up to them and asked if they knew where I might crash. They said yes, so-and-so has a nearby crash pad. They gave me the address. I simply needed to tell the woman who ran it that they sent me. The good ol' Sixties!

I walked over there, up to the second floor and knocked on the door. No answer. I walked around the block. With my heavy backpack and banjo strapped to it I didn't feel like walking anymore, so I sat on the front steps. No one came. Darkness set in. Streetlights lit. I didn't know what to do. I went back upstairs and knocked again, in case anyone had slipped by me. Still no answer. I put my hand on the doorknob and, uh oh, the door opened. Gulp.

I called in, "Hello?" No one answered. I said to myself, "Okay, I've got nowhere else to go."

So I wrote a note saying so-and-so told me I could probably crash here and I hope that's true, and I don't mean to freak you out but I'm inside on the couch and my name is Jack. I laid out my sleeping bag on the couch in the living room. My intention was to wait up for her to come in but, exhausted, I fell asleep.

In the middle of the night the crash-pad-woman walked in and jumped, startled. In the dark she hadn't seen my note. After gathering herself she said, "Oh, whose friend are you?"

I told her what my note said and asked if it was okay. She said, "Sure, you can have this room right over here." Great! My room must have been situated between her room and the bathroom because fifteen minutes later she paraded through my room stark naked. Beautiful body, too! I couldn't believe it. I had not experienced this at Clark University in Worcester, Massachusetts. Nothing like that ever happened there at that time—at least not to me. She then pranced through my room in the other direction as if it were the most natural thing in the world—and it was—and she bid me good-night. The good ol' Sixties!

I thought, "How wonderful to be so free!" Then I thought, "I wonder if she's trying to tell me something." I said to myself, "In the morning I'm going to find out." I thought it might be nice to experience a bit of the free love I'd heard so much about.

I awoke the next morning to three other people sleeping on the living room floor. Another stumbled out of her bedroom. Darn! Oh well—

But I digressed. Now the story really begins. I took a trolley as close to the Haight as I could get, found Haight Street and began strolling along it. I figured I would ask everyone I saw if they knew of a place to crash until I found one.

I walked all the way down Haight Street, past the "Haight is Love" signs, and didn't speak to a soul. Everyone there looked *so weird!* Women sat in doorways with vacant pie-eyed looks, tongues practically hanging out, babies slung over their shoulders, looking completely out of it. I couldn't believe it! Nobody had told me heroin had broken into the Haight with a vengeance and destroyed everything. It bore little resemblance to the so-called Summer of Love only one summer earlier. No more love at the Haight. The real hippies had escaped to the country. I walked straight through, stunned, ending up in Golden Gate Park. In a daze I sat in the grass leaning against my bag and banjo, not knowing what to do.

A hippy-looking black guy walked up to me and asked if I would play the banjo for him. I said, "No man, sorry, I really don't feel like it right now." Then I heard myself blurt out, "But do you know of any place I can crash." As soon as it came out of my mouth I regretted it. He said, "Yeah sure, man, you can stay with me and my friends." I said, "Okay, thanks."

I got nervous. I didn't know this guy from a hole in a wall. He looked freaky. But I found myself following him. He led me down two blocks this way, another few blocks that way, another block this way, all while my nervousness grew. But I was cool—on the outside.

"Here we are, man."

What? Where? Concrete stairs scattered with broken glass descended from the sidewalk down to a cellar door. Gulp again. He went down ahead of me and opened the door. Inside looked like a black hole.

He said, "Come on in and close the door." I hovered at the top steps for a few moments, not knowing what to do, then inched down slowly. He said, "Come on," walked into pitch blackness and lit what could not have been bigger than a birthday candle in the back of the room." I peered in and saw the outline of three other guys lying on a mattress on the floor, smoking. Uh oh.

Every word of that story is true. Then he said again in a gruffer voice, "Come in and close the door!" and I took off like a bat out of hell. Not true! He did not demand gruffly that I come in and close the door. It is true that I took off like a bat out of hell, but that was after what really happened. Yet that became my story. What really happened was I kind of tiptoed into the darkness, stayed fairly close to the door and they cajoled me to play the banjo for them. I was afraid not to. Quite nervous, I sang a few songs, then excused myself. I said I had some stuff to do but would be back, grabbed my pack and banjo, opened the door and walked up the stairs to "freedom." That's when I took off as fast as my backpack would allow, screaming inwardly to myself. I kept looking behind me to see if they were coming after me. They weren't. How had I allowed myself to get into a potentially dangerous situation like this? I'm sure they meant me no harm—they looked too out of it anyway—but what if they had?

I had the contact number for a friend of a friend of a friend somewhere up the hill from the Haight, which I didn't want to use but now would. I got severe shin splints trudging up and down the steep San Francisco hills with my heavy pack.

But what for so many years could possibly have made me not tell the story exactly as it happened? Why the slight exaggeration? Someone very close to me is an exaggerator, and I never wanted to be that way myself. So why did I?

In a word, embarrassment. I was afraid to let people know what a fool I was for putting myself in that dangerous situation. I'd made a really dumb move. I'd embarrassed myself and was afraid other people would look down on me for doing that. (Some readers may be thinking that right now.) What amuses me now is it was dumb enough just following that guy in the first place. But what I felt most embarrassed about was actually walking into that black hole where if they meant harm I could have been robbed, beat up or worse. Walking into that hole is where I drew the line at my own stupidity.

So what was behind my exaggeration? Embarrassment, obviously, but the embarrassment came out of ego—my poor sensitive little ego—and fear that I would be judged poorly for doing something that stupid, because even I looked down on myself for doing it.

Ego and fear together conspired to make me stretch the truth, and stretching the truth is a lie—no whitewashing it. The humbling part is I'm the one who made up both the ego and the fear.

Looking back at the times in my life when I lied, all were due to fear. Fear makes people do things that in their right minds they wouldn't normally do. Innocence, once again. I didn't know any other way at the time, and neither does anyone else. People can only see what they see at the time.

I'm not talking here about fear occurring in a moment; for example, the time I took a walk in the Vermont woods with my then little puppy, Gypsy, and suddenly we came upon a pack of coydogs. For readers unfamiliar with coydogs they are the offspring of coyotes mating with wild dogs. They run in packs and don't have the fear of humans coyotes usually do. I quickly grabbed Gypsy, picked her up in my arms, then froze with fear as I watched them slink low and slither by me about 25 yards away. Luckily they didn't go after either me or my puppy. But that kind of fear is understandable, fictitious or not (obviously, I didn't have to be fearful in that moment because nothing happened), but I'm okay with being afraid in that situation; it readies me for fight or flight—or freeze.

The kind of fear I'm talking about is fear that lasts well beyond the moment, that drives us without our even knowing it, fear that rules our lives in various ways, that makes us act counter to wisdom, counter to love, fear that makes us be less than who we really want to be or who we really are deep inside. If we can see that kind of fear as fictitious, as Syd Banks said in *Island of Knowledge*, then we see something of vast importance for our lives.

And not only exaggeration; almost every problem we have can be traced back to fear and ego. They are co-conspirators because they work together, feed off each other and cause some of the biggest messes of our lives. Yet we created both! They wouldn't even exist but for that creation. We live our lives at the mercy of our own creation.

Most humbling.

18. DOES FEAR SERVE US?

When my son Dave was in middle school he won a spot on the Vermont state AAU (Amateur Athletic Union) basketball team. Vermont wasn't supposed to send a statewide team to the national AAU tournament in Kingsport, Tennessee, but because Vermont is so small and would be competing against much-greater populations, and because excellent basketball players in Vermont are few and far between, we somehow slid by. In Kingsport the Vermont team played against some fantastic inner-city teams that completely dominated and overwhelmed them.

One team, from the Cecil-Kirk Recreation Center of Baltimore, had the quickest little guards I've ever seen. Purposely they would let you dribble by them, then reach around from behind and just when you thought you were home free would knock the ball out of your hands to their waiting teammates. One of these guards, Shawnta Rogers, later starred for George Washington University at only 5'5" tall, and ended up a two-time all-star in France's top professional league. I bring this up only to illustrate both the quickness and competition Vermont faced.

After playing against each other a few times, the all-white players on the Vermont team and the all-black players from Baltimore got along very well and became friendly—a pleasure to see. Before we knew it Mayor Peter Clavelle of Burlington, Vermont and Mayor Kurt Schmoke of Baltimore joined to sponsor the two teams playing each other in a good-will tournament. Several dignitaries got involved, including then-Vermont Congressman Bernie Sanders, a basketball player himself in his younger days—the very same Bernie who in 2016 made a huge splash running for President of the United States. First the Baltimore team flew up and played in Burlington. Bernie and both mayors made speeches; it was a big deal. The same then took place in Baltimore. The Vermont team and coaches flew down on a small, chartered plane, and we parents, Mayor Clavelle and Congressman Sanders flew on another.

We all had a wonderful time. This game was even slightly more competitive (Vermont still lost), and all was grand until the time came to fly home. At the last moment, I don't know why, Bernie Sanders switched planes with my son Dave. Bernie flew with the team and Dave came on the plane with us parents.

A sudden, eerie premonition overcame me. I couldn't put my finger on it, but I took it as a bad omen. Did this mean one of the planes would go down? I couldn't shake the feeling. This was well before I met the Three Principles. I couldn't let it go.

As we approached the Burlington airport to land, the pilot, who seemed like a real cowboy—don't get me wrong, cowboys are great, unless they're riding an airplane like a bucking bronco—turned in his seat and said to us, "I don't know why, but the landing gear won't come down, so I'm going to circle around and try again."

We flew around in a big circle. He tried again. Still the wheels wouldn't come down.

He turned to us again, "We're probably going to have to come in on our belly, and to do that I have to use up all our fuel, so I'm going to fly around until the fuel is gone so we won't start a fire when we land. I'm calling ahead and they're going to spray foam on the runway and have fire engines and ambulances waiting. But don't worry, we'll be fine."

I knew it was a bad omen! I became petrified. I got so scared I began shaking—literally. We flew around for what seemed like hours but probably only took a half hour. The entire time I could not stop shaking, absolutely certain we would all meet our maker. My life would be over, along with my wife, Judy, who sat one row behind the pilot, as well as our son and the Mayor of Burlington, who sat right in front of me and could probably hear my heart pounding. Our daughter, Jaime, at home, would be left all alone and I could do nothing about it!

The pilot announced we were going down, so we should all assume the crash-landing position, head down between legs.

This small plane had one seat at the window, then the aisle, then one seat on the other side. Dave sat directly across the aisle from me. He shot me a WTF look. I could only shrug my shaking shoulders. I couldn't say anything because I didn't want him to be as freaked out as

I was—I'm not sure anything would have come out of my mouth anyway. That Bernie and Dave had switched planes at the last second was an OMEN!

More minutes passed. I thought my bones would shake right out of my body. The pilot said, "Okay, brace yourself, we're going to land on the belly, but don't worry, there is foam all over the runway."

Yeah, right! Never mind worry; this was sheer terror! I never felt such all-consuming fear.

We headed down, down, down.

At the last second, just as we were about to hit ground, miraculously, the landing gear dropped down. We landed on wheels. Mr. Cowboy piloted a perfectly smooth landing as if nothing had ever happened, except foam flew all over the place. And we were fine.

Is there a point to this story? Well, for one thing, *we can never know the future*, even when the future seems imminent. For another, I could have saved myself so much consternation and potential heart failure had I known what would ultimately happen. Had I known, I wouldn't have been scared at all; it would have been more like a wild adventure thrill ride. Since I didn't know, what was the sense of scaring myself to death? Even if the worst happened, what good would a state of fear do?

Mostly, I experienced such terror because I thought I knew something. I was absolutely convinced it was a bad omen that Bernie switched planes with Dave. Such thinking made me a petrified, shaking mess. Apparently I wasn't alone. The mayor said he about pissed his pants.

Rule by fear and worry. Such wasted emotions! Am I saying I could now go through that experience again without fear? I don't know. But what good does it do? If we are going to crash, we are going to crash. I would have crashed (or not) with fear or without fear and a "whatever happens, happens" attitude. My experience of life would have been a lot healthier before death or before being maimed. But even if the worst happened, how would panic help?

Mr. Cowboy Pilot wasn't worried. He saw it as a challenge; he would corral his horse-plane and bring it down, cool as a cucumber, cocky as hell. And I'm glad. If he'd been in fear and didn't have his wits about him we could have crashed.

After that adventure, some people never would have flown again.

19. A DEEPER EXPLORATION OF CONSCIOUSNESS AND AWARENESS

As I implied earlier, probably because Syd Banks said it, many students of the Three Principles believe consciousness is *awareness*, especially awareness that we are the thinkers. While true, I believe Syd meant a lot more than appears on the surface. I believe Syd referred not merely to what we are aware we're aware of, but to awareness of our entire being and of Universal Consciousness itself.

We already said our consciousness always takes in the world through our senses via our thinking and brings our thinking to life. Is this not already beyond the notion of awareness?

Furthermore, what most people normally think of as awareness is already limiting. Consider the following: At age 17 my old friend, Jack Cullen—may he rest in peace—drove some rowdy teenage friends home from a party. As boys will be boys, oblivious to danger, they roughhoused in the back seat. An elbow cracked into the back of Jack's head. The rowdies in the back had no idea, except one of them must have had a sore elbow.

The next thing Jack remembered is pulling into his driveway. None of his friends were in the car.

Not only is this scary, it's puzzling. For years I've said that when we read a book and our mind drifts into other thoughts, while still allegedly reading, our consciousness leaves the book and follows our thinking, so we have no experience of what occurred on those three pages. I used to think our consciousness completely misses the experience of what we supposedly read. Jack Cullen's story calls this into question. Does what we read somehow register in our consciousness anyway, beyond what we would call our awareness? Could it be picked up by consciousness without thought? Impossible, right? What exactly went on with Jack, here? Somewhere within Jack's consciousness his actual driving still had to register or he would have been found in a ditch or wrapped around a telephone pole. If the elbow knocked Jack at least partially unconscious, where was his thinking?

Actually it is not as mysterious as it seems. Jack had thinking well beyond what we normally think of as thought, yet still within the realm of Thought! Jack had no personal conscious awareness of his thoughts, but thoughts of which he was unaware still altered his consciousness. In other words, after getting clubbed by the elbow, even though Jack had no awareness of his drive home, at a deeper level his consciousness still had awareness of the drive.

This is very consistent with the Three Principles. Consciousness gives us an experience of whatever our thinking. Once partially knocked out, Jack had no awareness of, or experience of driving—or anything—because he had no awareness of his thoughts. But at a deeper level his consciousness in its deeper awareness still picked up his thoughts and played them out. Tricky, yes? Complex, yes? But true.

I remember long ago reading somewhere that nurses who make fun of patients under anesthesia or when "unconscious" actually affect those patients. The so-called "unconscious" patients somehow registered what the nurses said. I forget how they measured this, but they did. Beyond being appalled that some nurses would actually make fun of patients in any way, this makes sense in light of Jack's story. If even a chance exists that this is true, nurses (and others) had better take heed.[14]

Beyond awareness, we could explore the realm of Consciousness still further. When we take in the world through our thinking, consciousness picks it up as a vibration. Here in this world of form, consciousness *is* vibration. This vibration occurs at different levels. Hence, levels of consciousness.

Our consciousness vibrates at whatever level we take something in, determined by whatever we think. Each level of consciousness vibrates

---

[14] In her book, *Dying to Be Me!* Anita Moorjani describes that during her experience of dying from terminal cancer and being in a coma she became aware of all sorts of things happening around her. She even overheard a conversation between her husband and a doctor outside the ward, too far away to be heard by her physical ears. She also picked up what her brother felt while still on a plane trying to get to her. Oh, the power of Thought!

like a different tuning fork. Our consciousness, then, is like a series of tuning forks almost appearing to stand on top of each other at each different level, each with a different vibration. We get a thought of whatever is happening out there, and—*ding*—molecules begin to move and vibrate. Thus begins the process of ultimately turning formless into form.

What we call a feeling or emotion is the vibration sparked by the movement of molecules created by a particular thought as it comes into consciousness. Uncountable levels of vibration are possible. Vibrations/feelings at the top levels are light and beautiful; vibrations/emotions at the bottom level are heavy and miserable. Many hidden habits of thought through which we see the world (without realizing it) vibrate at the middle and mid-lower levels.

Universal Consciousness itself, the Principle of Consciousness, is beyond vibration, for it is formless, pure, a clean slate upon which all experience becomes manifest, a gift from Universal Mind energy. Again, like the metaphoric blank canvas it is a piece of clay upon which anything could be molded, a chess board on which any game could be played. Before any pieces move on the board the game is all possibilities. Consciousness itself "contains" All possibilities, for it is connected to the pure formless energy of Universal Mind. Consciousness is the possibility of any energy vibration in form.

So we get a thought, often a thought we don't even know we're thinking, and—*ding*—we feel the vibration of that thought. We *feel* it! Guaranteed! If we get a sad thought—*ding*—we get the vibration of sadness. If the thought is of upset—*ding*—we feel the vibration of upset at a low level of consciousness. If the thought is of peace—*ding*—we get the vibration of peace at a very high level. Each is a completely different vibration, each a completely different feeling. A thought of depression—*ding*—is a very, very low vibration. Many accumulated depressed thoughts vibrate the molecules to such an extent it can actually change form and mess with body chemistry. Happiness—*ding*—is a high vibration. Within the unfathomable vastness of Consciousness all are equal possibilities. Our hands (thoughts) are on the dinger.

Which vibration of life will we accept for ourselves?

On one hand it's enough to know the only thing that can give us a feeling/experience is whatever we're thinking—whether we're aware of that thinking or not. On the other hand, with regard to what happened to my friend Jack, his unconscious thinking must have registered somewhere in his consciousness beyond the realm of what he experienced personally. What if a hypnotist hypnotized Jack Cullen and asked him to recall what happened from the time the elbow hit his head to the time he pulled into his driveway? Possibly Jack would have been able to recount the events. If so, the memory must be hidden somewhere within his consciousness and, if he can recall it, it must be thought. But he would have no personal experience of it *until* under hypnosis when actually realizing his thoughts about it. Consciousness, therefore, still picked up his thinking but on such an imperceptible level of thought at the time he never knew it. At least that's the way it seems to me.

This may be a stretch but I wonder if this is akin to a dog hearing sounds our ears are incapable of picking up. We have no awareness of the sound but our dog is going nuts, so the sound obviously exists. This is how Thought informs the senses. We humans do not pick up this sound even though it is sounding. We have no experience of the sound unless we have a thought of the sound, so the noise—of which the dog has a dog-thought-experience—is not part of *our* experience.

Does this give new meaning to philosophical question: If a tree falls in the forest and no one is around to hear it, does it make a sound?

The same is true for each of our senses; without thought we can have no experience of what those senses capture.

Thus, Consciousness is vastly more than awareness of which we are aware. Our consciousness must pick up an incredible amount not within our immediate awareness. But it must be *thought* of some kind, at some imperceptible level.

How can things get stored in our memory that we are not aware are there; for instance, sexual abuse trauma in childhood? How does this past hidden thought suddenly reveal itself in the present as if being relived now, when we previously had no awareness of that experience in our memory? Viewed through the lens of the Principles it makes perfect sense: present thought equals present experience.

What about consciousness beyond humans? A clam must have consciousness of water going through it, picking up whatever food a clam eats. We would never call that "thought," but the clam is probably having clam thoughts. It's tough to know what a clam thinks.

Many spiritual people believe trees and plants have consciousness. Does a tree have thoughts? A tree is part of Universal Mind. It is not out of the realm of plausibility that all things part of Mind have consciousness. Is there consciousness in every molecule? In every atom? In every quark? In every Higgs boson? Quite plausible. This would mean even rocks have consciousness.

All this, however, is the world of form. Does Consciousness exist within energy itself? Does formless energy itself have Consciousness? It is a mystery, but I'd guess true. Syd said Universal Mind and Universal Consciousness (along with Universal Thought) are really all One. It gets to a point, though, where Consciousness becomes way too complex and unfathomable—

—and the thing that counts most for our day-to-day lives is the simplicity that any experience we can possibly have is our consciousness picking up thoughts of our own creation in the moment, turning it into our "realty." This "reality" is what seduces us into believing the truth of it, and we can be aware of this phenomenon in general and see it happen in the moment.

20. SERENITY AND FEAR

The ocean rejuvenates me.

I've spent at least part of every summer of my life by the ocean. Born in Boston in June, 1946, my first home after the hospital was my grandparents' place on P Street at Nantasket Beach in Hull. My family, my aunt Bunny's family and my grandparents all crowded together in a fairly small two-story cottage; second house from the ocean. It was then passed on to my folks' and aunt's families, then bought solely by my parents. When my folks died it passed like a baton to my brother, sister and me, until my sister bought us out just before I'm writing this. It is a place for family gatherings and a Mecca for the beach.

Seeing the waves roll in, hearing the surf, watching foam wash upon sand, smelling the salt air, feeling the warm sand and wet sand-mud at low tide between my toes—everything about the ocean lifts me. Around it I feel calm. Around it I feel more alive. Around it I feel the aliveness of life. Serenity.

Or so it seems. Those feelings are within me anyway and in all ways. Those states are within my soul, built into me. I allow the ocean to give me the excuse to forget the rest of my thinking and feel one with the moment, to breathe in the air and experience life as it's meant to be experienced. By the ocean I allow my mind to temporarily cleanse of all its illusions and simply be present.

For many, many years I lived in the mountains or, more accurately, the hills of Vermont, and I love it there. It's beautiful, and it certainly feels wonderful, too, but the ocean is something else again. Same with Amy. She, too, spent every summer at the ocean, on Long Island.

Unlike Long Island, Nantasket Beach does not have a lot of big waves because it is semi-sheltered by Cape Cod, but big enough waves arrive in August when storms are on the ocean. I used to love it when those bigger waves rolled in, body surfing one of my favorite activities. I became a near expert at catching a wave perfectly just as it broke to catch the longest ride. Or I knew the split second I missed the perfect moment. When growing up, I thought, the bigger the waves the better. Bring 'em on!

Sometime around 1967 I saw the movie, *Endless Summer*. I loved that movie, the idea of people traveling the world riding surfboards, catching waves without a care in the world. No one surfed at Nantasket Beach then—most of the time the waves aren't big enough—so surfing never crossed my mind. But what enthralled me most in that movie were the three segments of enormous waves: "The Pipeline" and Waimea Bay on the north shore of Oahu, and "The Wedge" at Newport Beach near L.A. At The Wedge people didn't surf because the waves broke too close to the shoreline. But body surfing at the Wedge looked spectacular.

So after my adventure in the Haight I hitchhiked down to L.A. I made friends with a young panhandler and decided to spend one day panhandling on the streets, just to see what it was like. I didn't like it! Then I had a great time running around by myself at Disneyland (Disney World in Orlando did not exist then). But I really wanted to hit The Wedge and take in some waves. I found Newport Beach on the map, hopped on and off a bus and walked over a little rise to the beach.

Incredible disappointment. No waves! I did see a bunch of heads bobbing way out in the ocean about thirty yards from shore. Okay, even though there were no waves I had to take a dip. It was hot.

I waded out into the water, got about waist deep, and out of nowhere, by far the biggest wave I had ever seen materialized quickly in front of me. I froze. I looked up and stared at this wave towering over me at least twice if not three times my size. I was used to jumping over waves I was not ready to take in. In this case, a very stupid move.

I jumped as high as I could but the wave pulled me under. Suddenly I was in a blender under the water, flipping me this way, pulling me that, churning me, spinning me round and round, helpless. Just as I was about to lose my breath the current subsided and I came up sputtering for air, stumbling to my feet waist-deep in ocean again. I took a step toward shore to get out of there fast, glanced behind me and another wave at least that size crested high above me, smashing down upon me with a thunderous crash. I tumbled again in the washing machine until I felt my face pressed against the sandy ocean floor, holding me there until I had no choice but to breathe, then mercifully let me go. I came up gasping for air once again, stumbled out of the water and collapsed on the beach, knowing I would never again attempt anything so stupid.

Later I learned that all those heads bobbing way out in the ocean owned boogie boards, and they each wore one flipper, which allowed them to kick out back under the wave with force when about to be pulverized. My attempt to jump over the wave was worst thing I could have done.

Not that any of this advice would help me in the future. No way was I ever going to try that again.

In fact, I now found myself afraid of big waves—even waves way smaller than at The Wedge. I had never experienced that kind of power, and I never, ever wanted to experience anything remotely close to it again. Now when confronted with big powerful waves, such as on Long Island when visiting Amy's family, I'd get nervous and couldn't go in. I even tried once but found myself begin to panic. Even writing about it now I can feel the fear in the pit of my stomach.

Okay, yes, I know where my fear of big waves comes from, I know it's just my thinking, but it still looks like reality to me. And so long as it looks like reality I am stuck with the experience of fear. So, does knowing it's only my thinking help me at all?

If I am truly honest with myself, in this situation I'd have to say no. Knowing where my fear of big waves comes from doesn't help me into the water. I'm stuck with my "reality" at a low level of consciousness. This does not look like an illusion to me. But other people are out in those waves. It's got to be an illusion! Yet I cannot bring myself to do it.

What is helpful is to see it is just another example of being seduced by consciousness, another example of an illusion that looks so real it has me by the throat, another example of how the Three Principles are always working perfectly. Sometimes I feel a little sheepish not being able to go out into big waves when everyone else is doing it, but it's okay. I don't need to. I'm also pretty sure if someone were drowning in big waves and needed me to save them I probably would try because in that moment I would (hopefully) forget my fearful thinking and spontaneously act.

But let's face it, if in this circumstance I had deeper grounding in the Three Principles, I would truly see the fear as an illusion and would be able to ignore the nothing it is (because others are out in those waves having a grand old time), and relax, as I'd helped Richard do in the caves.

From the serenity I feel by the ocean to my fear of its big waves, all are brought to me courtesy of my own thinking and brought to life by my consciousness.

* * *

Not too long after I met my good friend, Gabriela, we walked and talked around Santa Cruz, California. We came to a steep gorge where, well below us, the ocean rushed through an inlet. No way around it, except over a train trestle. Were we going to walk all the way back around for God knows how long, or were we going to walk across this train trestle? We decided on the trestle.

Engaged in wonderful conversation, oblivious to all else, at once we both realized where we were: on train tracks in the middle of a narrow bridge above water swirling twenty or thirty feet below us, which we could see through the openings and cracks in the railroad ties at our feet.

Instantly, we both froze.

I had another one of those "Oh [bleep]" thoughts. My legs would not budge. They were welded to the tracks. No matter how hard I tried to move them I could not lift them off the tracks even a quarter inch. I looked over at Gabriela; the same thing had happened to her. She couldn't budge either. Our feet were encased in iron, immobile. I couldn't believe it.

Next I had the thought, "Okay, we can't move. What if a train comes?"

We had no choice; we had to get out of there! But there seemed no escape. If a train came we couldn't just jump into the cold roaring water twenty or thirty feet below. I tried to lift one leg. I couldn't. I was like one of those horses who refuses to have her leg lifted. No matter how much force one applies it is impossible to lift, until and if one is gentle enough the horse decides to allow it.

Since my will didn't work—I was still cemented to the tracks—somehow, some way another thought gently came along. Oddly, Gabriela simultaneously must have had a similar thought. This new thought, of which we were unaware, ever so slowly at first allowed us to barely move our toes, then our feet, then our legs a centimeter, then an inch, then we were able to pretty much—not totally, but pretty much—get started like a cold engine finally turning over.

Here we were, on the same trestle, same tracks, same water way below us, but now we were moving again, walking again as if nothing had happened, just as when we'd started across it.

Different thinking. At first we had no thoughts of danger, and our consciousness complied. Then fear-thoughts came along and consciousness complied again, paralyzing us. Finally we somehow shook off our fearful thoughts, and consciousness once again complied by allowing movement to be possible again. Works perfectly every time. Nothing else is going on ever, only Thought coming into Consciousness, thereby creating "reality," which is really an illusion.

And we think we're stuck. But we're not. For example, I really could jump into big waves if others are doing it, couldn't I?

21. KIDS

One evening, second grade teacher Ms. Amy received a phone message from a mother about her son, Joey. According to the mom, all evening Joey had been crying, mad, upset. He told her that during math partner games Margie had called him "fat."

But, the mom said, Joey made it very clear that he didn't want her to come in and have one of their meetings, of which they'd had plenty in the past. Yet, despite often being supersensitive, he was really upset and she didn't know what to do. This was her son! Nobody wants her son to be called names. Could Ms. Amy help?

"I'll look into it," said Amy.

When Ms. Amy arrived at school the next day, there sat Joey—he always showed up first. She offered a cheerful, "Good morning" and first let him settle in before saying anything to him. Since Amy knew that Joey knew his mom had told her he was upset all night, before any other kids arrived she squatted next to him.

"I heard you had a rough night."

Joey said, "Yeah" and got a little breathy, as he sometimes did when about to cry.

Ms. Amy realized she walked a fine line here. "Is it because someone called you a name?"

"Yeah."

"Did Margie call you a name?"

"Yeah." Joey did not offer what she called him.

"Did Margie call you fat?"

"Yeah."

"I heard you really had a rough time of it at home."

"Yeah."

Ms. Amy had taught her little pupils the Three Principles, not by using those names but by reading the children's picture book we coauthored, *What is a Thought? (A Thought is a Lot),*[15] doing the lesson plan activities in it and holding class discussions about it.

"Do you remember that you're in charge of it all, and our own feelings come from what we're thinking?"

"Yeah. She hurt my feelings."

"Yes, when people call names it might hurt. It may not feel good when you hear someone say something mean about you. But you have to remember that you get to decide how much it's going to affect you, like how much it is going to ruin your whole evening."

Joey nodded.

Ms. Amy had a gut feeling, but she didn't know how Joey would react if she said it. She took a chance.

"The other thing is, I'll bet that when you go into a tizzy at home, you get a lot of attention from mom."

Joey's mouth betrayed a sly little smile and he nodded quickly.

"I know. Just remember, Joey, you are the one who gets to decide when someone calls you a name how much it's going to affect you, or how much you just want to forget about it. And you can always, always, always just let it go, just let it pass by like those bubbles we talked about, or putting it on the train and watching it go down the tracks. You are in charge of that part, not Margie. She may have called you the name—that means she has something to work out on her own and I'll be talking to her to help her figure out what made her feel she had to be mean to you or to someone—but you decide how much it affects you. Margie doesn't have superpowers over you to ruin your whole night. You decide that part."

Joey seemed okay with all that, so Ms. Amy moved on and went about her business. When the other kids walked in she noticed Joey doing fine, talking with his friends, engaged in his morning work. Margie walked in and they seemed to interact well.

After Margie settled into her morning work, Ms. Amy now squatted down next to her. Although a lot of action swirled around them in the classroom, Ms. Amy said very quietly, "Margie, Joey said you were being mean to him during math partner games yesterday."

"No, I wasn't being mean."

---

[15] Subsequently, we wrote *What is Wisdom (and Where do I find it)*?

"He said you called him a name, and the name was 'fat.'"

Margie went to deny it, but Ms. Amy shot her a knowing look. Stopped Margie in her tracks. Margie nodded shyly.

"So Margie, I'm a little concerned. I'm just wondering if you're okay. Because when someone calls someone a mean name it means you're trying to hurt them in a way. And when someone tries to hurt someone, to me it's a signal that they're hurting inside. So I'm wondering, are you hurting inside?"

Immediately tears came to Margie's eyes and ran down her cheeks. She couldn't really speak. Ms. Amy placed a gentle hand on Margie's back and rubbed a little.

"It's okay, Margie. I just want you to know that I'm here. I'm here to help you when you have hurting thoughts. Or if you have happy thoughts. Or when you're fine, or when you're not fine. Just try to keep those thoughts in a way where you can talk to me about them instead of hurting someone else. Okay?"

Margie nodded.

"It's okay. I know you have an older brother and a younger sister, and things get crazy here and there, and you're trying to figure it out, too, like we all are. But just remember, when you have a thought of saying something mean to someone, you can keep it inside your head instead and know that it's just a thought and you don't have to put it out there. But then you could think, 'Huh, I wonder what's bothering me that would make me want to do that?' And you can even say to me, 'Ms. Amy, I don't know what's bothering me but I'm just not feeling right.' And it's okay, because those pass too."

Margie nodded. She went back to her morning work. Before long, things went on as they do in second grade as if no incident had happened.

Margie and Joey interacted with each other beautifully for the rest of the year.

* * *

One day when Ms. Amy picked up her class of fairly new first graders from recess Tex started to scream and cry and shriek uncontrollably. This was completely out of character for Tex, who prided himself on being cool.

Another little fellow, Jasper, appeared very concerned. With his slight speech impediment that sometimes made it difficult to understand him, he yelled to Tex, "I said teeth! I said teeth!"

Seeing this, Ms. Amy became quite concerned. Tex seemed about to have a seizure or something. She couldn't console him. He couldn't get out what was happening to him.

She asked Jasper what happened.

Apparently worried Ms. Amy would come down on him for doing something very wrong, Jasper said, "I said teeth! All I said was teeth."

"What do you mean? I don't understand."

"All I said was he had teeth coming into his mouth."

"Then do you know what he's so upset about?"

"He thought I said bees were coming into his mouth! I said teeth!"

That's why Tex freaked out. I'd freak out, too, if bees were coming into my mouth.

Ms. Amy looked into Tex's mouth through his shrieks and jumping around. Sure enough, two little adult teeth peeked up in the spaces where his baby teeth had fallen out. No bees in sight.

Amy could barely hold it together to keep from laughing. She had other classroom plans but this had to take precedence. Once Tex realized he didn't have bees in his mouth and had calmed down Ms. Amy couldn't resist creating this teachable moment for the whole class.

"Look how powerful thoughts are!" she said. "See how thought creates feelings! Even when something isn't really happening, just thinking about it can make us think it is—so much it can totally freak us out."

Kids… and a wonderful teacher.

22. THE INTELLECT

A medical doctor phoned me. He knew something of the Three Principles and wanted to see if it could help him with a personal issue.

I obliged.

Dr. Harry had an extremely impressive intellect. It served him well in so many ways—except for what he called me about.

"My wife rages at me all the time and I have such a hard time dealing with it," he said.

"Just out of curiosity, Harry, if you can't handle your wife raging at you all the time, why do you stay in this relationship?"

"Because people are so unpredictable, and they do really bad things sometimes, and you have to be so careful, and I get depressed about it. My wife feels the same way and she rages about it, so at least we have something in common to commiserate about."

Harry had something in common with Ray from Chapter 16: You just can't fight logic like that.

Then he added, "And it would be unsafe to live alone."

Oh. With this added little phrase I could sort of see his internal logic. I could understand his fear from his perspective.

Except none of it held water. His wife lives in New York City. He works at Boston hospitals, so mostly he lives in a rented apartment in Boston for four or five days a week. Then he travels back to NYC, gets raged at for three days, then heads back to Boston.

"Harry, according to my calculations, you're not living with her for four-sevenths of the time anyway."

"But there's a certain comfort in those three days a week."

"You mean comfort in being raged at? Didn't you call me because it was driving you crazy?"

"But at least it's familiar. Otherwise, it's too dangerous."

It didn't take me long to realize I didn't have a prayer of cracking Harry's intellect. He had a logical answer—at least in his own mind—

for everything. He'd even taken in the Three Principles through his intellect, which means nothing for one's life. But he thought he knew something, and it got in his way.

I talked about going into a state of "not knowing." This kind of unnerved him; he did not want to go there at all.

Puzzled about where to go with Dr. Harry, I reflected a bit, hoping wisdom would speak. Something hit me.

"Look," I said, "I don't pretend to know anything about the medical profession, so you tell me if I'm off base, but let me ask you this. Let's say someone comes to you with a symptom, and through your intellectual analysis you go through all the possible things you think it could be, all the common things and even some uncommon ones, but something just doesn't sit well with you. Something doesn't feel right. When that happens, do you go into more analysis, bear down more with your intellect, or do you get a little puzzled, get quiet, and something comes to you?"

"I get a little puzzled and something comes to me."

"That's what I'm talking about! In dealing with medical issues when you need to find a solution, past a certain point continued intellectual analysis doesn't work. Why wouldn't the same hold true in the rest of your life?"

"What do you mean?"

"I mean, for so many things in your life your intellect has served you extremely well. You've got an incredible intellect. Where it has served you well you definitely want to keep using it, but when it comes to the other things in life, such as your raging wife and your dilemma of thinking you're not safe without her, your intellect doesn't work. In fact, it blocks new insight from coming through. See what I mean?"

In that moment Harry got scared. Was I trying to take his intellect from him? What would be left? If I took away what he'd relied upon all his life, he didn't trust what would remain.

"Harry, it's the exact same thing you do naturally in your work when you bump into a symptom that's not easily diagnosable. You told me at those times you didn't apply your intellect further to figure it out. You know it won't get you anywhere. I'm saying it's the same thing. At a certain point in your work your intellect no longer serves you well.

Here in your relationship it doesn't serve you well either. You're depressed because you think you're trapped and there's no way out."

"That's true. I do feel trapped."

"I'm saying applying your intellect to get you out of the trap will never work. There's no way out through your intellect. It's useless for this. You're wasting your time."

"But if I can't use my intellect, what can I use?" Harry's fear showed palpably.

"Harry, as a doctor in the diagnosing situation you described, is it scary?"

"No."

"Then what would make it any different in the rest of your life? When you get stuck, when you feel trapped, all you have to 'do' is go into the same kind of 'process'—more like a nonprocess—that you apply at work when you're stuck. The way you get new insight in diagnosing an illness is so natural you don't even think about it. What's scary about that? Besides, you can see that the intellect route in your home situation isn't getting you anywhere. What have you got to lose?"

Harry became quiet for the first time. A good sign.

Something occurred to me in the silence.

"Harry, I just got something. You don't have faith that without your intellect an answer will be there for you, do you?"

"That's right. I don't."

"But you have that faith in your office."

"Hmm. I've never thought about that."

"Well, where do those new insights come from? You don't go out of your way to think your way to them. Where do those answers come from?"

"I don't know."

"But they show up, right?"

"They do."

"So what does that tell you? Why wouldn't the exact same faith apply in real life? Maybe it's only scary because you've never tried it before. How would you know? I say again, what have you got to lose?"

Deep listening told me Harry had little regard for the spiritual. I didn't think it would pay to talk with him about the Source; it would send him right back to his intellect, so I left that alone. Harry had to deal in very pragmatic terms. This was so interesting to me! Dr. Harry considered it simply true that when he got puzzled and quiet at work something usually came to him; Mr. Harry, at home, believed it a fluke if something ever occurred to him without his intellect. He didn't see his intellectual approach at home when stuck was as ineffective as at work when stuck. But he had never tested it out in the rest of life. That's all I wanted him to be open to right now.

By the end of our conversation Harry's mind had quieted a lot.

He said, "I think you put a little crack in my intellect."

Good enough for me.

* * *

Coincidentally, almost immediately after my conversation with Dr. Harry I spoke with a psychiatric medical doctor-in-training from Sweden named Fredrik, a delightful man who had joined my Extended Professional Training in Spain. Fredrik told me he got annoyed when he had to talk notes into a voice recorder for his supervisor after conducting a psychiatric session.

I asked what about it made him annoyed?

Fredrik reflected. He realized he saw the activity as meaningless. His reaction resulted from spending his time on "meaningless."

Ironically, I myself talk into a voice recorder a lot. I don't view it as meaningless at all. I use it to help me remember things for this book, or just to vent, or talk to myself about anything on my mind at the time, which feels good. Furthermore, Frederik's supervisor needs to know how well he's doing. Yet out of All possibilities Fredrik landed on "meaningless." He didn't have to.

Puzzling, too, Fredrik also told me he'd had a huge insight that feelings don't come from the outside world. Yet when I asked him what bothers him, he said, "When I'm with a bunch of alpha males. I don't like it and I get tense." Um, that's not the outside world?

When growing up Fredrik felt it was really important to his father that he think faster. Though his father never really said it, in Fredrik's mind his father sat on his shoulder barking, "Come on, think faster!" Fredrik was a slow but steady thinker. Unable to live up to his alpha male father's expectations Fredrik wondered if he was stupid. No wonder alpha males triggered Fredrik's thinking.

Based on our own unique thinking, which often stems from how we think about our upbringing, we all get triggered by certain unique things. But each trigger is so much a part of our being that we could have a big insight, yet still completely believe in exceptions to our insight. We don't call it an exception, of course; we call it reality, but no matter how one slices it we still believe it's an exception. To Fredrik, alpha males causing him to feel tense was an exception to "feelings don't come from the outside world." Talking into a voice recorder was an exception to "feelings don't come from the outside world."

Ironically, the very same intellect Fredrik's father insisted was not fast enough or adequate enough turned out to be plenty fast and adequate enough to get him through medical school and become a successful psychiatrist.

It is also fast and adequate enough to convince himself there are exceptions to his insight.

23. FEELING DEPRESSED[16]

As of May, 2011 my 86-year-old mother was doing remarkably well. Amy and I visited her and her partner in Delray Beach, Florida that February. She seemed slightly more tired than usual but still was her old self, still involved in many activities, still moved around well, her mind still sharp as a tack. She had slowed a bit but at age 86 this was not a big surprise.

Later that month she learned she had pancreatic cancer. Very bad news! Doctors presented options. They kind of talked her into undergoing a huge Whipple operation, where they removed part of her pancreas, part of her liver, part of her intestine and her entire gall bladder—an awful lot for an 86-year-old body to handle.

When the surgeon informed us how the operation went he said they were unable to get a "clean perimeter" around an artery. Her partner Charlie was very optimistic—good for him; it kept his spirits up—but to me this did not sound promising.

My mother's recovery crawled like a snail. Her first major problem: she couldn't keep any food down. She spent a month at Mass General Hospital in Boston, then got moved to the Spaulding rehab facility in Cambridge for another two months. Her quality of life deteriorated, literally going down the tubes hanging out of her. Lying in the hospital and rehab facility her body, too, began to deteriorate. After three months she finally got off the feeding tube. To say she was not a happy camper was a vast understatement. She desperately wanted to get back home. We moved her close to her home in Amherst, Massachusetts at Amherst Extended Care.

My brother, sister and I encouraged the physical therapists to set some realistic goals for her to get home. Jointly we came up with five

---

[16] I do not pretend this Chapter is about serious depression. It is about the type of depression in which anyone can find themselves for short periods of time. More on serious depression later.

goals, toward which she started working. But she felt very lethargic. She seemed to peak, then began to slide in the opposite direction.

We started weighing options. I'd been giving up about 40% of my life to regularly drive the three hours from Moretown, Vermont to Amherst, stay over, then drive three hours back.

In the midst of this my daughter's partner discovered he had a serious heart condition and immediately needed massive triple-bypass heart surgery. His recovery proved to be excruciatingly painful at times and slow. I now split my time driving back and forth between his hospital in Burlington, Vermont and my mother's rehab in Amherst.

My daughter, Jaime, took care of him constantly. She had been scheduled to help staff a West Virginia "Hero's Journey" retreat but decided she couldn't leave him during his recovery, despite being a wreck and worn down. She needed it. He told her to go, so she did.

While away, as he recovered from his operation, he decided to leave her. Literally he had a change of heart. Recently they'd bought a house together, mostly with his money, as he is quite wealthy, they furnished it together, they enrolled Jaime's daughter in an expensive Waldorf school. They loved each other very much. Everything appeared fine in their relationship, except Jaime now felt tremendous pressure having to continually tend to him during his recovery. His Venezuelan family flew in to be with him; now they lived with her in the house and were fairly demanding. One day Jaime lost it. Soon after, he called the whole thing off. Could her one freak-out be reason to leave her? It didn't make sense. Dumbfounded and completely devastated Jamie needed tons of support, which I attempted to provide.

In the midst of this, my contract ended with the State of Vermont as State Coordinator of all its regional Child Protection Teams, so I lost a good chunk of my income.

On its heels came the Vermont flood, courtesy of Hurricane Irene. Amy and I watched helplessly as the aptly-named Mad River on which we lived rose, overflowed its banks and swallowed up the road and mailbox. Luckily, Amy's house perched high enough on a hill to be in no danger, but when the flood waters receded we discovered canyons where the road used to be. Stranded for three days. We scrambled into and over the canyons to walk the mile into town to discover the entire town had flooded. The river had overflowed its banks so quickly people couldn't get out in time. Lives torn apart. Homes lost. For three days we helped people move soaking furniture, books and papers out of their houses. In one house we had to empty an entire, still-sopping-wet basement, with all kinds of ugly things floating in it. Bookcases and furniture lay in a crumpled heap, crashed into each other. Next we helped Amy's friends strip their lower floor walls of soaking wet sheetrock down to the studs.

Then the father of my close brother-in-law died.

Somewhere in the midst of all this I realized I felt kind of depressed, an uncommon feeling for me. Sure, I have my moods like everyone else, but this one I couldn't shake. I became unpleasant to be around. My low spirits started to get to Amy.

Driving back to the house one day after visiting my mother I realized I felt so low because I experienced everything as *pressure*.

Why pressure? Because I didn't know the right thing to do! I felt pressure about –

- What kind of conversation was I supposed to have with my mother, who by this time had stopped all communication?
- Clearly, my mother no longer wanted to live life this way anymore, but how was I supposed to help her with that?
- We had to make a decision whether to put her in rehab or in hospice, and I had no idea which would be best.
- How could I help her get home? She wanted to be home! It looked less and less likely she would make it. Somehow I had to get her home.
- Since I couldn't be in two places at once, should I be with my mother or with my daughter?
- Now that I'd lost my financial cushion along with my state contract, how could I continue to afford the gas to visit my mother all the time?
- How much is one supposed to sacrifice themselves for their loved ones? I saw my mother do it with her mother for years and begin to resent it.

Interestingly, I didn't even realize I asked myself these questions.

Yet seeing my head full of pressure made an impact on me. It didn't pull me out of my funk, but realizing this seemed to take the edge off. My consciousness rose a notch. Then I realized I actually wanted to wallow in self-pity for a while. I knew I was making up this feeling I couldn't shake, but knowing that lifted me only one more notch.

We realized our mother didn't have long to live. Finally we got her transferred back to her house with 24-hour nursing care.

On my drive to Massachusetts to visit her one day I listened to a CD I'd found of a psychic reading given to Amy and me by Jean-Jacques Guyot of Montreal a year and a half before. I couldn't believe how lighthearted I sounded on that CD. Amy and I sounded like newlyweds. I realized right then and there I liked being that way better than the way I now felt.

In that moment an insight struck: If I don't feel like being depressed, I don't have to be! Whoa!

Life is too short. Did I want to waste my life being depressed? Who is in charge of this?

Instantly my depression lifted.

Here's the thing: Nothing about my situation had changed! Everything in the outside world remained exactly the same, yet at one point I was depressed and now I wasn't. Things were still hard but now I no longer added to the difficulty, creating an extra burden with my own thinking.

The same lesson again and again, which I seem to forget again and again. It's so easy to blame our problems on what's happening in the outside world, when the outside world is incapable of making me feel anything! We blame our emotions on those external things, but are we stuck feeling the way we're feeling?

Nope.

Do other levels of consciousness exist that we might possibly be able to see it through?

Always.

The only thing that can ever lift us out is a big-enough new insight, which is always right around the bend. We only need to see it. As Syd Banks said, we're always only one thought away. We just don't know when that one thought is coming.

24. WISDOM

Low tide. I watch a seagull grab a clam in its beak, pick it up, fly high in the air and drop the clam on the hardest part of the beach to get into the shell. How do seagulls know to do this?

I look more closely. I thought they were trying to crack open the shell, but all they want to do is jar the clamshell open just enough to stick their beaks into the edge and pry it open. Where do they learn this?

Seagull wisdom.

Among the junk brought in by the ocean waves after a storm, once in a while they deliver a treasure. Today I find a beautiful light blue-green piece of seaglass.

Same with thought. Among the stormy junk sometimes thought delivers a treasure in the form of wisdom.

From where do thoughts arise that give us phenomenal ideas? Steve Jobs realizes how to change the way the world entertains itself. Bob Dylan writes a type of song no one had ever written before. Michael Jordan flies through the air, basketball in hand, a defender comes at him and at the last moment he shifts his body to make an impossible move nobody ever made before. Mozart hears a brilliant musical composition in his head that sounds nothing like any composer before him. Van Gogh sees a new way of painting no one had ever painted before? The list goes on.

But it is not just them. It is also us.

Among the junk thoughts of despair, destruction, anger, worry, anxiety, frustration, judgments of others, jealousy, fear, ego, sometimes appear thoughts of invention, of brilliance, of love, of gratefulness, of compassion, of thoughts never thought before about a particular situation, or ever. To have a greater chance of hearing the latter thoughts it is unwise to hang onto the former. To hang onto the first set of thoughts is to accept those for our lives; our lives becomes those thoughts. When we allow the second set to rise forth out of clear nothingness, our life becomes peace, love and wisdom.

Our life becomes what we think. Amazing!

Which type of thought will we give importance to? Which are we willing to accept for our lives? Will we accept a life of misery, worry, anger? Or will a yellow-golden brick road open before us?

If we want a life guided by wisdom, all we need is a clear mind. Wisdom speaks with soft voice, but also with clarity and certainty. We need only listen closely. We can only hear it when the mind clears.

Wisdom is speaking right now. Can we hear it? Here I must make a distinction between wise thoughts and Wisdom itself. Wisdom is the Intelligence behind life. Wisdom is inherent within the spiritual energy surrounding us. It is Universal Mind itself—or a part of it. It wants to share with us. It is feeding us wise information all the time in the form of insights, intuition, gut feelings. Another way to put it is, we borrow from Wisdom to get wise thoughts.

Will we listen?

A woman finds herself in an abusive relationship. I ask if at the beginning she saw any warning signs. Invariably she says yes. She chose to ignore them. The warning signs were wisdom speaking! Other louder thoughts overrode it. She chose to ignore wisdom. It got her into trouble.

Wisdom is unmistakable. It is not a function of our personal, thinking mind. Wisdom comes to us seemingly from out of nowhere. We *know*. We feel it. It feels different. It feels unshakable.

Some people wonder whether what they're thinking is wisdom or not. Rule of thumb: If one is confused about whether it is wisdom, it isn't.

[*More on wisdom in the final chapter—47.*]

25. RELAXING VS. TIGHTENING

I am pretty much a mid-intermediate cross-country skier. When I lived in Vermont, as soon as the snow fell I went out nearly every day, skiing out my door. Cross-country skiing is perfect for getting and staying in shape, plus it gets me out into the great outdoors and into the backwoods.

When I'm at my best I ski completely in the flow; I can feel the ground beneath my skis, my legs giving and adjusting to whatever hills, valleys and bumps I encounter. My legs and knees feel loose; I simply feel great.

The challenge comes when I encounter a steep downhill. Cross-country skis do not provide nearly the control of downhill skis. It is a completely different sport. When heading downhill on cross-country skis faster than I want, I must have my wits about me. But it's kind of a relaxed wits. The feeling is being one with the moment, feeling everything happening in that moment. If I tighten up even a bit I am more likely to crash. Tightening can only happen with thought. I'm not aware I'm thinking, but I am.

As I approach the farthest bridge I built over a stream beyond Amy's backwoods I must be really careful there. A slight slope drops down onto my narrow bridge. If I'm not alert I pick up more speed than control.

Across the other side of the bridge two trees have fallen across the path. Over the bridge it flattens; then about thirty feet or so from the bridge come the downed trees—plenty of room before them to stop. The first log lays on the ground about a foot high; the second fell onto another tree and crosses the trail about chest high. I had skied there the day before, stopping in time to step over the first log, then duck under the second. I needed to be careful, but no big deal.

Oops, today the snow is a bit icier, faster. I pick up more speed than yesterday, a lot more than I want. I did not prepare my mindset for icy conditions; meaning, on downhills I don't often stay on the trail. Our neighbors often make beautiful snowshoe trails, and in heavy or high snow those paths help a lot. After a storm I love when they go out before I do, so I don't have to break trail all the way. But when conditions get a little icy those snowshoe trails on the downhills can become treacherous. So I ski off the path into the deeper snow and zigzag back and forth across it with semi-control at least, so I don't kill myself. Sometimes that's tough when trees line either side of the trail. Nevertheless I make adjustments. This day I didn't.

But no worries. If I make it over the bridge I'll slow down in time before I hit the downed trees. The snow is fast but I feel relaxed speeding across the narrow bridge. I make it over, but holy cow, I'm heading toward the downed trees too fast! I tighten up. Cardinal sin. I am not slowing, certainly not stopping.

A quick thought: "How am I going to ski over the first tree then duck under the second one at the same—"

It happens so quickly I don't even have time to finish my thought. My skis hit the first tree log on the ground. They don't make it over. They stop, but I don't. I fly forehead-first into the second chest-high tree.

I sprawl out on the snow and ice in a daze. Luckily I'm wearing a thick toke hat double-folded across my forehead, which cushions the blow.

How could I have let this happen? Two reasons: 1) I didn't slow my mind down first and assess the situation so I could hear wisdom speak, "Jack, because of ice, you need to zigzag across this downhill path." 2) Once I knew I was in trouble I had thoughts of fear. Fear equals tightening. Tightening equals less control. To escape without harm my thoughts needed to be one with the moment, with the skis, the snow, the conditions, the downed trees. Fear thoughts are off the moment! With my wits about me at least I could have bailed out and thrown myself to the ground before my forehead hit. But no.

Not listening to wisdom can hurt.

26. BLIND SPOTS AND HIDDEN THOUGHTS (Saga, Part I)

Note to readers: I tell a lot of stories in this book on purpose, so you, the reader, will lose yourself in the story, which allows you to forget about your own issues and problems, which allows your mind to relax, which enhances the possibility for you to have your own insights. In that respect the story you are about to read here is no different, except this story is an autobiographical account, a saga in three parts spread throughout the rest of this book. Though this saga is personally embarrassing to me I include it here because it is the perfect illustration of how any of us who believes in the reality of our own thinking can at any time be seduced by that "reality," as consciousness makes it look like truth. No matter how much we allegedly know about the Three Principles, any of us can be caught by a blind spot we can't see. This saga also represents my own cutting edge of understanding; I bump up against myself. So, first, I write my story as it unfolded from the low level of consciousness I saw at that time; then at the end of my saga in the last chapter of the book I look back at it from a Three Principles perspective. Because I don't want to interrupt the flow of the story as it unfolded I ask you, the reader, to be patient and bear with me for its truths to be revealed by the end. At the beginning of the second and third parts of the saga, Chapters 33 and 46, I say more about my intentions for including this story as I do, as I know it is quite different from the rest of the book.

By this time, astute readers of *Somebody Should Have Told Us!* or *Parenting from the Heart* may be wondering who Amy is and what happened to my wife Judy who appeared in those books. In a word (or six): wisdom obscured by hidden blind spots.

Before going there, I need to say something in general about blind spots. A blind spot is thinking we can't see that acts upon us without our realizing it. We don't even know there is anything to be seen. Unlike common hidden thinking, a blind spot drives us, directs us, without our knowing it. Everyone has them.

A car slows in front of us on a three-lane highway. We want to pass. We look in our rear-view mirror. All clear. We check our left side mirror. All clear. We turn our head and look left to be sure no car is there. Clear. We pull out left to pass. BEEEEEEEP! Whoa! Whew! We nearly hit a car about to pass us. Where did it come from? We looked! We were certain no other vehicle existed. But it was in our blind spot, just out of view. We didn't know, we didn't see it and it nearly killed us because that car existed nowhere in our consciousness because we were blind to thoughts of it. Yes, we could have been more careful, but we can only see what we can see.

No matter how much anyone knows about the Three Principles and lives life through this understanding, no matter how knowledgeable or skilled a Three Principles practitioner, no matter how wise a human being, no one is immune from having blind spots. Why? Because a blind spot, by definition, is not known, or at least the totality of a blind spot is not known.

This should not be scary news to anyone; it's so common. All that's going on, really, is with a blind spot we get caught up in strong sensory data and forget what's behind it is only thought, not reality. When caught in such thought, which we don't know we're having and we believe it, we easily can be taken for a ride and become blind to anything other than that thought. For example, if someone is lustful he becomes seduced by the senses and it really feels like truth. If someone has a phobia she becomes seduced by the senses and it really feels like truth. If someone is defiant he becomes seduced by the senses and it really feels like truth. Same with everything. What we don't realize is in all these cases our senses are giving us information about our own thinking, not about the outside world. When I was a kid I used to be afraid of bees. I was so blind to the role of thought it really looked as if bees, themselves, were really scary because I could get stung at any moment. But the bee could be near others and they wouldn't be scared.

Blind spots take many forms. For example, being ruled by ego one does not realize one is ruled by. Being ruled by a fear one does not realize one has. Being ruled by greed when one believes only that it would be beneficial to have as much money as possible. Harming someone we wouldn't harm in a million years if we knew we were harming them. We can be blinded by so many different things. No matter how much we live through the eyes of the Three Principles in nearly all aspects of our lives, we are not immune in certain other areas. No one is.

Yet, curiously, we may judge or look down upon others whose blind spots get revealed and who harm themselves or others in the process, especially when involving colleagues whom we believe should know better. Why do we do this? Because their blind spots are different from ours. We may not like the blind spots we see in others, and we use our creative power of Thought to pass judgment, even while blind to our own—until our blind spot reveals itself; then we're not blind to it anymore.

Since we can't see them, blind spots are innocence. Innocent or not, blind spots unfortunately can do harm to ourselves or others or both.

I am about to reveal a huge blind spot of my own, which eventually came to light probably too late. I am not proud of being seduced by this blind spot, courtesy of consciousness. As I said, it's very personal and embarrassing to admit publicly; it makes me cringe even thinking about it. But I couldn't see it then; it wasn't in my consciousness. Even if someone had pointed it out—and some probably did—I would have denied it. How could I admit to what I couldn't see? I wouldn't even write about it here if it didn't have implications for everyone who has a blind spot (and that means you; only yours are different, if you're lucky).

Over the years this blind spot partially reared its head several times and got me into some trouble. After a while I sort of caught on to it and decided to change. I thought I had set it aside. Unbeknownst to me it merely took another form. So when it appeared again it took me completely by surprise—

It happened innocently enough. I'd been hired to conduct a Health Realization/Three Principles training at a Vermont elementary school. I set up the training room in a semicircle the way I like it. As I sat immersing myself in last minute preparation I noticed a few teachers trickle into the room. A woman caught my eye.

The strangest thing then happened. I heard a voice in my head. It sounded loud and clear. Only I could hear it. I didn't know where it came from. I didn't know what it was.

The voice said, "She's the one!"

What?! This took me completely by surprise. I had sworn off women—one of my major blind spots. In retrospect, my blind spot looked like this: When alone I sometimes had an uneasy feeling, as if something wasn't quite right, almost as if I had a hole inside myself that needed filling from something external to myself. Specifically, women. Nothing made me feel better than to be in the presence of an attractive, wonderful woman who cared about me, with whom I could totally be myself, who completely and utterly accepted me unconditionally for who I am. Since it made me feel so good I sought it out, particularly with female colleagues with whom I worked in the field of prevention. All thought, of course, but I couldn't see it then. Back then I never could have described it like this. I simply had an uneasy feeling when alone. I wasn't looking for sex; I was after a feeling of closeness and unconditional acceptance.

Over the years my blind spot resulted in one full-blown illicit affair and a few close encounters. Needless to say, this did not do wonders for my marriage. It got to the point where I knew it was wrong; it had to stop. So I did. When I did I felt like something died inside me. But I accepted it as life. Since I became exposed to the Principles I felt happy in pretty much every other way. So imagine my surprise when I heard that voice—

Since I couldn't conduct a training with that on my mind I let the voice-thought pass. I set it aside for the six months I conducted the training, though Amy clearly was my favorite student and the one who caught on most quickly and deeply to the Three Principles. I set it aside for another seven months of a Long-Term Professional Training I conducted with Lori Carpenos, which Amy attended unrelated to her school. Despite her again being my favorite student we had no contact outside the training or classroom; neither of us thought about the other in any way except professionally.

A month or two after the last training ended I had the opportunity to run a Health Realization workshop in Killington at the BEST Institute, a Vermont education conference. I asked a few of my top former educator-trainees if they wanted to run the workshop with me, Amy among them. I found myself really looking forward to spending time with her.

The day before the event they cancelled our workshop; not enough people pre-registered. I found myself very disappointed—not because of the workshop but because I wouldn't be able to hang out with Amy. When I contacted Amy to tell her the bad news I heard myself ask if instead that day she wanted to go on a hike with me up Camel's Hump.

She said, "That sounds even better than BEST."

Something happened to me on that hike—to both of us, actually. I hadn't planned for this. Maybe it was the wonderful conversation and energy that flowed so freely between us; maybe because it was the most beautiful first time I'd ever spent with anyone, but we both felt an astonishing connection. We found much in common. We both loved music, sports, being outdoors and in nature. Being with her felt uplifting. We practically flew up and down that mountain. When we came down, to relax our weary legs Amy asked if I would like to jump into her hot tub.

"Okay," I squeaked.

In retrospect, the wise thing would have been to never contact her again. She held too much of a charge. It felt too good. Already it felt almost too late. Pandora's Box had opened. Instead, we arranged a second hike, then a third. Although I didn't think so at first, now I couldn't believe how beautiful, intelligent and deep she was. Soon we fell madly in love. Years later when I saw an interview with Bob Dylan and he said with a wry smile, "You can't be in love and be wise at the same time," I knew what he was talking about.

Way before that, though, I got really scared. We both knew this was wrong. How in every other way could I understand how Mind, Consciousness and Thought worked to create reality, but not see it here? The seduction felt too good, the magnetism too strong. I found myself unable or too weak to stop—an addiction rekindling the part of me I thought had died long ago. In our stolen moments I felt alive again. This didn't look like thought to me; it looked and felt like reality.

While visiting my mother at Nantasket Beach, with the moon especially full that day, I took an early morning run at low tide—the lowest tide I'd ever seen. As I ran along I noticed a sandbar far out in the shallow ocean where I'd never seen one before. I couldn't resist wading knee-deep out to it. I climbed up onto the sandbar and stood a while breathing in the salt air, gazing at the shoreline far across the water, feeling so happy, so alive, lost in natural mindfulness.

Suddenly I felt water lap at my heels. The tide had started to come in. I didn't want to leave. It felt too good out there.

I felt water at my ankles. The sandbar disappeared. It felt like I was standing on the ocean. At that moment I realized the full moon and the sandbar were the metaphor of Amy's and my relationship. From the very beginning and at every point along the way we could leave the island we created. But we said, "Oh, just a little while longer. It feels too good!" All while the water keeps getting deeper. Up to our knees. The deeper it gets the harder it becomes to pull away. Up to our waists—even harder to stop. Up to our necks. Once up to our noses, it's too late.

I waded off the sandbar belly-deep in ocean. Had I waited any longer I might have been in trouble. Shouldn't I do the same with Amy before it's too late? The sooner the better. Time to get out. Best not to really get going (we had not made love). But, "Oh just a little while longer, please!"

I told Amy the story of the full moon and the sandbar.

She said, "We can always swim to shore."

Ya' gotta love her.

What she said sounded great to me. She sounded so certain. I wanted to believe her. But I had grave doubts. I thought she was kidding herself. Love is the strongest force in the universe and in the face of extremely strong personal love all bets are off. I couldn't resist her (or so I thought, and what I thought, consciousness seduced me into believing true; therefore it was truth to me and I felt it as strongly as I'd ever felt anything in my life). I knew someday we would be in deep trouble. The more we got together the greater our love would grow and the less possible it would be to stop, to break the bond, to even cut back a little, which was the feeble route we chose.

I had by far the best year of my life, fulfilled to the max in every way possible. It took eight months of resisting before we fully made love. This relationship felt like perfection, lifting us to realms I never thought possible. I have never been happier.

There was one catch. One huge catch. This was an illicit relationship! We both felt extremely guilty. Life on the run isn't real. We both knew we couldn't go on like this, yet the thought of leaving my soulmate felt impossible. Life without her looked too scary. I felt so torn. I would not have traded it for anything, but did that include hurting others? Neither of us were the kind of people to hurt others. So we went into denial, into fantasy; we simply believed somehow it would all work out and no one would get hurt. Yeah, right.

We couldn't tell our spouses for one reason. Fear! Raw fear. Fear of losing everything we had. Besides, we had no good reason to give up what we had; we had no idea what a long-term relationship with each other would be like. We hadn't lived together. We had no idea what we would become over time; we were too new. It is extremely rare for couples who have affairs and leave their spouses to make it together in the long run. There's a real good reason. Thinking changes, because the entire foundation on which the relationship is built changes. We only knew we were deeply in love, too afraid to give it up and too afraid to spill the beans because we were too afraid to lose the lives we had. Fear makes people behave in ways they wouldn't if they had their wits about them.

The inevitable happened. Almost one year to the day of our first hike we got found out. Caught! Nailed. The details aren't important. I got kicked out of my house—not immediately but soon after. I drove off, not knowing where to go. That night I slept in the back seat of my car. I awoke on my birthday, cramped and stiff. I went to back the car out to leave, but something didn't feel right. I got out to look. Flat tire!

Happy birthday to me.

Over the next few months some very nice friends put me up in their homes. I drifted from room to room, totally lost.

Odd timing, but I had to fly across the continent for Syd Banks's 75th birthday celebration, an invitation-only surprise party held for him on Salt Spring Island. I wouldn't have missed it for the world. I arranged to meet Gabriela before the event and told her my sad story. She kindly consoled me. Then I walked into a room filled with love. Syd touched so many lives. I had the thought that Syd may never know the full impact he will have on the world; how this understanding is guaranteed to keep growing and spreading. George Pransky got up and said, "Someday people will look back on these days and say, 'Remember when there were so few people involved in this understanding.'" Extremely moved, Syd said it was the best night of his life.

Sitting listening to everyone pour out love for Syd I realized that for an hour or two I had not thought about Amy. Shocking! My mind had been all-consumed with her. A realization came to me, and I leaned over to whisper it into Gabriela's ear: Life consists *only of moments*. That's all we have. One after another, moments come like pearls strung on a necklace, only no string holds them together—just thoughts. A moment of thought comes, it passes by, is gone, and a new moment comes. That's all life is.

Gabriela whispered back, "That is huge."

I thank Gab from the bottom of my heart for being there for me. I thank Syd from the bottom of my heart for changing my life. I realized if it wasn't for Syd I would never have met Amy. He didn't know and never would. If it weren't for Syd I never would have met Gabriela or so many wonderful others. A string of pearls.

I rented an apartment and settled into a new life. Meanwhile, Amy and her husband divorced after an uneasy marriage. Amy and I still saw each other and together went through all the pain involved in hurting other people and disrupting families. Both of us felt horrible about what we had perpetrated.

Lo and behold, after being on my own for a while Judy decided she wanted me back. By this time I felt a great deal of peace. I had never experienced such peace of mind. I cherished it. I relished it. I loved it! I wanted this kind of peace for the rest of my life. I didn't know what to do; I was torn. I knew the "right" thing would be to go back to my marriage, back to the life I'd experienced for forty-two years (thirty-six married).

Judy and I had met in a registration line at Clark University. I was 19 years old. She was so bubbly, friendly, full of life. I liked her smile. I was a kid then, pretty insecure. My uncle, a fantastic if quite troubled beatnik artist and wonderful man whom I loved, had just jumped in front of a subway train. I had arrived at Clark feeling terribly upset and lost. I needed a strong woman to take care of me; I had grown up with a strong woman who took care of me. It wasn't until three years later in 1968 when I hitchhiked around the country by myself, then spent a year in VISTA living and working by myself in an African American community in Centralia, Illinois, that I came into my own and felt much stronger. I no longer needed a strong woman to look after me. But I had one, and by then I was in love with her, and though our relationship was rocky at times, it became life to me. I knew nothing else—until she forced me out on my own and I experienced such peacefulness. Should I do the "right" thing and go back to Judy, or should I follow my heart. I was in a quandary; I had no idea what to do.

Gabriela said to me, "Wait for clarity." In other words, wait for wisdom to speak. Don't make any moves until absolutely certain wisdom is speaking. So for two or three months I waited. Finally, one day I heard—the clarity unmistakable and unshakable. Wisdom said: "Your relationship with Judy has run its course. You need to choose peace for your life at this time in your life. You can't go back; it is time for you to live in peace." I felt it so strongly. My decision was now crystal clear. This had nothing to do with Amy. I felt prepared to be alone.

My decision upset my kids, who were well grown. I was the bad guy. I can't blame them for seeing it that way or wanting to protect and support their mother. When I told Judy I wouldn't go back, she turned on me. For years she could not get over it.[17] Neither could Amy's ex-husband.

Amy wanted to live on her own for a while. I respected that. Instinctively we both knew something needed to change but we didn't

---

[17] Judy and I now get along fine, by the way. But here's something interesting. A woman friend said to me, "I don't really know how I'd handle this if I were in Judy's shoes, but I hope I'd say, 'I love you, so I want you to have what your heart yearns for, and if it's not me I wouldn't want you to stay with me just because you thought it was the right thing to do.' For example, if at some time a different person brings out a better side of our partner than we do, wouldn't it be wonderful to make space for that to happen?" Meaning, when we really love someone we want what is best for that person and want to set them free. There is always another way to see it.

know what. The fact was, my blind spot had not been fully unmasked; only its effects.

Although I now had beautiful, wonderful Amy and truly felt our souls tied together in a process of discovery, that we had somehow been thrust together for a reason, over time could I potentially even put us in jeopardy if I did not fully overcome my blind spot? When I first met Amy I'd been attracted to two other women, and although I didn't seek them out because I became so fulfilled with Amy, I couldn't say for sure what would happen if either had come on to me. I knew something needed to heal, but I didn't know exactly what or why. So I sought a healing with my daughter's friend and fellow student at the Barbara Brennan School of Healing, Melissa Whittaker. I lay on Melissa's table as she began working her way up my body. She reached my solar plexus.

"I'm not feeling like you're letting any love in here. I feel some kind of block. I'm not sure what it is."

Then she reached my heart.

"Wow, I'm *really* feeling like you're not letting any love in here!"

It felt true but I couldn't put my finger on it. Then she started to work on my heart. I have no idea what she did. Her fingers began to move seemingly independently over my heart in rapid twitching movements. She told me to picture "honey droplets of love" dropping into my heart.

Suddenly I became overcome with emotion. I began to cry. It became uncontrollable. It wouldn't stop. In a flash I knew where it came from. I grew up feeling love conditional on whether I did it right or good enough, and it seemed I could never do it quite good enough. I'm certain my mother never intended this; she was a wonderful, loving woman. But I could not stand it when she became disappointed in me and I let her down. At those times her supreme disappointment seemed to supersede her love for me, and I would feel horrible. In that moment on that table I realized my need to be with other women was simply a way to mask that pain through feeling closeness and being appreciated and accepted unconditionally for who I am.

The session ended. As the excellent healer, Melissa, went to write her notes, she told me to take my time and lie on the table awhile before I got up. Suddenly, I felt surrounded by a golden cocoon of love—literally. And I knew the source of that love was me. I felt love coming from within myself for myself completely, utterly, unconditionally, for the first time in my life. I knew when I got up off the table I'd be a changed man. I didn't feel it as typical thought with words; it was more akin to what I experienced with Syd—thought at a much deeper level of consciousness. I now vibrated at a higher level.[18]

It didn't take long for it to be put to the test. Amy went away for the weekend, and I met an attractive woman at a meeting and learned she lived right up the block from me. I felt compelled to pay her a visit, not even sure what I was after. I walked by her house. I felt truly compelled! But given what I experienced on that healing table I knew I was at a major crossroads. If I followed my compelling thoughts I would have learned nothing. I would have let Amy down, let myself down. I was dying to go over there; it had been such an insatiable habit for so many years—

I literally forced myself not to go. Instead I went for a walk by myself. I knew at that moment the spell had broken. I have never felt that need or urge since. I had changed. Wisdom won.

As for me and Amy, I never felt more at peace in a relationship. It helped that she understood the Three Principles. It is so wonderful when neither partner takes the others' moods seriously or personally, when one respects different views as separate realities, when one truly listens deeply, when one only speaks with love in one's heart. We

[18] Important Note: I need to be very clear that readers do not get the wrong idea here. I don't want anyone to come away from this story thinking my insights came from a healer or from any psychic, shaman or whomever; my insights came from within me, period. My talking with or having an experience with any of these practitioners coincidentally may have precipitated or triggered my insights, but it was not because of them or what they said or did. They could have said the same thing to a hundred people and only one or two of us may have had an insight. I might have had the same insight talking with someone in a grocery store, watching a TV show, or by myself from out of the blue. I wouldn't even mention them but for my intent to report historically, autobiographically, what happened to me. What people do in these realms happens to be a personal hobby of mine; I am fascinated by what they see and tap into, but I am not recommending that anyone go see any of them to gain new insight. The Three Principles show unequivocally that no one has any more wisdom or answers than we ourselves do, embedded within everyone's pure consciousness. I say more about all this in Chapter 34.

simply loved being together. I considered it the best move I ever made, albeit a confusing and treacherous one.

But it was not without consequences, not without heartbreak. People got hurt. In turn, some went out of their way to hurt us. I do not recommend having affairs. They're too painful, too filled with fear and deceit. They send unhealthy energy out into the world.

When most people hear "affair," looking from the outside they tend to see "terrible," "immoral," "poor victim." Innocently they think and talk out of that stance. It becomes their perspective. They know! They don't listen to the alleged perpetrators; they listen through that filter. Communication cuts off; discussion goes nowhere, no new understanding possible.

What I can't figure out is, how I could possibly have ended up with the best relationship of my life had Amy and I not acted as we did? I know it wasn't right. I know the proper thing would have been, at the first sign of strong feelings, to say to our spouses, "I don't know what's going on here, but I have feelings for this person and I don't know what to do with them," talk about it and let the chips fall where they may. At least that would have been honest, which is always best. But would I have been willing to give up a thirty-six-year marriage for what at that time would have been only a fantasy? No! I didn't know enough about Amy then. I will likely remain baffled about this.

Personally, I think Amy and I lucked out. Our fantasy worked out exceptionally well in reality. This is extremely rare. Most such relationships fail, because once the "new" wears off and the new isn't new anymore—it is impossible for the new to stay new—a relationship often changes, and whenever the eros stage ends and people enter this second stage, most often what they thought they knew in the first stage doesn't hold true anymore. They start seeing differences; they begin arguing, even fight, and it often portends the end of the relationship and the people in the affair end up with nothing—a far more common experience.

Nine years later we were still going strong—

27. MINDFULNESS

From the ridiculous to the sublime—

The ocean is very peaceful this morning, very still. Quite foggy. Sunrise. The sun attempts to peek through the fog. The ocean is silvery blue, turning mostly silvery as the sun begins to rise. A golden pathway appears on vaguely rippled water, a direct path from shore to sun. Gorgeous.

Surrounded by peace and beauty like this it is not hard to be in a mindful state. It reminds me of the end of the movie, *Grand Canyon*, when with all the craziness in people's lives, their ego-driven minds swirling a mile a minute, suddenly they appear at the rim of the Grand Canyon and instantly stop in their tracks in awe, amazement, one with the moment. The world simply stops. It's like, in spite of themselves, they were slapped in their faces by the angels into a state of complete mindfulness. And they didn't have to do any mindfulness exercises or activities to get there.

The ocean is gray-blue now. Clouds have entered the picture. The golden path fades to a silvery gray. Way out on the horizon I see one patch of gold, the sun finding a tiny opening through the clouds, shining through.

Would it not be amazing to be in this same state of mindfulness in nearly every moment of our lives? We do not use our thinking to bring us to this state; it is the other way around. When all extraneous thoughts cease we automatically fall into a state of mindfulness, of peace, of seeing beauty all around. Our use of Thought is the only thing keeping us from being there always. It's the only thing that can. Merely thought entering consciousness, inhibiting this natural state. In every moment we don't feel mindfulness it's because we are creating non-mindfulness with our very own thinking. Otherwise, a mindful state would be there automatically. Because it is.

To clarify, I'm not saying a mindful state is not also thought; I'm saying it is thought aligned automatically and completely with the moment, and there's nothing we need to do to get there.

Many who profess mindfulness appear to have it backwards; saying we have to do something to become mindful. Not so. We *are* there already. We can only get in its way. But for our thinking we are one with the moment. When confronted with beauty such as I see on this beach, all other thoughts disappear. Some people, on this same beach at the same time confronted with the same beauty, might be so caught in personal thinking they may not even notice.

Here on this beach in this moment all my senses are fully engaged. I see a vision of beauty. I hear the sound of the waves. I feel the sand on my toes, light wind on my skin. I smell the salt air. I breathe it in so deeply I can almost taste it.

This possibility exists in every moment. We don't often take it. Our minds work hard instead.

We often make the mistake of thinking we get direct experience from the senses. Yet, I may not even notice, therefore have no experience of what comes through my senses. Busy mind interferes. This has happened to me many times. Same beach, same beauty around me, same water lapping at my feet, yet I barely notice, ruminating over a problem I can't figure out, going over and over it in my mind. Getting nowhere. Missing the rest. Missing the moment. In my dilemma over Amy I missed a lot. The power of Thought.

Thought decides what I experience through my senses; not the other way around.

The cutest little sandpipers dart about, tiny legs moving so fast my eyes can't even register their movement. Thousands of clams spread across the wet sand today. Seagulls take advantage. Clam massacre. White seagull poop splattered along the beach. The pathway to the sun is all silver now. My field of vision changes constantly. In a new moment a different picture appears. It looks the same for a while, then I realize it's different, changing imperceptibly moment by moment.

Same with our thoughts. Changing constantly. Almost never stopping. Why do we latch onto a particular thought giving us an unhealthy feeling, crushing peace of mind, not serving us well? We latch; we get stuck. The state of mindfulness departs. But it's there for the taking in the very next moment, because it never really went away.

The tide goes out little by little by little. At some point it reaches its limit and takes a turn. We can't see that exact moment. But so imperceptibly we don't even notice, we see the change after the fact. I see water barely trickling down little crevices in the sand. In between are tiny little sandbars. Water surrounds a tiny sandbar almost unnoticeably, then swallows it up. The tide now creeps in.

Same with our thoughts. They creep in, they go out. We can't stop them. Just like the tide and New England weather, thought simply changes.

The sun is bright now rising above the horizon, the golden yellow pathway on the ocean now too bright to even view. I'm told that from the beach we can see only twelve miles out to the sea horizon, but there's so much beyond. A long time ago people looked out at this same ocean, same horizon, and believed ships would fall off the edge. We can use our power of Thought to create anything. It took visionaries like Columbus to realize something else could exist beyond what people could see, beyond the prevailing "conventional wisdom" (which is completely different from true wisdom.) It takes a visionary to venture beyond what people know. Visionaries almost always meet resistance. Most people feel compelled to hold onto what they know at all costs. It feels safer. At least they think it does. It's not like the earth wasn't round before people discovered it. The only limitation to seeing Truth is our own thinking. Until someone like Columbus or Sydney Banks comes along, sees something beyond, takes the chance, and it changes everything.

We don't create the beauty around us—although certainly we can use our thinking to create actions that destroy it, such as polluting the waters, soil and air, cutting down the rainforests, spilling oil, usually through thoughts of greed—we create the realization of beauty around us. That is, until we get caught in a thought, then the beauty surrounding us disappears from our consciousness. In other words, the beauty already *is*. Only a thought can wipe it away—for us; a thought we created.

My thoughts drift to a couple of nights before. Amy was not a Bruce Springsteen fan—except for one song, the live version of

"Thunder Road" that began his *Live/1975-85* album, a song that held great meaning for the two of us—but I dragged her and her son to a Springsteen concert at Fenway Park, the first time I'd seen him perform. He was incredible! Almost more so were the 37,000 people all one with the moment, singing along with Bruce. Put most crowds of 37,000 in the same location and you get 37,000 separate realities, 37,000 different worlds. But in Fenway Park at that moment with all 37,000 singing along with The Boss, everyone merged as one. Everyone's extraneous thoughts flew out the window. Of course I have no way of knowing about everybody's thoughts, but I would guess most. Amy got hooked. Amy, her son, me and 36,997 other people all at one with Bruce, singing and dancing along to his power and compelling lyrics.

Then all 37,000 people tried to get out of Fenway and Boston at once and just as quickly lost their mindfulness to traffic. But they didn't really lose their mindfulness. Underneath it, the exact state still exists as when everyone sang and danced along as one. The only difference? Different thoughts crept in, distracting them from their natural mindful state, creating the illusion of separation from mindfulness.

I suddenly notice I am no longer in the sun. It has turned a bit chilly. Fog and clouds have again taken over. No more silver-gold path. Lost in my thoughts of Springsteen and his audience I didn't notice it change. My consciousness busily followed my thinking. I can either experience being one with the moment or I can have an experience of my own thinking. Consciousness graciously brings me whichever I apparently want at the time.

It's quite humbling to know I can use my gift of Thought to create forgetting I'm in this beauty. Or it can bring me a feeling of Oneness with the beauty. The path is realization—simply seeing how it all works. When we're not in the moment we could be, because we already are; we only don't realize it at those times. The only reason I do not experience the waves, the foam, the sand on my feet—which are always there for the taking on this beach—can only be because of my own creation in the moment.

Yes, humbling!

28. UNDERSTANDING, TRUST & FAITH

I don't do much downhill skiing, and when I do it is with a lot of effort. I learned skiing way back in 1964 as a teenager with the Shaker Village Ski Group. I love it but it got too expensive. Every once in a while I go, and whenever I do, no matter how well I stretch my legs beforehand, the muscles on the top front of my legs—I looked up the name: the rectus femoris—become very painful. The last time I skied all day they got so painful I wanted no part of skiing downhill anymore.

But when I arrived in Morzine in the French Alps on my European Tour, Anthony really wanted me to go skiing with him. Anthony says the entire ski industry teaches skiing the wrong way and he prides himself in knowing the right way. I had not skied downhill for a couple of years, but in the French Alps, how could I not? Besides, I had a chance to get a ski lesson from an expert, so with great trepidation I got onto the slopes.

My goodness, going up on that chair lift was beautiful! Anthony first brought me onto an easy slope. He observed my skiing for a while, watching me turn with great effort by pushing my leg out to the side, straining, especially when I went a little too fast for myself.

Anthony said, "You need to ski more relaxed."

Easy for him to say. This is how I had skied my entire life. I could ski on intermediate, even some expert trails; it was just tough for me. Now Anthony was trying to tell me to ski relaxed! I didn't know how.

Anthony would not let me off this easy slope until I skied relaxed. He kept me on that easy slope for the entire day. I didn't like staying on an easy trail for so long. I knew I needed to relax but I couldn't because whenever I went too fast fear blocked the way.

Anthony said, "You've got to use the whole mountain, the whole width of the trail." I had been skiing as if I was on a narrow trail, taking sharp short turns with great effort. Sometimes one does have to ski on narrow trails, but this was not one of them.

Observing more, Anthony said, "You're skiing flat."

"What?"

"Your skis are flat on the snow. When you go to turn, your ski is still flat."

"How else are they supposed to be?"

"The skis are contoured, so when you tip your skis a little to one side or another, you turn automatically."

"I'm not used to skiing like that. The skis I have are pretty straight. They're old."

"Skis are different now. They're curved like the rented ones attached to your feet right now, if you notice. All you have to do is tip your skis a little and you will turn. Trust me."

Who knew this? This was entirely new information. I decided to try it.

As I headed down and came to where I needed to make a left turn, instead of kicking my right leg out, as another good skier had once taught me, or doing sidesteps from one side to the other as an even better skier had taught me, I simply leaned and my skies tipped to the left and, lo and behold, I turned! Then I leaned to the right and my skis tipped to the right along with me and, amazingly, I turned again! I leaned to the other side and tipped to the left—wow! I couldn't believe it. For the first time I understood! I could relax—

—except when I got to a steeper place going a little too fast. Then I would tighten up and go back to my old habits. I couldn't believe how many times I reverted to old habits.

Right there on the slopes I had a realization. First, one has to see it—have the experience of it. Second, one has to trust it—trust that whenever the skis tip, one actually will turn. Third, one has to have faith—that even in sticky situations, such as going too fast for oneself, tipping the skis will still make the same turn happen no matter what. It might mean one only has to tip them more.

Yet whenever I went too fast for a turn I would go into fear and, habitually, my leg would push out hard to turn me. Anthony would not let me off that easy slope until I didn't. Finally he was satisfied. We would try again tomorrow.

The next morning the lovely Kay the wedding celebrant joined us. Anthony, Kay and I took off and skied all over three different interconnected mountains—the most beautiful day of skiing I've ever experienced.

Still I was amazed at how often, when I picked up too much speed I would slide back into my old habits. But I apparently skied relaxed enough so by the end of a full day of skiing on some fairly steep slopes, my rectus femoris did not hurt. I couldn't believe it.

Skiing and life. To change, first we have to *understand* and *have the experience* of it, which cements the understanding. Something like, "Wow, when I lean and tip my skis they really do turn me!" Or, "Wow, I see life really does work from the inside out!"

Once we understand and have the experience and see it happen enough, we come to *trust* it. "Wow, every time I tip my skis, I turn!" Or, "Wow, every time I have an experience, it really does happen as a result of my own thinking, not from what happens to me out there."

Once we have the understanding and experience and come to trust it, then we can have *faith* in the fact that it always happens, even when we find ourselves in sticky situations. "Uh oh, I'm going too fast and I need to turn. Yikes! Do I revert to my old habit or tip my skis?" I tip and I turn the exact same way. "Wow! There really are no exceptions!" "Wow, even when fears come up in life, even when I get caught up in my thinking without knowing it, it's still just consciousness making my thinking come alive in the exact same way! There really are no exceptions! Amazing!" We can have faith in that.

Not one single feeling does not come from our own creation of Thought. There really are no exceptions! See it, experience it, trust it, and faith comes.

Every morning when I walk or run on the beach, the sun comes up without fail. I suspect this happens everywhere. I have complete and utter faith the sun will rise, not one ounce of doubt, even on mornings when the sun is hidden behind a thick veil of clouds. I never question the sun's existence, even if I can't see it in pouring rain. Complete and utter faith—no matter how it looks.

Sometimes it feels as if it's raining in our hearts, in our minds. Sometimes our brains are full of clouds, hurricanes even. We can feel those thoughts, taste them. They overwhelm us. We become lost. Seduction at its finest. Yet, if we have the understanding and the experience, if we trust the existence of our own innate mental health deep within our souls and realize it never disappears just as the sun rises each day, we also can have faith even when things feel at their lowest, even if we can't touch it then. Faith in the essence of who we truly are—our spirit, our soul, which came into this life with us, which brings us automatic peace, automatically fills us with love, automatically allows us new insights from wisdom when our minds clear. Answers exist for us always, even when we cannot yet see them. Faith! Each of us can see new at any moment, see into realms we've never seen before. This is the promise of each new day, each new moment.

No matter what the seduction, to understand, to trust, to have faith that our inner spiritual essence shines like the sun and can never be destroyed no matter how hard we try, is our saving grace.

In fact, it is grace itself.

Even a hurricane has an eye of peace.

29. EGO RULES

Russell told me he gets irritated with his five-year-old. Russell understands the Three Principles. He knows getting irritated with his kid is not the best thing. He can't help himself. What is he missing? As a Three Principles counselor and coach, how would I help him?

First, I want to be sure I'm in a healthy state, myself. I certainly don't want to let Russell's predicament bring me down, even if I can't help him. That would be silly. His problem has nothing to do with me. I don't have to take responsibility for whether he sees beyond it or not. All I have to do is my best.

Second, Russell and I have very good rapport, a good feeling exists between us. Together we have a good time. Thus, our relationship is conducive to his mind relaxing enough to potentially hear new insights.

Third, I want to clear my head of all preconceptions and sink into a nice feeling with nothing on my mind, listen as an empty vessel. I want to feel or tap into the energy that exists between, around and through us. Wisdom, including the solution to Russell's dilemma, is hidden within this intelligent energy. All I have to do is listen deeply for it. I want to become as receptive as a radio antenna picking up signals, almost as receptive as a psychic. But the signals are subtle; they don't come in the form of words.

Out of this state I realize I'm puzzled. I am not consciously aware of my puzzlement. I don't say to myself, "I'm puzzled," yet somehow I drop into a state of puzzlement. Unknowingly I ask myself, "How can someone be irritated with his son when he understands the Three Principles and therefore allegedly knows his experience is created not from whatever his son is doing, but from within himself?" Furthermore, Russell wants a good relationship with his son, and frustration and irritation are not it. In light of all this, what would make him get irritated? That's puzzling. But I don't keep that thought on my mind; I let it set with me quietly, until and if I see something.

And I do. Out of that state I realize something.

I realize that the problem is how Russell is *seeing* his son. He sees his kid as "in my way" and disobedient, someone who doesn't do what he's told. Russell is very busy in his work, often works out of his home, and he doesn't want to be interfered with. I realize if he wasn't seeing his kid as "in my way" he would not be irritated.

I say, "Russell, if you see your kid getting in your way and not cooperating, of course you're going to be irritated, no matter how much you say you understand the Three Principles."

To Russell that made sense. Then he hit me with the all-too-familiar killer line, "But what am I supposed to do about it?"

"Russell, it's not a question of doing. It's a question of *seeing*. It's about how you see your son. If you happened to see your kid as someone excited to explore life who wants to show his father what he's been discovering, you wouldn't be irritated; you would get a warm, endearing feeling for your child in the process of exploration and trying to make sense of this world. Or, if you saw your child as, 'Oh, isn't that cute? He doesn't know how to respond when I'm telling him to do something. I have to help him patiently understand it at a five-year-old level,' you wouldn't be irritated; you would be intrigued about finding a solution. I'm not saying go out of your way to think these things. I'm saying, if any of those other thoughts about your son happened to pop into your mind, you wouldn't be irritated; you would feel something else about your kid. So it's got nothing to do with your son, because nothing about the way he's acting would have changed."

I thought what I said was brilliant. Russell remained unmoved.

I plowed ahead, "So if you realized, 'Wow, I could see my son in a million different ways, and I'm inadvertently just picking one to land on, therefore the way I feel about my kid is always up for grabs, always my own creation,' then you would not be stuck in irritation."

Still Russell was unmoved. Why? Because I had stopped listening deeply! By being caught in my own idea I left Russell in the dust. I had to drop back into deep listening.

This brought me into an even deeper state of puzzlement. "What would make Russell see his kid as 'in my way' in the first place? Why 'in my way' instead of something else?"

Out of nowhere I flashed to the man I affectionately called my witch doctor, Dr. Michael Billig, who, sadly, had died suddenly. I loved going to him for any physical ailment. He performed Contact Reflex Analysis (CRA) and kept me healthy for fifteen or twenty years without relying on Western medicine. CRA is a way of muscle testing via pulses of the body. Dr. Billig told me, "The body never lies." He'd say, "Hold your arm up as strong as you can," and he would press various points on my body, and when he pushed on a certain trouble spot, as hard as I tried I would not be able to hold my arm up. It would go down like a knife through butter. He said, "This is about some condition or deficiency in your body in this moment causing this physical condition [or disease] to materialize." Then he would muscle test me for what I needed to take (often various doses of certain megavitamins over a set period of time) to overcome the condition. I don't understand what he did, but it sure worked for me. I got a charge out of how the body can heal itself so the condition could no longer exist. The dominoes would then fall so I would not experience the problem that would be diagnosed by a medical doctor.

Why in the world did Dr. Billig and CRA suddenly occur to me while deep listening to Russell about what made him see his kid as "in my way?" Wisdom sometimes operates in very strange ways.

The connection came to me in a flash! Russell's mind harbored a condition that caused him to see his kid as "in my way." He only saw his son as "in my way" because of that condition. I simply needed to uncover the condition in his mind, much like Dr. Billig uncovered the physical condition in my body.

I became puzzled by what it might be.

Bingo! The reason he saw his kid as "in my way" is because, behind that, he is thinking "me, me, me" thoughts. His ego is engaged. His kid is interfering with the "me" being allowed to perform its illusory dance. Then Russell would get scared that he wouldn't be able to protect himself.

I asked Russell if that might be true. Instantly he knew. He told me the story of how when he was growing up he was raised extremely Christian. Between the church and his mother he felt his "self" pretty much denied. He was living for God and living for his mother and he had to sacrifice him*self* to that.

"Isn't it perfect?" I said. "Isn't it pure innocence that you would pick up a habit from childhood about having to preserve and protect your 'self' at all costs, and carry it into today and have it be like a veil over the beauty of the moment with your son? You can't appreciate the moment with your son because a 'me, me, me' veil stands between you and the moment with the two of you. As soon as your kid does something you perceive as getting in the way of 'me,' you get irritated, and it's got nothing to do with what he is doing. It's not him irritating you; it's that you interpret whatever he is doing as getting in the way of what you think you need to protect. And it's only this veil of 'me' overriding your appreciation of your own child in that moment."

Russell saw it! That's all it was? Unbelievable! It unlocked a ball and chain from his leg. Freedom. But not freedom from having those thoughts, because they are such a habit he will keep getting them, guaranteed. It's about how he will now see those thoughts when they arrive. Will he be caught in them, ruled by them as he has been, or will he notice them and see them for what they are—just innocent thoughts from childhood that mean nothing now, interfering with the moment—and be amazed how often they show up? If he sees the latter and simply notices them playing tricks on him and is attuned to picking up these thoughts and not letting them rule, over time they lose their power. With this new perspective from a higher level of consciousness, his thinking, feelings and actions change automatically. Instead of seeing "in my way," he realizes "in my way" is only a figment of his imagination, only his own self-protective ego at work. What remains is the pure experience of seeing his kid lost in enjoying life. Then, wisdom naturally arises about how to deal with the situation so he has both time to get his work done and time to enjoy his son naturally. This comes out completely differently than when acting out of irritation. Something like, "Buddy, I'd love to play with you. Just give me twenty minutes to finish up what I need to do for work, and then we can have a really fun time together."

Very often a hidden layer of ego, "me," fear, hovers over everything like a veil. The veil stands between us and the moment. Seeing new pulls off the veil, allowing our innate health and wisdom to appear, because it never went anywhere.

30. MONEY AND CONCERN

Vicky called me, concerned about money. She hadn't had a job in a while but just found one. Now she worried it didn't pay enough for her to live on. She also said the company she works for is so concerned about the bottom line it overrides everything else, and that troubles her.

Interesting. When Vicky didn't have a job she had concern about money. Now that she has a job she has concern about money.

Will Vicky be concerned about money whether she has income or not? Vicky also has concern over her employer's concern about money. What if her problem isn't so much about money; what if her real issue is *concern* in general? What if she goes through life with concern on her mind? As I listened to her, these thoughts ran through my mind. I wondered if she harbored a hidden thought that things needed to work out a certain way in life and, if not, she experiences concern.

Before I could ask, Vicky asked me, "Well, how are you about money?"

"How is that relevant to you?"

"I really would like to know."

"Well, Vicky, if you must know, I used to be very concerned with money. I grew up with a mother who lived through the Depression and was always concerned about money. It's funny, though, because my father also came through the Depression and he never seemed concerned about money—he was always so generous—so obviously it wasn't growing up in the Depression; it had to be separate realities. But my mother spoke with a much louder voice, so my thinking became more influenced by her. It's also funny to me that even though as a kid I worked for my father in his electric motor repair shop [I stripped armatures, wound wire coils, helped him with bookkeeping], my first real job was working with low-income kids doing anti-poverty work. This is how I got into the field of prevention, which is anything but a lucrative profession. So I always struggled with money, felt the lack and that lasted most of my career. But now I'm not nearly so concerned about money. And it's not because I have a little more now than I used to, because it's not all that much more."

"What happened, then?"

"What really changed me about money was I had a big insight."

"What was it?"

"When I would complain about not having enough money, people used to ask me, 'Why don't you get a job where you could make a lot more money?' My answer was, 'Because money isn't important to me; I'd rather do what I love.' One day I heard myself and I realized, 'Wait a minute, I'm saying money isn't important to me, but I'm worried about money all the time. That means it *is* important to me! If it wasn't important to me I wouldn't be worried about it.' That was a big insight for me."

"So are you saying you no longer think about it?"

"No, money concerns became such a habit those thoughts still show up from time to time. But now when they show up I know I'm at a fork in the road. I know I have equal potential to have thoughts of lack or thoughts of abundance, and many more in between, and I inadvertently pick one and latch onto it as if it's truth. I had been choosing 'lack.' I could just as easily have picked 'abundance.'

"You mean you now go out of your way to choose abundance?"

"No, that's not what I'm saying. I'm saying so long as I know *abundance* is an equal possibility, then I don't have to be so attached to *lack*, because they're both made up. See, what I and you actually do to earn money is one thing, but we could do the same thing to earn money and do it with concern and worry, or we could do the exact same thing without concern and worry, and the same amount of money would appear. We would be in the exact same position financially with or without the concern, but the feeling we experience about it is something else. Does feeling lack or feeling abundance give me a better feeling? Which would I rather experience? Since I am the creator I get to experience money in any way I want."

"I think I'm getting that now."

"When I say I'm the creator I want to be clear I'm not talking about choice. I'm saying that from a higher level of consciousness I see the possibility of 'I don't have to take lack seriously because I'm making it up.' This means realizing that 'lack' thoughts and 'concern' thoughts are an illusion not doing me any good, not serving me well. They're not getting me any more money or getting me money any faster. If I need more money I have to do whatever I need to do to get more money faster. Thoughts and feelings of either lack or abundance have absolutely nothing to do with whatever I actually get, but I'm the one who gets to live with the feeling of it."

"Oh, I see."

"But Vicky, I'm not even sure concern over money is your problem."

"You don't? What is?"

"Concern in general. No matter what it is, you'll find something to be concerned about. Do you think that's true?"

"Ha! Now that you mention it, probably."

"Well, the same thing I was saying about money also holds true about any concern you have."

"What do you mean?"

"The fork in the road. Seeing from a higher level of consciousness. Knowing whichever path we pick we're making it up."

"I think I see."

31. JEALOUSY

Ty from Europe joined a webinar I conducted. Toward the end he asked a question about jealousy. I didn't have time enough to adequately address it, so I asked him to email me a specific incident where jealousy reared its head, then ask whatever questions he had and I would do my best to answer. Up front I told him I might be interested in including our email dialogue in my new book. Ty agreed. What follows is our edited email conversation. When I saw what he wrote—well, shocked is an understatement—

Ty: [This is about] my relationship with my girlfriend…We really love each other and enjoy the other's company. It's just when she has dark feelings all hell breaks loose…One thing we've been having problems with is music. I love music; music is something close to my heart. If I listen to music where females are singing she feels really bad. For a while I gave up music. I couldn't listen to music anymore…"Oh shit, now she feels bad. I have to turn this off." Movies, TV, same there. If there is beautiful women there we can't watch it, most of the time at least…And if there's a naked woman or females in bikinis I have to turn away and not look at the TV screen…I can't say anything positive about any woman, like "She is funny, good person, helpful." Sometimes she doesn't have any bad feelings and sometimes she has them. Even if I THINK that a female looks good, like if her friend dressed up to go to a party and she asked if she looked good in this dress, that would be a nightmare…. I don't mean "She looks so good I want her instead" kind of thoughts, just a quick thought, "Yeah, she is physically attractive," and poof that thought goes away. My girlfriend can't handle those thoughts…What she has said to me in those situations are, "They have a better voice than ME. They look better than ME. They have a better body than ME. Funnier, smarter, better than ME ME ME," and she gets anxiety and can even get panic attacks.

I think I only really have 3 questions:

1. How can I help her realize that these ideas are made up? She understands that she should not feel this way but can't stop feeling bad. Or, how can she realize it's her that I want, nothing "better"?
2. What can I do when I get the "stick"? I hate feeling that I'm the one who makes her feel bad. I know it's not really true, but...I hear from her, "You can't do that or that or that. If you do I will feel bad." What can I do when I get sucked into my emotions and can't be strong for her?
3. Something she has a hard time understanding is why it should be OK for me to think that people look good; it's not something I have any control over either way…

Whoa! I was taken completely by surprise. Before I received this I thought we would be talking about Ty's own jealousy. Ty definitely had a big jealousy problem, but he was not the jealous party. This was the most extreme case of jealousy I'd ever heard. That was my first thought. My second thought, thinking about his girlfriend, was, "Poor thing!" I felt for both of them. But okay, I committed myself, so I went into reflection.

JP: Thanks so much for writing that. My first thought was, "Do you really want to live like that?" That's real extreme. I wish you were the one having the jealousy issue, though, because then our dialogue would pertain to something you would have direct control over. Do you think this is something your girlfriend would be willing to talk to me or write to me about? Meanwhile, I'll attempt to answer your questions.

1. *How can I help her realize that these ideas are made up?*

The problem is her fear and ego are very real to her; to her they are not an illusion of her own creation. I'd ask her questions such as these:

"If I'm watching a movie with an attractive woman in it, what are you really afraid of?" I'll try to answer for your girlfriend but I'm just taking a wild stab here. She might say something like, "She's got a better body than me."

"What are you afraid of about that? So what if she's got a better body?"

It's not a question of what you can *say* to her, Ty; it's a matter of asking her questions like that and deeply listening, and based on her answers asking her more questions until you understand what her world looks like, and then respond out of that.

Another question comes to mind: "A lot of men are better looking than me—bodies, faces or whatever. How come I don't mind you looking at them? [If that's true.] What is the difference between you and me about that?"

I had to stop writing. Later I sent a second email:

JP: To your second question: *What can I do when I get the 'stick'?*

Ty, you cannot make her feel bad. That is impossible. Only she has the power to make herself feel bad—or feel good. People can only feel bad when they use their own power of thought against themselves. If what you're telling me is true, you are not the problem here. So if you think that way, you will be using your own power of thought to make yourself feel bad. Then you have two down people instead of one. Let me be blunt: The way your girlfriend is acting is not normal. This is the most extreme case of jealousy I have ever heard. You can't even listen to music because she makes it about herself and gets jealous? That's crazy thinking. You can't watch a movie with a pretty woman in it? I don't care how much you love her, if you sacrifice yourself like this and walk on eggshells around her it can only lead to disaster. She has huge control issues because she's got huge fear and ego issues. Jealousy is only the by-product. But the fallacy is she thinks she gains control by insisting you don't do these things. Here's the thing: You noticing other women is not what will ultimately make her lose you; her trying to control you like this is what will make her ultimately lose you.

I usually refuse to give advice, but this case is so extreme. If it were me, before I said anything to her I would get my mind right first. I would feel solid in the knowledge that losing myself in a relationship, even for someone I love, is not healthy for me. I would see her kindly, because she is a lost soul about these issues and can't help herself. I would see her with love. And out of that frame of mind, I would tell her this cannot go on like this. I would offer to help her get some help about this because it is not possible to sustain a normal relationship in the face of it. And if she is unwilling to get help, then I see you have three options: 1) Keep doing what you're doing and slowly eat away at yourself; 2) Do exactly what you would like to do—listen to music, watch movies, everything normal regarding other women—and tell her you're going to do that and she's going to have to deal with it (or get help) if she wants to keep you; 3) leave the relationship. Number 1 is unacceptable for your own well-being. I see this issue as way beyond jealousy. Your own well-being is at stake! You've got to take care of yourself first.

Now that I'm writing this here I thought of a fourth option: No matter what she says, do not take it seriously and ignore it. But I didn't think Ty could pull that one off. I had to stop again before I could respond to question 3, and I sent off what I'd written. I got a response from Ty.

T: I'm grateful of your answers. As you can imagine, our situation is not the easiest one. But I wanted you to know I've read your words and I have less confusion than before. I will have a big talk with my girlfriend to get some priority straight. It's not like she does not understand that her thoughts are damaging to our relationship; she hurts as much as I do when she "destroys my life" like this. She genuinely wants to be free from these types of thought. I always tell her, "It's not YOU who make me feel bad, it's my thinking." Still, sometimes it's hard to get back to that viewpoint as I haven't realized it fully yet.

Our emails crossed in cyberspace. Meanwhile, I wrote a response to his third question.

JP: 3. *Something she has a hard time understanding is why it should be OK for me to think that people look good…*

No matter how attractive someone is, there is always someone more attractive. So what does that mean for the jealous person? That she (or he) can never be happy? In other words, so long as someone carries this idea with them, unless they completely isolate themselves, cut themselves off from everyone else in the world, they've had it! The hope is it's only thought and thought can always change.

I've been thinking about the difference between jealousy and envy. There is a very important difference, and it's hard for me to articulate. Envy is something one keeps within oneself; jealousy has to do with attributing a motive to someone else about what that person is up to. For example, let's take it off your girlfriend and put it onto you. Suppose she met David Beckham [the soccer/football star model]. Some men feel envious of Beckham's looks and body. Envy is not a healthy emotion—comparing in general is unhealthy. Envy I can understand, but even though it's not healthy it's kept within oneself and doesn't really mean much.

Now suppose Beckham asked your girlfriend to hang out with him, and she wanted to. Is that something to get jealous about? Why would it be? At this point you have no idea what is in her mind about it. Any jealousy would be you using your power of Thought to make something up about what she's thinking about him and then get fearful over what you've made up. So that doesn't make any sense.

Now suppose you see that your girlfriend really is turned on by Beckham. You're not making it up now; she really does feel that way! Is that something to be jealous about? First, what good would it do? Could it possibly serve any purpose to anyone or anything to feel jealous? I think not.

What if a man says, "I can't help it, I feel inadequate in Beckham's presence and I know my woman would like to be with him because I can see she's turned on by him." But isn't that also thought running wild? The man would be using his power of Thought to make himself feel inadequate and therefore bad. Perhaps even more important, what do her feelings about being with Beckham have to do with you? Is she saying she would rather be with him than you? You wouldn't know that at this point. You would be making that up completely. So unless she actually says she'd rather be with Beckham than you, or unless she leaves you, or unless she cheats on you to do it, or unless she starts wanting to be with you less or is less turned on by you, it really has no bearing on your relationship at all. So being jealous still makes no sense.

But now suppose she really does think those things and wants to have an affair with him or to leave you because of it. Is that reason to be jealous? It still makes no sense to me, because it just means your own relationship wasn't as solid as you thought it was, and is that the kind of relationship what you really want? Wouldn't that mean trying to hold onto a fantasy that isn't what you thought it was? And what are you going to do about it anyway? Out of jealousy try to stop her? Will that work? Will stopping her from doing something she wants to do work for the benefit of your relationship? No, it will start to kill it. What I'm trying to say is, built into the emotion of jealousy is the seeds of its own destruction. There isn't one thing helpful about it, and taking action out of it means disaster.

"But I really love this woman and I can't imagine losing her!" If you really love her, set her free. If she finds someone else it means you weren't meant to be together, no matter how much you want it. If she is free to experience whatever she needs to experience, she may find that experience isn't what she thought it would be and may end up appreciating you even more. Or she moves on. But you've loved her so much you just want the best for her, no matter where it takes you. If a relationship is really, really solid it can withstand even attractions to others. Again, there are always people more attractive or fantasized to be more appealing—in lots of different ways. Is that what we want to rule us?

Of course all this assumes everything is talked about up front, respectfully, with listening, kindness and caring, because betrayal is another matter entirely and doesn't have anything to do with jealousy.

In summary, jealousy can't work. It's an illusion and a complete fallacy that if someone is jealous it will help him or her keep one's partner. It achieves the opposite.

Ty: I wanted to write and say, in a moment of clarity I saw what life should look like for me, and how to dissolve my ego and hers. I'm not there yet, but I do know where "there" is and how I will get there. If she wants to follow I will gladly walk hand in hand with her to the ends of the earth. I wish to thank you for your help; you did help me with this process to clarify what I believe to be true for myself. Where tomorrow takes me, if it's with or without her I don't know. Whatever happens it is for the best. I can no longer suffocate myself like I have done. Thank you. Much love, Ty

32. HOLDING ON AND LETTING GO

Shortly after my email conversation with Ty, while busy working on a project, I received a call from Mikki, a woman. I didn't know. I don't usually take cold calls, but I had been at the computer too long and needed to change my energy, so she caught me at the right moment. I didn't even have time to say a little prayer, which I usually do before each session to get my mind right, so I had to say it silently while she began to talk. Once I was able to drop into deep listening the conversation went something like this:

M: I first got exposed to this stuff by listening to Michael Neill's TED talk, "Why Aren't We Awesomer?" and it really resonated with me. Then I picked up your book and read it twice. I really feel like this is the direction I want my life to go in. I want to be able to help other people with this.

JP: So how can I help you?

M: I know all this intellectually; it just resonates with me so much. But I can't seem to let go of this thinking that swirls around in my brain. I have a really good intellect, and it serves me in every way except for this.

JP: Oh, you're one of those, eh? A big intellect. I know I'm in trouble now.

M: [laughs] I have a whole bunch of questions.

JP: Why does that not surprise me?

M: [laughs again.]

JP: Okay, go ahead.

M: Well, I know all this is true but when it comes to things in my life like relationships I just get so caught up I get into trouble. My relationships have been very abusive. Probably because I was raised by abusive parents. They were not good people.

JP: Give me an example of what you mean by ‘abusive relationships.’

M: Well, I was in a relationship with this guy who was emotionally abusive. He would put me down all the time. And I just couldn’t take it anymore, so I finally dumped him, which was good, but I can’t seem to let go of thinking about him. He is on my mind constantly. And I know it’s not good for me to keep thinking about him, but my brain won’t shut off.

JP: What does it say?

M: It says, “Why did you let yourself get involved with him? Why didn’t you listen to what your intuition was telling you? Why did you listen to him instead? How could you put your faith and trust in him when he was seeing other women and not telling you?” He was just bad for me. “How did I let myself get involved in that kind of thing again?” It’s happened to me again and again. I know it’s just my thinking. I know I’m creating it. But I can’t seem to let it go.

JP: A lot of times people know they’re creating their own reality, but once that reality is created, then it’s real to them. No one can let go of something that’s “real.”

M: But intellectually I know it’s not real. I know I’m doing this to myself.

JP: No matter what your intellect says to you about it, it’s still real to you.

M: So what can I do? How do I get it to stop fucking with me?

JP: It’s not a question of what you can do. It’s a question of what you see. If you’re able to see with new eyes then this whole thing will end up looking different to you, then what you need to do will fall into place naturally.

M: Well, I don’t understand how to overcome what I’m seeing as reality.

JP: When we’re stuck in a reality from which we can’t seem to loosen our grip, it’s really helpful to call that reality into question.

M: What do you mean?

JP: Well, for example, I was just talking with a guy who is with a woman who has the most extreme case of jealousy I have ever experienced. [I briefly told Mikki of the conversation in the previous chapter.]

M: Wow, that's really extreme! I experienced jealousy in my relationship with this guy, but nothing compared to that.

JP: I only brought it up because, in her case, whatever she sees looks totally real to her and, as I said, you can't talk someone out of their reality. But when you look at what she was thinking, is it true?

M: Not likely.

JP: So we both know her "reality" isn't *Reality*, right? But to her it looks like such reality. So if we were asking her questions we'd ask, "Is it really true that when your guy is listening to a female singer this means he is going to want her instead of you?" Or, "Does him watching a movie with an attractive woman really say you're not good enough for him physically or any other way? Does it really have anything to do with you at all?" "Do you think that kind of pressure you put on him because of your neediness and demands is more likely to have him want you and stick around?" Questions like that.

M: Yeah, I get that.

JP: So it's obvious to you about her "reality," but it's not so obvious about your own. You're doing the exact same thing she is, except a lot less extreme. We all do. For you a question is, "Is it really true that if I keep thinking about this guy it's going to help me in any possible way to feel better about myself? Am I just giving up my power and well-being to him?"

M: But it won't stop. I can't get my brain to stop.

JP: That's what I'm saying. You can't stop because you're still seeing the "reality" of it! Tell your brain to shut the bleep up.

M: [laughs]

JP: Whatever your "brain" is saying about your worth is totally meaningless. It's a lie! The truth is who you are really within your spiritual essence. That's the only real truth. Everything your brain is telling you about yourself is your own creation. It would not exist if you weren't making it up. All that stuff puts a veil over your essence, and the veil is a lie. There is no truth in it about you, despite how much your intellect keeps telling you there is.

M: But my brain is what has helped me make it through all these years.

JP: The brain is only a vehicle through which thought comes. No matter how helpful it's been to you over the years, and I'm sure it has been in lots of ways, has it been helpful to you concerning your own well-being? Has it served you well in your relationships?

M: No it hasn't. I know I have so much to offer in a relationship. I know I'm a beautiful person. I can give so much. In fact, I am one of those "absorbers" that you talked about in *Somebody Should Have Told Us!* I keep doing that. I keep giving myself up to them.

JP: What do you think you get out of that for yourself?

M: [pauses, gets quieter] So they'll love me.

JP: Yes! And does that really work?

M: No.

JP: Can love for yourself come from anyone else outside yourself?

M: No. But I keep going there.

JP: I can relate to this—in a minor way compared to you. I grew up thinking that the love I got from my mother was conditional on whether I was a good boy or not. And I brought that with me into my adulthood just like you, and it caused me to look outside of myself to feel loved. So I was doing the same thing you did.

M: Yeah. So how did you get out of it?

JP: [I told Mikki the story of being on the healing table and feeling love from within myself for the first time]

M: I'd like to feel something like that.

JP: But Mikki, don't miss the real point of my story. That's who you really are! It's what is in you. It was in me all along. I didn't see it. I didn't need a healer to bring it out. She just helped me see what I already really am. It's the same for you. That is you! Everything else is your own creation that puts a veil over it and doesn't allow it to be experienced. But you can't get away from your essence even if you wanted to, just like I couldn't. Because it's there, and all that's necessary is for the veil to be seen for what it is; then it drops off on its own and what is left is total spiritual well-being and automatic love for yourself from within.

M: I tell myself over and over again that it was because I got abused that I'm not able to overcome getting involved in this stuff over and over again—because of what happened to me.

JP: Wow, I just realized something.

M: What?

JP: That you need to forgive yourself.

M: What do I need to forgive myself for?

JP: Your intellect really helped you when your child. It protected you. And that is such innocence!

M: [quite touched, begins crying]

JP: I feel for you so much right now. But it's okay, Mikki. It really is.

M: Wow, I never realized that my intellect is what saved me when I was a kid. It really did save me! That's what I used to escape from the sexual abuse and other abuse I was experiencing from my parents. Like I knew I could get by because of my intellect.

JP: Yes, that's what I mean by innocence. It served you so well then. It's like, of course, if it served you well as a child you would take something that worked and apply it to your adult life. [*That recurring theme again.*] That makes perfect sense. Of course you would do that. Total innocence! And that's what you can now forgive.

M: [deep sobbing now]

JP: You're seeing something really big for yourself right now. Things will likely look different to you after this.

M: What really got to me was seeing that what I've been doing to myself innocently served a wonderful purpose back then, but it doesn't have to be that way anymore. Wow, I feel released from it now.

JP: That's wonderful, Mikki. But just remember, because it's such a habit you're likely to experience those kinds of thoughts coming at you again and again. The key is to just see them for what they are—

M: And have compassion for them. That's what I really see. Compassion for what I kept getting trapped in because it was so valuable to me to save me when I was a kid.

JP: Yes, that's huge.

M: [Mikki started intellectualizing about something again and the feeling began to get lost, but she caught herself] I just realized that I was going into my intellect again.

JP: Yes! But you caught it! You could tell by the feeling of it that it stopped serving you well. That's what you want to see: the futility of going there—even when it comes back on you again and again. That's the lie about who you are and, as you said, you can have compassion for yourself in the face of that. Right now I'm thinking we've had enough for today. You just need to sit with it for a bit, see how it sets with you. See if things look different now that you've gone through this. See what happens to you now. If you need another session later, if you run into any difficulties, you know where I am.

M: Yes, I agree, it feels right to stop now. Thank you for deep listening to me. Thank you so much! This is big!

I never heard from Mikki again.

33. A WORLD SHAKEN TO ITS ROOTS (Saga, Part II)

The saga, continued, with a wholly unexpected turn. This happens in life sometimes. Sometimes we can be completely thrown for a loop and remain blind.

After encountering Syd Banks and the Three Principles, as I describe in Chapter 4, for the most part I experienced a beautiful life. I felt happy, high-spirited, hopeful. I had very good relationships with my peers. Life felt pretty easy; I generally took what happened to me with a grain of salt. When I did get reactive, which happened from time to time, it lasted only briefly.

During the editing process of this book, however, well after initially writing this autobiographical saga, I had a huge insight: I realized to my utter shock that I saw one area of my life—my own love relationships—as an exception to the Three Principles, when there can never be exceptions to the Principles. Unlike in other areas of my life, with relationships I took things very personally. My ego got triggered. I would go into fear. Because of this I sometimes became trapped in a bad dream of my own making. Everyone is blind to some aspect of life where they do not see the Principles in action. This is mine.

The intent of this book is to point to what Three Principles understanding can bring to our lives. Not so with these three autobiographical saga chapters; they are very different from the rest of this book. I purposely describe the saga in detail to provide a stark example of and feeling for how it looks when one loses one's way—in contrast to when one sees Three Principles understanding. When it came to relationships, I admit humbly, I forgot all about the Three Principles. I got trapped. I got lost. This is how it looked to me then. In the final chapter I revisit this story to show how it looks from a higher level of understanding.

"I think I need space."

I could not believe my ears. These words came out of the mouth of the love of my life, the woman with whom I was certain I'd spend the rest of my life. Shocked to the roots of my very existence is (to me) the understatement of the century.

Didn't we have the most beautiful relationship—for nine whole years? We never fought; almost never even quarreled—only very rarely when both of us got into low moods at the same time. We had very few differences in general. I loved everything about Amy and about our relationship. Now she, my soulmate, needed space from me?! I didn't get it. Talk about a kick to the stomach.

To fully absorb the blow I needed some space of my own. I grabbed my bike and pedaled down the road, tears streaming down my face. I could not fathom this happening to me.

"It's got nothing to do with you," Amy said. She felt something deep within her soul. Confused herself, she had no idea why this was happening.

I wanted to believe her but felt suspicious. Was she interested in another man? She assured me that was the last thing she wanted. She loved me, she said.

Out of our massive confusion we called the great Jean-Jacques Guyot, our favorite psychic,[19] who'd helped each of us gain needed perspective a few times over the years. Our two-and-a-half hour drive to Montreal was anything but pleasant. My thoughts—therefore my feelings—bounced around the car between hurt and anger. Anger at what, I wasn't sure. Amy didn't know what this meant. She didn't want to hurt me.

We decided to each get separate readings but in each other's presence. Amy went first. At the beginning of Amy's reading, before she said a word, Jean-Jacques turned to me and said, "This has got nothing to do with you."

Within five minutes of listening to Amy's reading I felt relieved, as if a weight had been lifted. He said Amy had reached a point in her life where she had to find her freedom and discover her personal power,

---

[19] Why in the world, you may ask, did Jack Pransky, who supposedly understands the Three Principles, go to a psychic? For the answer, you'll have to wait until the next chapter.

and she couldn't do that with me right now. She needs space so she can. What Amy is going through right now is written in the stars, he said, embedded in the cells of her body. It is so necessary for her to follow this, he said, that if she resists or fights it she will become physically ill. Her relationship with me has strengthened her to the point where to fulfill her soul's purpose she now needs to be on her own.

Lucky me.

Okay fine, I thought, if she needs space I will gladly give it to her. I came up with the idea of going on a two-month European Tour. She would have her space, while I would go on a big Three Principles work adventure. We decided to take a formal hiatus and officially separate. We would reassess when I returned.

One catch. Amy needed double hip-replacement surgery. Inherited from her father she contracted osteoarthritis at a young age, exacerbated by all the kicking she did to win her Tae Kwon Do black belt. No matter what happened between us I wanted to take care of her in her recovery After all, I still loved her beyond all else. Amy decided to get both hips operated on at once to get it over with. Talk about impaired mobility! She was a trooper, so brave. She just put on her game face and plowed through. I took care of her for a whole month. Caring for her turned out to be more difficult than I'd thought, but nothing compared with what she went through. When she recovered to where she could finally hobble around well enough, at the end of February, 2014 I flew off to Europe.

I thoroughly immersed myself in my European Tour, which Sue Pankiewicz and Sheela Masand had helped me think through and gain courage for on the beach in Albir, Spain. As much as possible I had to set aside thoughts of Amy and us. I traveled from Colchester, England to Paris, to Brussels, to The Netherlands, to Denmark, to Sweden, to Germany, to Switzerland, into the French Alps, to Italy, down to Sicily (where I got sick and had to get out of there fast), to Spain (where I ran my Extended Professional Training), to Portugal, back to England, to Scotland and back to London. Originally when planning it I had only a few trainings and a bit of individual coaching lined up, but I only had to ask people in the Three Principles community in various European countries if they wanted me, and everyone did. By this time my book, *Somebody Should Have Told Us!,* had become fairly popular in Europe (in small circles). I had a fabulous time and wrote a daily blog of my journey and adventures.

Ironically, being on my own like this I felt stronger. My European Tour did wonders for my inner strength and spirit. Jean-Jacques said this would be important for me, too, and he was right! Being with Amy I'd inadvertently lost myself a bit. Early on in our relationship Amy had showered me with such love and affection and we were so in tune with everything it was like living the most beautiful, peaceful, loving dream imaginable. I'd gotten lost in the love of her. I let it sink its claws into me and never wanted to let go. Even in our later years when I felt her total desire for me wane a bit I still clung to what I knew because to me it was still the best, and I believed I'd never find anyone even close.

Then I realized something. Even after my healing with Melissa when I'd freed my need to feel love from other women, I could now see that Amy had replaced "all other women" in my mind. I had not let go of my need to feel whole and complete now *through Amy*, so the thought of possibly losing her became too much. Then came a most humbling thought: Oops, maybe the gripping energy emanating from me was no small contributor to why Amy felt she needed space from me. Yes, humbling!

Halfway through my tour I had another realization. I realized I didn't *need* Amy anymore for my happiness, yet I *wanted* her as much as ever. Amy or no Amy, my inner core of health and strength remained intact. People liked and appreciated me. I helped them. They wanted to be around me. I had the thought, "I really *am* helpful to humanity in a small way! I am fine being by myself, not needing anyone." But I still *wanted* Amy because she was the best. Why wouldn't I want to be with the best?

Just before leaving on my trip I had a session with Wendy Halley, a shaman (shawoman?) I knew in Vermont.[20] I came upon the notes she'd sent me after the session, which I'd never read. Truth be told, I don't know what to make of this shamanistic stuff; it never really resonated with me, but I'm open to it all because, to me, it's all within the realm of Universal Mind. Reading her notes stunned me. Wendy said she had

---

[20] Why in the world, you may ask, did Jack Pransky, who supposedly understands the Three Principles, go to a shaman? For that, you'll have to wait until the next chapter, also.

connected with me "in the dreamtime," with the part of me struggling to feel solid about the state of my relationship with Amy. There she encountered a five or six-year-old me, alone and scared, clinging to a teddy bear in a pink dress, which represented the vulnerable parts of him (me) and gave him comfort and security. Wendy's spirit helpers sent Grandmother Moon to help Jack release the parts of Amy he'd been holding onto. Grandmother Moon explained that Jack had important work to do and it was time to let his stuffed bear friend go back home. Very sad, Little Jack placed the bear in Grandmother Moon's outstretched hands, whereupon she held the bear up high above her head and sang an ancient song, making the bear quiver and transform into a hundred colorful butterflies, which flew away home, some reuniting with Amy. As Grandmother Moon held Little Jack on her lap, rocking him and stroking his head, a majestic male penguin emerged who said he would help Jack manage the time of separation and heal his heart. The penguin's spirit merged with Jack's dreambody, lifted its feathers and revealed a glowing rose-colored egg. The penguin said, "That's your broken heart, and I'm going to take care of it until it's ready to hatch." He gave Jack a dose of lightning medicine, a big boost to his personal power. At the end of the healing Little Jack had the sweetest smile on his face; he had already grown stronger.

Okay, too weird, right? It certainly was for me. But the astonishing thing is that stuffed teddy bear actually existed! My mother had kept it since my childhood, and when she died I decided to hold onto it—I have no idea why—and I set it on a closet shelf in a plastic bag. And even though it is terribly battered and has lost its eyes I recalled clearly, for the first time in sixty-three years, that the teddy bear originally had a little pink lace dress! No way could Wendy have known that! Hmm. Plus, the outcome sounded as she described: I did feel much stronger. Did Wendy really set this stuff in motion? I'll never know. Okay, I'll accept this—um, maybe. You go, Little Jack!

Anyway, the trip went great—I met wonderful people, did some of the best trainings I had ever done to that point, visited many countries I had never been to and helped propel Three Principles understanding throughout Europe. I felt stronger independently. I had no idea what would happen upon my return. I figured only three options were possible. Amy could say: 1) we're on again; 2) it's over; or 3) I need more time.

When I arrived home Amy presented a fourth option I did not imagine: "Why don't we see how it goes?"

Oh! Sounded great to me. To give her even more space I spent some more time alone at Nantasket Beach to write. Then Amy and I spent nine or ten more wonderful months together—at least I thought so.

Around Thanksgiving we took a little trip to Florida to look at houses or condos for me to buy. Amy had the idea that we could have a long-distance relationship where we would live apart for a while but each visit each other. This made no sense to me. This could never work, I thought, unless we lived our own completely separate lives, then came together and were completely with each other when we did, an idea Amy didn't much like. She said we would still be together; we just wouldn't be living together all the time, which would give her the space she still needed. If this was the only way I could keep her, could I handle this? We looked for places around Delray Beach, an area I really liked when visiting my mother. I settled on a condo in neighboring Boca Raton, within walking or biking distance from the ocean.

Eight or nine beautiful months later the time came for me to go to Europe again. Before flying off to Spain and the U.K. again something seemed amiss. I felt Amy distancing herself again. So we sat down and talked about our relationship.

She realized now, she said, that she really needed her independence—her new word. I heard her say our relationship had to end.

She said it. But it wasn't so clear. As I took my cramped seat on the plane I knew we were pretty much over—not altogether unexpected—but it felt kind of vague, so I wasn't as upset as I could have been. Again it sounded like we were both free to do whatever we wanted. I still harbored fantasies that when Amy and I visited each other occasionally we could still be "friends with benefits." After all, we were still in love with each other; she just needed her independence.

Ironically, my scheduled topic for my first evening presentation in Spain was "relationships." Gulp! What could I now say about relationships? I knew nothing about relationships anymore! The audience would see right through me. I decided all I could do was be completely real. I told them exactly what I was going through.

Participants sat on the edge of their seats.

I told them what I had realized to date. "When Amy gave me the news I went through all kinds of different, very powerful emotions, but because I also know something about the Three Principles, my understanding kept me from being utterly devastated by all this."

What did I know? I knew each emotion resulted from my own creation of Thought. Each time my thinking changed, my emotions changed. But my big insight was I realized *each emotion lasted only as long as my thought about it!* Once any particular thought-emotion stopped, it *no longer existed* for me in that moment. This split-up did not mean any one thing; it continuously changed each time I had a new thought. This breakup did not mean "devastated"; it only meant I felt devastated for as long as I had that thought. Then it would switch to something else, like upset, and the breakup would mean upset for the length of time I thought that, then it would mean anger, then it would mean gratefulness, and then it might jump back to devastated, etc. Furthermore, as painful as this seemed, *because of my innate health I knew I would be okay no matter what.* My talk went very well.

My Extended Professional Training went even better. Next I had a fabulous experience on Yoga Mark Jones's soul trek expedition (where Richard had his cave experience). The best training of all followed, with my new "Breaking Free of the Known" retreat. I was flying high. Because my mind was so engaged, my relationship woes were not.

Until the events ended. Suddenly I had time to think. Always dangerous.

The night before I left Spain for the U.K. I woke up at 4:00 in the morning unable to get back to sleep. I don't know what possessed me, but I turned on the computer looking for an email from Amy. Nothing!

I thought, "Of course! What do you expect, Jack? This is the way it's going to be now, and you'd better [bleepin'] get used to it!" My mood descended into sarcastic bitterness. "Great, Amy is getting exactly what she wants, and I'm getting exactly what I don't want, and I'm the one left holding the bag." One part of me stood outside myself knowing this was remarkably unhelpful thinking and wouldn't last; another part of me stood encased in the cement of it, courtesy of consciousness. Time to face reality; it was over! Who was I kidding?

A low came immediately before the 2015 Tikun/Innate Health Conference. I noticed a sentence buried in the middle of an email from Amy: I don't know what happens to love; I never thought I would change, but I have. Whoa! Wait! Was she saying she didn't know if she even loved me anymore? Our break-up wasn't supposed to have anything to do with me, remember? Now I not only lost the love of my life, I lost her love for me as well? I plummeted.

In that state I had to speak the very next day at the conference. I arrived shaky, but immediately felt showered with love. When I first walked in, while standing in the registration queue, a fellow I didn't know approached me. He told me his 84-year-old mother had told him to find me to tell me I'd saved her life as a result of reading *Somebody Should Have Told Us!*. It ripped me right out of myself. My eyes filled. At least five other people told me my books had done similar things for them. My books have changed lives! Such an honor. So humbling! Total gratefulness.

Phew, such highs and lows!

I knew my state of bitterness from my low was worthless, so that thought alone lifted it. But my emotions again began jumping all over the place, much like each different song on Bob Dylan's superb album, *Blood on the Tracks*, about the breakup of his marriage. I could relate. But I also knew something Bob probably didn't, that every different emotion stemmed from each change of thought: So when I believed I gave a lot more to the relationship than Amy did, I felt incredulous; when I thought she tuned out from me to make it easier for her to let go, I felt annoyed; when I saw our time together as the best of my life, I felt grateful; when I thought of her being with other men, I felt envious (as opposed to jealous); when I thought it might be possible to find this complete love again with someone else, I felt hopeful; when I doubted I could ever find anyone that great again, I felt despondent; when I thought I would still be thinking of our relationship as the best while she would no longer feel that way, I felt sad; when I believed something had been wrenched from me, I felt hurt; when I thought I won't be able to share my life with her anymore, I felt pained; when I thought how confused Amy has been through all of this, I felt compassion; when she said she would always treasure all she learned from me and would always love me, I felt comforted; when I realized I would ultimately make it through all this craziness and be okay, I felt relief. Each change of thought caused a new emotion. None would exist if I didn't think them up. There was one catch: Each time I had one of those emotions, consciousness seduced me into believing it unarguably real in that moment. But if I realized that and recognized it in the moment, I'd be fine.

I also knew, if I could see every one of those changing emotions simply as experiences flowing by, courtesy of my own thinking, I'd be fine. If I could allow myself to simply experience each of those emotions, feel them knowing they can't harm me and not wallow in them too much, I'd be fine. If I could appreciate them simply as life experiences and accept them as such, I'd be fine. If I could observe them instead of being caught in them, I'd be fine.

Then came a bigger thought. Something lies underneath all these emotions, more powerful even than the love I have for Amy. I could transcend all these emotion-experiences by realizing my spiritual essence, my innate health, the Oneness of All things. Therein lay the answer. If I truly knew that I'd ultimately be fine anyway, I'd be fine now, in spite of myself. There could be no other answer!

Only I couldn't find it yet—

34. KNOWING?

Sometimes I hear people say, “I know this stuff already,” or “This confirms what I already knew,” yet their lives don’t seem to be going so well. This doesn’t compute.

I ask, “Who among us can know everything that can be known or seen about Universal Mind?” As I said, when it comes to full and complete understanding we are babes in the woods. Sydney Banks said this even about himself. He said no one could totally understand.

Who among us can even know the true power of creation of Thought? The Noetic Sciences discovered not only are thoughts form but, as form, actually have mass. Accordingly, they claim that thought holds the power, literally, to alter things on this earth, to alter life, to change the universe. While the Three Principles does not take a stand on whether our thinking determines external reality, but only states with certainty that our thinking determines our own “reality,” I bring this up only to illustrate that we can’t begin to comprehend how *huge* Thought may be.

Who among us can know all there is to know about Consciousness? In Chapter 19 we explored, to some extent, that the “awareness” about which Syd speaks is Universal—the complete and utter awareness of All, of the One. Again, so huge, it is incomprehensible—Consciousness within everything on this earth and beyond. Further, no matter how much we say we know, when we get seduced by consciousness in any way and get lost in false “truth,” obviously we have so much more to see.

What we “know” places a ceiling on what we could Know. What we know limits us.

I hear some fairly new Three Principles practitioners act as if something other than the Three Principles is needed for people to get healthy, as if understanding these Principles themselves is not enough, so they fall back on their old, outside-in practices. If a client isn’t "getting it," it simply means his or her understanding is limited, that she or he doesn't see it deeply enough—yet. The Three Principles are everything about how our experience is created; how can *everything* not be enough?

I hear others saying they've got to "work the principles." There is no work! There is no doing! There is no practice! Only new insight of enough magnitude will cure. Only deeper understanding.

I hear some try to make a distinction between the Three Principles and "the source" of the Three Principles, implying something exists even more deeply spiritual behind it all. There is no difference! Universal Mind—the energy of All things—*is* the source of the Three Principles. The Three Principles themselves are the source! What could be deeper than that?

I hear others say "The Three Principles" has become a form, and they feel constrained by the form. The Three Principles are formless! To some, the practice of the Three Principles may have become a form. But the "practice of the Three Principles" is made up by people's use of the formless Three Principles. The only purpose of the practice is to help people see the formless true nature of life and how things really work. It is not the practice of the Three Principles that gets people off the mark; it is some people's interpretations of what Three Principles practice is that gets people off the mark. The practice itself is always in the process of evolving.

Astute readers may be wondering, "Jack, especially given what you just said above, if you claim to know about the Three Principles enough to teach and write books about it, why in the world would you go to a psychic, shaman or healer? By doing that, aren't you mixing other things with the Three Principles, even though you say it is unwise?"

I'm so glad you asked.

To me, *everything* is the Three Principles in action; everything makes perfect sense in light of the Three Principles. I can read any spiritual book and see the Principles written all over it, even though the authors themselves may not know or see only parts. I can see where what they say fits within the realm of the Principles, and I can see what they miss. As I reported in Chapter 4, after I had my experience with Syd Banks my entire spiritual search screeched to a halt; I stopped reading spiritual books, stopped paying attention to other spiritual approaches. Then, about eight years into my Three Principles learning I entered a doctoral program that forced me to explore the relationship between the Three Principles and other spiritual approaches and practices, and with science and quantum physics. During this examination something clicked; I had a huge insight about how the process all fit together, which I wrote up for my doctoral program, then included it as Chapter XXI and the end of Chapter XIX of my book, *Prevention from the Inside-Out.*[21] Once I received my Ph.D. in 1999 I again stopped looking in that direction. A decade and a half later, a few years prior to writing this book, I again got curious about what other spiritual thinkers were saying, this time with my deeper level of understanding. As I said, I now see everything through the eyes of the Three Principles. Now I consider it fascinating to see where what they say fits and what they miss. Many spiritual authors speak or write within the realm of Universal Mind, and their various cuts on it are quite interesting to me. Occasionally they even say something that strikes me in a new way, expanding my own limited view of Universal Mind and Universal Consciousness. That said, I consider myself an absolute purest with regard to the Three Principles because I have never read or heard anything that contradicts it; in fact, it all corroborates it, except where they don't see the connection between Mind, Consciousness and Thought. What sets the Three Principles apart and what Sydney Banks offered new to the world is how all three fit together to become our sole experience of life.

What about spiritual practices? I would only ever consider going to a non-Three Principles practitioner for one of two reasons: 1) Out of curiosity—just to learn and see what it is all about, or to see where it fits into the Three Principles; 2) When wisdom guides me there. I went originally to see psychic Jean-Jacques Guyot because of #1, because early in my relationship with Amy a friend of hers told her about him, she went to see him, had a great experience and I got curious. Then I had a great experience with him, myself. Thereafter, #2 kicked in, as

---

21 Pransky, J. (2003). *Prevention from the Inside-Out.* Bloomington, IN: AuthorHouse. In addition, as of the date of this writing, Dr. Tom Kelley and I have written this as an article titled, "How the Formless Comes into Form," to be published in 2017 in the journal, *Cogent Psychology*.

wisdom guided me to him a few times. If I hear wisdom say to me, "Jack, you need to go to see Jean-Jacques," I believe I would be a fool not to. And without fail every time I've seen him it has paid off big-time, I'm guessing because I did listen to wisdom. Because of what I know about the Three Principles, automatically I see how my new insight fits, which arises in me out of a session with him. Sometimes I see how, ooh, I got lost in a particular way. I am not suggesting that others should go to Jean-Jacques or any psychic. I am only talking about my own experience.

What I believe happens with psychics (real ones, that is) is they are able to tap into the energy of Universal Mind that Knows All. They are brilliant deep listeners. I am fascinated by anyone able to tap into another realm, whether it be psychics, clairvoyants, mediums, channelers, shamans, Yogis, Rinpoches, swamis, sages, healers, alternative health practitioners, or the great spiritual masters—anyone. I can say this, however, because I know beyond a shadow of a doubt that it's all about the Three Principles anyway.

I also know if I get an insight as a result of listening to any of these spiritual people or exposing myself to their practices out of curiosity or whatever, I know it's not them! I know *the insight comes from within me*—no matter who or what it is. Same with Sydney Banks or any Three Principles practitioner. It's all within each and every one of us. It's an inside-out job. As Syd used to say, you go to your church, you listen to anyone you want; it's all about your own insight from within and it always comes down to the Three Principles.

The great spiritual teachers from all times taught this. Syd kept saying over and over, it's not about me! We could read or listen to any spiritual teacher or teaching—Joel Goldsmith, William Brenner, Ralph Waldo Trine, Mooji, Adyashanti, Thich Nhat Hahn, Lao Tzu, Buddha, Jesus, *Conversations with God*, and so many others—and see the same things over and over expressed in different and sometimes beautiful ways. Reading those other teachers doesn't diminish us. It doesn't say we are looking for answers other than through the Three Principles; it means we could listen to anyone and know how it fits precisely into the Three Principles. They may say it differently than Syd but it points to the same thing. Personally, I think there's an absolute treasure in listening to Syd, especially his older tapes that are so beautifully spiritual.

However, while an insight can be triggered from anywhere, no matter what spiritual or other practice anyone uses, the question is whether people come out of that teaching or practice understanding what will help them most, which I believe is this: 1) that it is all one big illusion of our own creation from within, that what we believe to be reality isn't; 2) that we are already everything we seek—our spiritual essence/true nature connected to the Oneness of All things—and it only looks as if we're not because we use our thinking combined with consciousness to obscure it, and we access it with a quiet mind or when our head clears. Do people come out of any practice understanding these? If they go to a Freudian psychologist, a humanistic psychologist, a Gestalt therapist, a Narrative Therapist, a cognitive-behavioral therapist, an NLP practitioner, will they get there? Doubtful. I don't care where people go; I care that they get there, because I know this is what will ultimately help them most in their lives beyond their presenting problem, especially in the long run.

An insight can be triggered from anywhere, but do people understand that insight comes from within them, not from the one who sparked the trigger? Further, people can get an insight that helps them overcome a particular problem or resolve a particular issue, but when the next problem arises, do they realize the same internal, spiritual process is at play? Do they realize no matter what the problem it is created by their (usually inadvertent) use of the Three Principles, and that the solution is understanding and seeing in the moment how it *always* works the same way? *If* we have a very solid grasp on this and naturally walk through life seeing through the eyes of the Three Principles, then we could go anywhere or to anyone because we will see always where it fits. If within our hearts and souls we don't know this, we can be easily distracted by the external practice, person or teaching, which in my view indicates it would be unwise to go there.

What I am absolutely *not* saying is that it is okay to mix the Three Principles with other practices; for example, when a practitioner is having difficulty getting through to a client with the Three Principles and is tempted to fall back on some other approach or practice. No! The answer always lies within the Three Principles, and *the answer to helping a client lies in deeper listening.*

In summary, I am an absolute purist when it comes to the Three Principles because I know there is nothing that is not the Principles in action. No one could ever talk me out of that because I see unshakably that it is how life works always. Am I a purist about the practice of the Three Principles? I am in the sense that, in my empirical observation now backed by research,[22] what heals people is when they understand how illusion is created and how it tricks us into believing it is reality, and how our true nature or spiritual essence always exists, is available to us always and can only get covered up by our own thinking. About this direction I am an absolute purist. I am not a purist about a particular pathway people use to get there; I am only concerned that they get there. I firmly believe that working with a good Three Principles practitioner—and a growing number of them now exist out there—is the best way to realize this.

Again, I am talking only about the way I, personally, see it.

---

[22] Kelley, T. M., Pransky, J., & Lambert, E. (2015). Realizing improved mental health through understanding three spiritual principles. Spirituality in Clinical Practice. 2(4), 267-281; Kelley, T. M., Pransky, J., & Lambert, E. (2016) Understanding spiritual principles or using techniques to realize and sustain optimal mental health. *Journal of Spirituality in Mental Health,* 18(3), 217-238.

35. LONELY VS. ALONE VS. SOLITUDE

When I began writing this book I knew it would come out best if I wrote in a state of solitude.

I drove the four hours from Vermont to the Pransky family cottage at Nantasket Beach. As I write this, here I am. Except for a few neighbors to whom I say a polite "hello," I know no one. I am alone. Recently I came back from my European Tour.

The first night I find myself lonely. Amy is off at a conference in Oregon; we are extending our hiatus. I find myself longing for her. My desire for solitude somehow morphed into loneliness.

How did this happen? New thoughts, of course. For two nights I feel this loneliness strongly. It is discomforting, disquieting. During my European tour I hung out with wonderful people in every port, almost never alone except when traveling from country to country. I didn't feel lonely at all. Now I do.

By my third day at Nantasket I find myself no longer lonely. Now I am simply alone. A big difference exists between being alone and being lonely. Alone is simply a fact: I am not with anyone I know. "Alone" is neutral.

On the seventh day, my mind rests. I drop into a state of solitude. I love this feeling. In the morning I awake. I head to the beach for a walk or run. Sometimes I talk into my voice recorder. Sometimes I simply take in the sound of the waves and become attuned to the sights and smells. Sometimes I listen to music. It all depends on what I feel in the moment. I come back and eat gluten-free granola with coconut milk. I settle in to write. If the weather is beautiful I stop writing by 10:30 a.m. and head to the beach; if it's nasty I keep writing until lunchtime. After eating I write more because I try to stay out of the sun at midday. At about 3:30 p.m., if the weather holds, I head back to the beach, this time to relax, sunbathe and read. Depending on ocean conditions I might jump in to take a dip, ride some waves or swim. Dinnertime. I watch a Netflix movie or documentary or a Red Sox game. I go to sleep, then start all over again. I love this feeling.

Solitude is a state of peace, the state from which wisdom is heard. Comfort. Complete contentment and satisfaction with life. Occasionally a feeling of bliss, as I allow everything in mindfully, no extraneous thoughts.

Alone, as I said, is more neutral.

Loneliness comes with a feeling of unsettledness, dissatisfaction.

I realize in each of these states no difference exists in my physical being. I am in the same location and no one I know is around. The only difference is my state of mind.

In the exact same situation I can feel lonely, alone or in solitude—each my own creation of illusion—then I get to live with the feeling of whatever illusion I created. I have equal opportunity to create any of these states. The one I inadvertently pick becomes my life in that moment.

As usual, my creative power of Thought is at play, sometimes causing mischief. Once again, consciousness obeys whatever my thinking dictates. With no discrimination it gives me a "real" feeling of whichever state I want, even if I don't think I want it.

I don't mean to create loneliness, but occasionally I do. I don't want to create loneliness, but who is the creator? No one but me allows it into my head. "Lonely" is thought in a moment, off the moment, sprinkled with thoughts of past and future. Thinking of what I had. Thinking I want something I can't have right then. Longing for something else. Longing for what is not now.

"Alone" has no longing attached. If I go off to the store alone, even if I live with a partner, in that moment am I not still alone? But in that case I wouldn't even think about it. I could go off alone for a day, for a weekend, for a week, even a month and think nothing of it because deep down I would know I am going back to her. That one thought is the only difference. Sometimes when alone I feel a tiny twinge that something is missing. I'm not desiring anything different, yet something feels slightly amiss, like being cut off from the familiar. That one little thought breaks the neutrality of the simple fact that no one is around me. But in this case I am not looking for what I don't have, so it does me no harm.

In the face of continual potential for immersion in peaceful solitude, both loneliness and alone are pretty foolish ways to be. If I wasn't thinking something else I would experience my own spiritual essence connected to the moment, connected to the Oneness of All things. But for my own extraneous thinking, automatically I would be in a state of peaceful solitude. Only my own creation can take me off exactly where I want to be, which is already where I really am.

Humbling! Does that make any sense?

We are one thought away from loneliness, from alone, or from solitude.

36. DEPRESSION AND THE UNIVERSE

Now, to real depression.

"My name is Rob Somers. I was in a band called The Samples. I left that band after about eight years.

"When I left the band I didn't know what to do with myself, and over about six months I got very, very depressed, until I reached a point where every day I was actually praying for death. I wanted to die.

"I was seeing a psychiatrist who was trying to help me with the depression. I lost about a hundred pounds and she said that was because of the depression. I didn't go see a regular doctor because we didn't have insurance yet. When we finally got insurance and saw a doctor he sent me to the emergency room where they did some tests. They found out I had Stage Four cancer spread throughout my body and through six or seven different organs. The doctors looked very glum.

"I said, 'Okay you guys, just give it to me straight. What is the real deal?' and they said, 'We think at best you have about six months to live.' And, believe me, that's kind of a shock. We all know we're going to die, but most of us don't know when.

"So I was being told I had a six-month window, and something really interesting happened to me. Instead of freaking out and going crazy I felt myself get very calm and very peaceful. I felt myself say I want to spend more time with Amy, my wife. [*Another Amy; don't get nervous.*] I don't even know if it was my decision—something happened, something changed, where I just knew I was going to live. I was going to do whatever it took to live. And the moment that happened my depression dropped instantly. There was no process, there was no trying, it just immediately dropped away and something else took its place, which I believe was just the will to live.

"From that time on through the great help of my wife and my family and doctors and everyone, I lived. And when I went back to see the doctors they couldn't believe it. I could see the shock in their faces, and they said, 'You are a miracle!' I never really felt that way, myself. I felt more like the universe was very generous and said 'Okay.' It wasn't like a miracle to me. It was, like, that's what happened."

I [*Jack*] asked, "What was it like for you to be inside the depression?"

"I think it's very, very difficult for anybody who has never had depression to understand what it's like. It's an absolute denial of life, that anything could ever be good, that anything would be better. It's so hard to describe to somebody who has never felt it. It's the most nihilistic feeling. It's like a black hole of nothingness. There is absolutely zero hope, a place of zero hope. If you can imagine that, that's what it is. And I think one of the main things of being alive is simply to have hope—even for the next moment, to the next day, or the next year. When you have zero hope it's just an unbelievable thing."

"When it shifted, was it in a moment or—?"

"It was in a moment. This happened to me once before. In that moment I was very calm and very peaceful, and then it just went—[*snaps fingers*]—and it shifted."

"What did it shift to inside your head?"

"I had an absolute—it wasn't even a hope—an absolute *knowing* that I was going to live, even though they told me I wasn't. I knew I was. I think a religious person might describe it as grace. What I'm trying to say is it was nothing I did. I didn't do it. It was something larger, just like that—[*snaps fingers*]. You could call it the Universe, you could call it the T'ao, whatever you want to call it. But I feel that whatever that is, that very loving presence is very, very generous. I decided I wanted to live and that presence said, 'Okay, you'll live.' It's like, whatever you want, it's okay. There's no good or bad; that's just a human construct."

"That moment you speak of kind of reminds me of what happened to you at my kitchen table when you were in that intensive session with me. Can you describe what happened?"

"Well, what happened at your kitchen table was that my mind was running crazy like a computer out of control, racing, racing, racing, racing. At the same time you were pushing me. The combination of those two things, I believe, made my conceptual mind collapse, and I had a glimpse, for a moment, of enlightenment, of the true nature of reality. It was a very short glimpse because I believe I got frightened of it, so I instantly jumped back to the conceptual mind. But the actual moment, even though short, was incredibly, incredibly deep. Very, very deep."

"I vaguely recall that you saw salt and pepper shakers, or something like that, in a completely different light."

"I don't remember the specifics. Honestly, I think I glimpsed Reality at your kitchen table—very briefly, but long enough to be a harbinger. Like, 'Okay, you saw that, and that was real.' It was a very, very profound experience. I told you before, Jack, that I really believe—and it's one of the reasons that I want my Amy to sit with you—that in a session where you're helping people, it's nothing that you say to them. It's the presence of your health that cures those people and helps those people. I believe that it was your presence that brought me to that spot. You pushed a little, but my mind was already crazy, and it cracked. I really believe it's the innate health of the person you're with that heals you. I think if you're in the presence of Jesus or Buddha or L'ao Tzu, or Syd, just being in that presence is what heals."

Rob Somers is now a shaman practicing in Big Sur, California. His website title reads, "Find Your Way Back to Your Healed State."

* * *

In Chapter 19 I spoke of how each level of consciousness is a different vibration brought to our consciousness by different thoughts; that when we inadvertently create depressed thoughts upon depressed thoughts upon depressed thoughts the vibration gets so thick and heavy body chemistry can change and, before long, someone needs depression medication. I'm not going to say it always happens this way—because I don't really know—but it happens a lot. The point, here, is the power of Thought is so commanding it is possible for one enormous insight in an instant to change body chemistry. Rob experienced such a moment, and in that moment everything changed. This is the hope for each of us, and it can happen at any time. We just don't know when it is coming. Syd Banks kept insisting, "We are only one thought away!" This is an example of what he meant. For many, many years someone could be depressed or be filled with anxiety or be violent or be terribly troubled by the break-up of a relationship or a myriad of other things, and in one instant, *poof*! Gone. Never to return. A miracle? Or simply Universal Mind sending a monstrous new insight-thought our way through grace, which infuses with our consciousness, which changes us across the board. This is the hope for all. Thought can change! In fact it does, continuously. Am I saying we can go out of our way to make this happen, to try to make this happen? No!

Remember the quote from Syd at the beginning of this book: "A mind searching for itself can never find itself." Our little minds do not stand a chance. In fact, the little mind can only get in the way. But we could have hope by knowing this possibility exists for anyone at any time and, of course, each of us is included in the category of "anyone." We could set our intention for it (then take it off our mind), and see what happens.

Hope uplifts the soul.

* * *

Toward the end of this book's final editing stage, another miracle happened. John Doorbar (he elected to use his real name) from the U.K. but living and working in Germany, had been one of my two or three most difficult clients. I thought him a really sweet guy but I could not get through to him. Unbelievably depressed and suicidal for many years he had studied the Three Principles with some wonderful teachers for seven years to no avail. Sometimes it seemed I made some headway, but he always slid back between sessions.

I had a feeling. Maybe if he attended the November 2016 "Cultivating the Art of Working with People One-to-One from the Inside Out" retreat, conducted by Gabriela Maldonado-Montano and myself in Albir, Spain, it might shake him up and rip him out of himself. At this most powerful of retreats John had a wonderful experience; he opened up and got real (prior to this he had always put on a front with others in a group) and he forgot about his depression. It seemed he made tremendous progress. When he returned home it took him only a few days to become even more depressed, if even possible.

His partner had had it with him. They had bought a house together. She needed a therapist to help her cope with John. Her therapist said it sounded like John needed medical help and gave a referral, which his girlfriend insisted he take. At his session John described himself as extremely depressed, anxious and on the edge of giving up. He had tried so many different things to get better for so long, he had no idea where to go from here. This made him very frustrated and sad. He desperately wanted to feel free and happy, and have some inner peace. Very concerned about his suicidal thoughts and the fact that he had not slept well for a year and a half (he always awoke at 4:00 AM steeped in worry and anxiety), the psychotherapist wanted to send him to a clinic or at least a psychiatrist. She said his ability to continue functioning at work must be due to his depression having a manic aspect to it, which provided him the energy to work. She told him he was ill and needed help. John retorted that he felt basically well but had a load of depressed thinking that he wanted to slow down so he could hear his inner wisdom.

At least I had helped John see that. I still held out hope for John. I suspected he needed medication, which is out of my bailiwick, so I referred him to the wonderful Three Principles psychiatrist, Dr. Bill Pettit, who graciously agreed to meet with him over Skype. Bill's approach: to read Sydney Banks's book, *The Missing Link*, with him and discuss it. At first this did not seem to take hold; John told me he was still anxious and depressed, but he did feel a little hopeful and would continue.

Then in February 2017 I received the following email from John [the capitals are his]:

> I think looking at THE MISSING LINK created a crack in my view of the world (and my APPARENT plight.) Yesterday (on 3rd February, 2017–a day now beautifully etched in my memory) I forgot a client and instead of getting angry I watched George [Pransky]'s tape on the Psychological NATURE of selling. I have watched these lots and lots of times before but yesterday was DIFFERENT. I heard something new. George was talking about: Why do placebos work…? Our thought that the sugar pill will help us CREATES the experience via consciousness. The EXPERIENCE! So you feel better because you think you will. Then George said it is the opposite of HYPOCHONDRIA. I [heard]

DEPRESSION. So it is the same as the sugar pill... My thought that I am depressed HAS BEEN CREATING THE EXPERIENCE that I am actually depressed, again via consciousness. Does this then actually mean that MY DEPRESSION is nothing more than a CONSTRUCT of my own mind that I have created myself? This is the conclusion I have come to. The implications of this are huge. My depression is/WAS just my own illusion. This makes 100% sense, Jack. It is a fact that my depression, dare I say, WAS (as it never really existed at all) a figment/no... rather an Embodiment...(i.e. I felt depressed and exhibited Depressed Symptoms) of my own thoughts and imagination. I would guess that these Depressed Symptoms are no longer in my body...or will start to fade... I have not experienced a blinding light or anything. Rather I have experienced a CERTAINTY of how I create my own experience via my thoughts plus consciousness... I am feeling a lot better.

I wrote back to John telling him how thrilled I am for him, and received this in return:

Yes, I am really, really pleased... I still have a normal life, but I do not take it so seriously. This makes what I do more enjoyable, more effective. I have hope and look forward to a really good future by being more present in the moment. THANK YOU, Jack. I really appreciate your support over the last months. You have been the best and kindest, most caring and generous person I have ever known.

That touched me. I told him so. Then I received this:

I wanted to tell you about what has been happening. On Friday I read pages 80-81 in *Somebody Should Have Told Us!* **AGAIN.** I have read these pages time and time again. But this time I SAW the point. *Whatever illusion we see is exactly what we get.* Then I saw the key point of Syd's truth. We see something outside in the world. We think something about it, e.g., my flat is a pain, I hate my job. Then this thinking is **INSTANTLY** transformed into a feeling. Because it is so **INSTANT** it looks as though it is the outside world doing it TO US. In fact, it is we who are DOING IT TO OURSELVES, via our thinking. This means that the outside world can NEVER make us feel anything. The system is not made that way. Our feelings are a signal to us that we are thinking stuff which is not helpful. To remind us to come back to our true self – **to come home**, as Syd said time and time again. The implications are huge. I am not afraid any more. I get on a lot better than I did before with close family members now. I am not worried about the future, as with this BRILLIANT system—in the universe everything is on our side. I thought I had to tell you this. If I had not met you I would have given up on the 3 Principles. Bill has also been a great help. Thank you for putting me in touch with Bill. TO SUMMARISE, Jack. Miracle. Thought and Feeling are inextricably linked. We think all the time/make it real INSTANTLY/see/look outside and presume that our feelings are coming from the outside world. In fact, there is NO CONNECTION at all. It only looks that way. My thoughts plus consciousness. Maybe this is even more useful than a blinding light from heaven…

Then finally—

I think this very positive change seems to be permanent. I do forget, of course, then smile to myself, and go back to knowing that the inside out reality is a fact. It only works one way. This means that nothing that happens out there can affect me (without my letting it). This means that lots of stuff (better, all) from my past has no power over me anymore. As I am creating everything, I can decide not to recreate memories and have them be real—unless they are nice/pleasant/joyous memories.

And they say miracles can't happen…

37. THE PAST AND FAR BEYOND

Cecilia is a most delightful person. She didn't think she was. I also think she's beautiful through and through. She didn't think she was.

I met her in 2014 on my European Tour. Cecilia and her husband graciously put me up and took me to see the sites. One day she and I took a long walk together and began talking about her life. Our conversation morphed into an informal counseling session.

Cecilia's presenting issue: When it came time to make any big decision in life she became paralyzed with all the options. If she went in any one direction a reason always appeared why it would cause a problem somewhere else. This caused circular thinking where nothing got accomplished, which became a source of frustration and worry for her and her husband.

I'll let Cecelia describe to you what she described to me.

Cecilia: Fundamentally I believed myself to be flawed and broken, bad and wrong, something intrinsically unloved, unlovable and unfixable. This was a fact. I lived with it. I coped with it. I lived my life anyway despite this undeniable knowing. I found ways around it. I was a great actress, exceptionally adept and convincing. But cracks appeared. The cracks grew. The cracks became gaping holes and I tried to fill these holes with "good stuff"–good thoughts, positive actions, a good way of looking at life, smiles and laughter. A few years ago, the filler was not enough anymore, and I completely fell apart and was lost to myself and the world. I had to face brokenness in all its ugliness and clawing rawness. I shut down. The façade had broken down; I could live no more with the lie.

Then I searched.

And I searched.

I studied. I learned. I looked in different places. I wandered. Not knowing. I went on courses and became certified in NLP as a Master

Practitioner. I looked into various therapies and tried a few out. Finally one day through fluke and luck and a knowing that something was still missing, I came across the Three Principles.

To cut a long story short, I've been deepening my understanding since I heard something mind-bendingly obvious, simple and beautiful in the Three Principles in 2011. I have had many, many insights, my understanding has deepened, and my internal life, my internal experience of life has shifted beyond recognition. Externally my life has not changed that much. I wasn't mean to people before, etc. and what people could see was not an unhappy person. But I was stagnant, missing something, paralysed. I've been living in all-pervading fear for as long as I remember, but it was so ingrained that it was almost invisible and actually normal to me.

Again I crammed. I learned. I listened. I opened my heart, watched videos, read books. I essentially filled my head with lots more information. I saturated my brain with thoughts, ideas, and concepts. This time they touched a deeper place but not the deepest place. Something fundamental felt amiss. I felt I didn't deserve happiness; that I was unworthy. Yes I knew I was making this up but it didn't seem to change anything for me. There was something I wasn't seeing and I knew it. I didn't know what, though–I just knew it was at the deepest level, and until I could see it the rest of my growth was on unstable ground.

Two or three months ago I stopped reading and watching videos and listening to different people's ideas and thoughts. I gave up trying. I'd been trying to be all the good things that I was hearing that you "got" by understanding the Principles. And it was true that I was experiencing feelings and beauty that I'd never experienced before. I did have glimpses of something more, something greater, something beyond. It just didn't feel grounded in anything substantial. It was enough to keep my interest and curiosity and longing to know. But I needed to give up all that I knew or all I thought I knew. That was what got me to where I was, but I wanted more. I knew there was more. Quietly somewhere within me there was hope, a knowing that there was more but it wasn't where I'd been looking so far.

As Cecilia described her decision-paralysis to me that evening I listened deeply. I immediately became puzzled. Our conversation went something like this:

JP: So you're saying you got a glimpse of your innate health while working with your mentor but that hasn't helped you?

C: Well, it helped me, but not with this major problem.

JP: So it helped you, but it didn't fundamentally change you?

C: Essentially, yes.

JP: And it doesn't help you to know that we're making it all up with our thinking?

C: I see that on an intellectual level but I don't think I really see it deep down.

JP: And you know that seeing it on an intellectual level means nothing?

C: Yes.

JP: Okay, so where did this paralysis of yours come from?

C: [*long reflection*]. Probably my parents. I felt like they were always criticizing me for what I did. They still do it today.

JP: What do you mean?

C: My family situation was very stressful from the start. My father was quite a changeable, controlling workaholic and is now very unwell. My mother has a big character and has always been very fearful and insecure, trying to control things in her own way mainly through criticism, getting emotional and being defensive, and not giving us any space. Currently she's getting to the point of not being able to cope with my father and his illness anymore. My sister has had her own issues and has given me a very hard time and gets really emotional over the phone—she uses her emotions to try to control others, a little like my mother. I won't go into all the details but at times I felt like I couldn't handle them and things in general anymore. Sometimes I've had thoughts that I've just wanted to end it all.

JP: I feel for you. I really do. And this way you've been treated, has this been going on your whole life?

C: Pretty much. I was criticized constantly—it was a high-strung environment. And I just wanted to escape and have some peace; just keep out of the way and try not to be seen or heard, not rock the boat, listening out in case I needed to understand what was going on during what felt like constant arguments. It didn't matter what I did or didn't do, there would be criticism and put-downs. Doing anything on my own initiative didn't make sense. I'd do what was asked of me in small insignificant ways but being creative or original meant that whatever I'd done would be wrong in some way. The longer I procrastinated the longer I would put off getting criticized.

JP: And that worked?

C: Well, it postponed the criticism, and maybe if I waited long enough it would die down a bit. It gave me necessary recuperation time. So yes it worked.

JP: Yeah, I can see how it makes perfect sense.

C: What does?

JP: That it worked when you were a kid. It worked to escape and keep out of sight. That protected you, to a certain extent. There's only one problem: It's not working anymore.

C: No, it isn't.

JP: See, that's what we do. We take a strategy that worked when we were kids and it becomes a habit and we carry it innocently into adulthood and we keep doing it even though it's not helpful anymore. In fact now it does us harm.

C: Yes, I can see that.

JP: But I'm picking up something else. It feels to me like there is some fundamental fear behind all of this that will not allow you to let it go. Do you know what it is?

C: No.

JP: I'll bet deep inside you really know. Just reflect on it for a moment. Don't think about it, but get quiet and see what comes. What are you afraid of, really?

C: [*reflects and sighs*]. That I'm not good enough. That I won't be able to do it. That whatever I do, it won't be right anyway. So if I procrastinate long enough I won't have to face fresh criticism—another area where I'm apparently doing something wrong. And even if I procrastinate that will be wrong too, but it's the frying pan I know as opposed to the fire that I don't yet.

JP: "Not good enough" and "won't be able to" sound suspiciously like your parents talking. Do you really believe that?

C: [*pauses*] Yeah, I kind of do.

JP: That you really are not good enough? Really?

C: Well, not really, but…

JP: Cecilia, you can't have it both ways. Do you really believe you're not good enough, not smart enough, not clever enough, and will not work hard enough to be able to accomplish what you need to? Or is that just your parents talking?

C: [*pauses*] It's just my parents. But at some level I believed them—it felt convincing. [*pauses*] But it's not really true. I see now that they were trying to motivate me, spur me on, force me forward in the way they thought was best, in the only way they seemed to know how to do. It just had the opposite effect.

Dusk gave way to darkness. The city exploded with lights as we continued our walk.

JP: For some reason, even with what you just said, I still get the feeling this is not penetrating all the way. Is it possible that you don't want it to be any different because if things stay this way then you won't have to take the responsibility? What's in it for you to keep up this fear that stops you?

C: It's easier.

JP: Easier to not do anything?

C: Yes.

JP: That was the way it was when you were a kid?

C: Yes.

JP: Same as now, right?

C: Yes.

JP: But here's the thing, Cecilia, is it?

C: What do you mean?

JP: Is it really easier? I mean, it sure seems easier at the time because you don't have to deal with anything, but what you end up doing is suffering from the consequences to the point of thinking of completely giving up on life. This is easier?

C: [*stops her in her tracks*] Oh—

JP: When you really stop and look at it, it's silly to think it's easier, isn't it? I mean it's pure innocence. No blame in doing it; it's such an innocent habit you picked up. But what would really help here is to see, "Of course."

C: What do you mean?

JP: Given that keeping out of the way and not being seen or heard worked for you when you were a kid—not totally, because it just postponed the inevitable to some degree, but enough so it took the edge off for a while—*of course* you're going to take what you believed saved you as a little kid, take that into the rest of your life and think it's going to still work today. So when you get into this kind of thinking today, if you can see, "Of course! It makes perfect sense that I'd be doing this now." But then ask yourself whether it still really works today, or if it is just an illusion that you think it's easier. Because in the long run there's nothing easier about it, is there? It may be easier in the moment but then you have to suffer with all those other moments. It doesn't make any sense.

C: Hmm—that just got to me a little.

JP: See, that's the illusion—that it's easier. And the amazing thing is, this is all our own creation. This entire business—that we're using our creative power of Thought to create this illusion not only that it's easier but also that we're not okay. This is why it would serve you well to forgive yourself for feeling this way. It's total innocence.

C: Hmmm—

JP: And that points to an even deeper part.

C: What?

JP: That underneath all this is formless, perfect health. That lying underneath all this innocent, illusory thinking that feels to us like reality is our pure spiritual essence that is perfection itself. It must be perfection because it is not of form. It is the purest of energy connected to Oneness itself, and we are a little tiny part of it, so we must be part of the perfection. Underneath it all, no matter what we think of ourselves, we are perfect.

C: Wow, I just saw something. I feel like I'm seeing something for the very first time. Whew, I feel lighter.

The next morning Cecilia wrote what she saw. I didn't get to see it until writing this chapter.

Last night I heard something that transported me to a fresh plane. I heard a simplicity, a freshness, a quiet logic that just made sense. It's common sense. It's pure and simple. It's unassuming but all pervading.

It's truth, and fundamental to life. Now nothing looks the same—even having slept on it!

This is the logic of oneness; this is the truth of what our spiritual essence is. Now, I've heard versions of this many times since 2011, but I believed deep down that there were exceptions—and I was one of them. I truly believed this. The logic of what I heard shifted my perspective 180°, although the shift felt so slight, but it was at a deep level of Consciousness.

Here is how I interpret what I heard: There is something greater than me. It is greater than each one of us—each one of us individually and as a whole; greater than everyone who's ever existed and who will ever exist and beyond...It is everything and it is beyond everything. It is the generator and catalyst for life. It is more than that. It is life itself, and it is more than that. It is intangible. It is formless. It comes before form. And it is form. It touches everything, is beyond everything; it creates everything; it is everything. And it is nothing. If it is everything that means it is a whole. It is one. It is indivisible. It is pure. It is more than perfection. It is whole. If it is everything and we are part of that everything, a droplet in the ocean of this pure life, of pure consciousness then this is our essence. Behind all we see, the illusion of imperfection, of separateness, we are purity. We are part of that essence. We are that essence. We are pure light. It is impossible to corrupt or contaminate what is formless. Nothing can remove the purity; nothing can dirty or divide the oneness. It is by its very nature untouchable. It just is. It is the fabric of life. Our very nature. It underlies and is all things. This is what our soul is made of. It is our essence.

This means that at our core, behind the illusion of the imperfection and separation of life, we are perfection in the guise of something else. Our essence is unbreakable, flawless, whole, perfect, ultimate peace, purity, light. It is neutral and natural. It is more than the concepts and ideas conveyed by the words on this page. It is beyond all things, untouchable, intangible, formless. It is wholeness personified.

Now, we can think we are separate but it is an illusion that we can be divisible from anything else. Our soul is part of the oneness. It is whole. It is pure. It is pure peace and Love. This is who we really are.

The illusion of Thought is picked up by Consciousness and this is powerful! Whatever our attention goes to, via the stream of Thought, is made so wonderfully real and staggeringly ordinary through Consciousness. This creates the illusion of life as we "see" or experience it in the flesh, in the form. We trick ourselves that we are afraid. We trick ourselves that we're not worthy or that we have a contaminated soul. Everything that we live as our reality is made up. We make it up and feel it and see it and believe it to be real through Consciousness. It is all-singing, all-dancing. It creates all illusion—every veil that sweeps over or covers up the truth behind life, the truth before life. It is all a lie except for the spiritual essence.

We are all playing the same game. It is the same game whatever the flavour. Each person is playing innumerable games and yet just one. It may be the game of wellbeing or of fear, of pleasure, of grief. Ultimately it is the same game. We play the game of something mattering, of something not mattering... It's all made up. It is like a layer over the top of our spiritual essence and yet it's part of the fabric of life. The only difference comes in the illusion of the difference we see.

Peace and love is closer to spiritual essence. When we stop doing the rest, this is what is left. Through deepening our understanding of what life is and what is behind it, we can live at higher levels of Consciousness. Our levels will fluctuate all the time but what we see is from the level of Consciousness we're at in any one moment.

Personally I've lived from very low levels of Consciousness—from fear, unworthiness, stress, and worse—I was living right up against these self-created realities with very little perspective that I was the creator. These reasons were created from within this same reality. It was like going round in circles within a closed maze, blindfolded. There's no way out until you stop playing that game and think outside of the confines and rules you've created.

It can be useful to know the reasons I created the habit of fear and unworthiness. It was a way that I saw to protect myself at a certain time, and it worked in its way for a while. Now, this same game no longer serves me. This is the time to remember what the truth is, what it really is.

I know now that I'm coming from a different standpoint, a higher level of Consciousness—There is more. There is always more—so much more that it's almost wild and beyond our little minds to conceptualise. The potential is endless, literally endless. Whatever that means! This is why people talk about spiritual essence being pure potential. It is endless and is therefore beyond our tiny minds. Talk about wild!

What I needed to see, according to Jack, if I've got this right, is:

1. *The reality I created for myself and I was living in.*
2. *The illusion and the fact that it is an illusion.*
3. *What's real. Truth at a more profound, deeper, higher level of Consciousness. What underlies my personal "reality."*

Now I am ready. Let's see how this game plays out.

Ultimately what I now know at a deep level, as a fact, is I am fundamentally ok, fundamentally whole and nothing can touch that. This is something so small, such a tiny shift and yet the potential this realization leaves me with is mind-blowing. The feeling of wholeness is (almost) tangible. This is a knowing that touches the essence of life and goes beyond my previous knowing and understanding. It is a gift. Thank you Jack!

38. SEX

The chapter you've all been secretly waiting for—

Donna from Europe Skyped me, troubled over whether she should get married.

After ten years she and Gary had a beautiful relationship. Warm and cuddly, very affectionate, they loved each other very much, loved living with each other and it showed. They listened to each other, enjoyed each other's company. It wasn't always that way. Their first two years were quite rocky. They argued all the time. Gary was very demanding. Donna rebelled. Since that time, however, they resolved nearly all their issues except one, and their relationship thrived. It should be time for her to take the next step into marriage, she said, but she felt really scared when she thought of it.

Donna began to cry.

"Why are you scared of getting married?"

"Because I don't trust that Gary won't go off and have an affair."

Oh. "What makes you think he might?"

She finally got down to it: Sex.

"On a scale from 1 to 10, our relationship is usually up around 9. When we move towards sex it drops to around 2. Once we get going it might get to a 5 and on rare occasions a 6 or 7. But on the whole I don't look forward to it. I have to psyche myself up."

According to Donna, Gary is extremely demanding in bed. He needs to have the act done a certain way. He almost demands it.

"It sounds like you feel sex is a great burden to you."

Donna cried again. "Yes."

She gathered herself. "Gary is heavily into porn. I think this has informed his sexual style. I feel like a sex worker sometimes, almost like I'm in a porn movie having sex with him. It was worse at the beginning, but I still feel the burden. Sex has to culminate in either

Gary masturbating on his own or with me [stimulating him in an unmentionable way here—sorry—in fact, I'd better use discretion in what I describe here; let's just say that Donna doesn't have the strength—you can use your own imagination.] We have not had penetrative ejaculation for years. That's boring for him and hard to achieve. He tried to stop masturbating a few years back but couldn't sustain it unless I had very regular sex with him, which still made me feel he needed my body for him to get his rocks off. It wasn't about love and connection and making love. So I don't want to do it. When we go without sex for a while the inference is it's my fault. But I'm not up for it, and why would I be? I don't feel fulfilled much."

Okay, let me see if I have this straight: If Donna doesn't take responsibility to please Gary in exactly the way he wants—and what he wants is unusual at best—she fears she will send him into needing other women, which is why she is scared, which is why she doesn't want to get married, which is why she feels guilty. Whew!

"It doesn't surprise me at all that you have no sexual feeling under those circumstances. Look, Donna, what Gary wants is not your responsibility."

"What do you mean?"

"I mean Gary has no right to demand of you that you perform to his satisfaction, especially since he can only get his rocks off in a very particular, unusual way. Then you develop an aversion to having sex with him. Then, if you don't do what he wants, you feel like you're letting him down. Then you get scared he'll go elsewhere to get it."

"Gary says he wouldn't do that."

Well, maybe, but to me it sounded almost like sexual blackmail. Normally I refuse to take sides but something told me, right now, here, I needed to.

"Look, it's not unreasonable at all for you to feel this way. What he is demanding of you is what's unreasonable. No wonder you fear getting married!"

I was right. Donna broke down again. She felt so relieved to hear that she wasn't crazy after all.

I asked, "Do you think Gary would be willing to speak with me? Then I'd like to have a session with both of you together."

To his credit, Gary was quite willing. He told me he'd been very insecure as a young person. Then he found sex. And sex, he discovered, was one thing he was very good at. It helped overcome his insecurity. In bed he became quite adventurous. Then he found himself bored when sex was not adventurous enough. He admitted he needed Donna to do special things to him so he could finally ejaculate.

"Gary, do you think what you're trying to achieve for yourself here is having the effect on Donna that you would like, or is it having the opposite effect? Like, what if pushing too hard might make you lose this woman you love? Is that really what you want? Does this make any sense?"

He admitted it didn't.

"Furthermore, Gary, what you say you 'need' is only thought masquerading as real need. I know it looks real. I know it *feels* like a real need. But, really, this so-called need is only self-created thought."

By the end of our conversation Gary had jumped a level of consciousness—enough that I believed he was ready for me to speak with both of them together.

When Donna returned from a three-week business trip, we all had a Skype session. The two were very lovey and cuddly and seemed to thoroughly enjoy each other's company. This was not put on; I could feel it.

When I work with a couple, first I assess whether a solid foundation of love exists in the relationship and whether both people really want to be together. If there is and they do, I do everything in my power to help them stay together by seeing each other with new eyes. If no foundation of love exists and they have no real desire to stay together and seem resistant to a change in thinking I help them split amicably. Clearly, Gary and Donna had a solid foundation of love and a desire to work out differences. I needed to help them listen to each other very deeply until they could each hear the grain of truth in the other's side. There is always a grain of truth in the other side that makes perfect sense to that person. Deep listening is healing in and of itself. If they still bump heads, I want to help them reach a meeting of the minds.

They did have a beautiful relationship until "bedroom" or "sex" came up, which bred fear in Donna, which sent her feeling down the tubes, which sent her running for cover, which upset Gary.

Interestingly, early on in our Skype conversation Gary brought up that he wanted lovemaking to be an expression of his love for Donna. Donna agreed wholeheartedly.

I said, "Gary, you're absolutely right! You're talking about the pure expression of love that automatically comes out between two people attracted to each other in love that naturally wants to express itself. This comes from within. And if you only have *that* on your mind when you want to make love, none of the rest of this stuff would even be an issue. But you've got other things on your mind."

Gary joked to Donna, "Jack must think I'm a 'perv.'"

I got feisty. I don't often jump into the middle and take no prisoners. But here, now, it felt right. Maybe it was the subject matter.

"Actually, Gary, I don't care one bit what your sexual proclivities are. What I care about is whether your own personal 'needs,' which you inadvertently make up but rule you, are getting in the way of what you say you want for your relationship. I don't care what you like. I don't care what you do. You can do anything sexually you want. But if you want this relationship to last and thrive you've got to realize that what you want for yourself is your own business, not Donna's. It's your responsibility to take care of it, not Donna's responsibility, and if you make it her responsibility to please you and satisfy you in the exact, unique way you want to be satisfied, this relationship is going to fail because it becomes a burden to her and she wants to run. So you need to take care of your own special 'needs' yourself—unless *she wants* to do it naturally as a pure expression of her love for you in a moment. Right now, nothing is happening naturally because she gets scared."

I turned to Donna, "This is not your responsibility!"

Gary jumped in. "In fairness, I'm not doing this so much anymore. I admit I did at the beginning, but I learned and now I'm taking more care with her feelings and trying to respect her desires."

"Donna, is this true?"

"Yes. It's true. He's not like he used to be."

"Well, Donna, if that's true, yet sex is still aversive to you and a burden, then you, too, are interfering with lovemaking being a pure expression of your love for Gary. Your habit is to jump back into the past, and when you do it can only get in the way. You keep saying how difficult it was for you that—'In the early years of our relationship

Gary did this and that,' and then you say, 'but he's not doing that so much now.' So why bring it up? It's got nothing to do with now! If Gary even tries to approach you purely now, he's got to plow through all the past things you're holding onto about him and what he did, and your antennae are way up to see if he's doing it again. How is that conducive to anything you're trying to accomplish here?"

Now Donna felt a little sheepish.

"And Gary, can you see that your habit of latching onto what you 'need' from her to be satisfied totally obscures your own intention for lovemaking to be that pure expression of love for Donna, because those thoughts, taken seriously, begin the downward spiral. So when you allow those thoughts to take you over, [I turned to Donna] then you, Donna, get scared and go into your habits of thinking about the past and how difficult the burden is for you to have to take the responsibility, then you feel an aversion to go to bed with him, which totally obscures your own intention for lovemaking to be solely an expression of your love for Gary. Then Gary goes into fear. See how this downward spiral works?"

They both saw it.

"Gary, would you say your sexual demands on Donna have been turning her on or turning her off?"

The answer was obvious.

"Right," Donna jumped in. "Gary goes after me right away very roughly—it hurts sometimes—while I need time to warm up first. If I'm helped to warm up gradually then sometimes I might actually be up for doing more of the adventurous things you want—especially if it isn't demanded and expected."

"Do you hear that, Gary? And you also talked about being bored in lovemaking. How is 'bored' even possible if lovemaking is simply an expression of love for Donna? You use your thinking to create extraneous thoughts of expectation, then with more thought you compare what is actually happening to the expectation, then with more thought you create dissatisfaction and boredom when the two don't match up. No expectations exist in 'pure expression of love.' It's people's true nature expressing itself.

"And Donna, if you were to take all the thoughts of past/future out of the picture, what would be left? Just pure expression of love for Gary through making love."

What a simple solution! I reminded them, though, as I try to remind everyone, because they both have been driven by these habits of thought the thoughts will likely continue to appear. When they do, the two of them will be once again at that proverbial fork in the road. One path is to keep being driven by the habits, take them as reality, get scared and let it get in the way of the natural flow of love. The other path is to help each other gently see when the other is sliding into the habit again—when they don't want to be. In a good feeling Donna could say something like, "Gary, would you say what you're doing now is simply your pure expression of love for me?" With a loving feeling Gary could say something like, "Donna, would you say what you're doing now might be going into the past again and losing the moment?"

Gently and lovingly helping each other move beyond. What would be left? The wonderful relationship they have in every other way! Pure love expressing itself through making love. Such a beautiful thing to receive—and to give!

A solid new ground. New hope. Both satisfied.

At the end of our couples' session Gary said this was so simple compared with all other therapies he had been to in the past. "What's humbling now," he said, "is we have all the responsibility. Before we could always blame the other person. We can't get away with that anymore."

So true.

39. TRAUMA

I hadn't heard from Monica in a while. One day she called me in a panic experiencing feelings of terror; traumatized. Though she didn't actually come out and say it I had the feeling she thought she might need to be committed; she could no longer trust herself.

This seemed serious. I jumped into my car and drove the thirty minutes to her house. Monica lives way up a dirt road at the top of a hill, with very few houses around, miles from the center of a very small town. Readers of *Somebody Should Have Told Us!* may remember Monica as the subject of one of its featured stories.

Monica told me she kept doing crazy things where she felt almost separated from herself. For example, she had a crush on her neighbor, spent most of her time avoiding him, and when she did bump into him she got all tongue-tied and froze. That wasn't the crazy part. One day she wrote him a letter telling him how much she wanted him. That wasn't the crazy part, either. The unwise part was she sent it. He stopped communicating with her. She became completely embarrassed, feeling she'd acted like a crazy woman, and ever since felt in a near panic. In another incident she'd walked into the workplace of her child's father and asked loudly if he had any smokes. Driving away afterwards she thought, "I can't believe I did that!" Another embarrassment from inappropriate behavior. Then came her ultimate extreme move of giving up both her kids to their father because she could no longer trust herself with them. She'd lost her job and couldn't find another; in fact, she no longer knew if she could handle working. Her life had become a mess.

I became so puzzled. Why would somebody who understands the Three Principles, who'd had such a powerful life-altering insight (see *Somebody Should Have Told Us!)* now lose it like this?

I asked, "When did all this start happening?"

After a long discussion it finally came out. She felt terror ever since her ex-boyfriend, who had once raped her mother, got out of prison. She couldn't be totally certain but she thought she might have seen him around her house. She got paranoid.

I became concerned for her. She lived out in the boonies, with only that other neighbor nearby. "This is not paranoia, Monica. He's out of prison now and you're afraid he'll do you harm."

"Well, he's not around anymore."

"What do you mean?"

"I found out he raped some other woman and was thrown back in jail."

Oh. "So now he's back in prison but you're still living in fear? You're still feeling terrorized?"

"Yes."

"That's puzzling to me."

"Me too."

We talked about seeing terror as reality when, given the current circumstances, nothing terrifying exists now.

"Well, I sort of have an inkling that this might be coming from my thinking."

"Sort of an inkling? Look, it's either all reality or it's all your thinking. No in-betweens. That you think it might be coming from your thinking is irrelevant because once it's there it's *real to you.* Then you buy into the reality of it."

"Do I need to see the thought driving me into terror?"

"You mean the specific thought?"

"Yes. I don't know what the thought is. Do you think I need to see the specific thought?"

"Well, if you happen to see that terror is the same as any other feeling and can only come from your own self-created thinking, then you wouldn't need to see the specific thought. Or, if you *see* that in the face of pure consciousness/innate health/your spiritual essence, none of our human creations in this form really mean anything, then you wouldn't need to see the specific thought. But if you can't see either of those, sometimes it does help to see the specific thought."

"Well I can't see those things. I'm not able to wrap my head around that. I think I knew it once but I can't see it anymore."

I could tell this was not getting through to Monica at all, so I went back to listening and reflection. Something struck me.

"Where do you think your terror comes from?"

Monica reflected a few moments. "It's all the sexual abuse I was subjected to as a kid."

"Well, that makes sense. But could you help that?"

Monica mumbled something about thinking she could have helped it.

All of a sudden it hit me with a flash: Monica does not see her own innocence! Not even at three years old when the horrific sexual abuse started.

"Monica, at three years old, what could you have done? What could you have done?"

Monica got stuck. Her intellect tried to hold on for dear life. She said, "But later I could have, maybe."

"Oh, wow, Monica, you feel guilty about what happened, don't you?"

"Yes—[*long pause, tears came to her eyes*]. I feel guilty that part of me, at least, actually liked it. Part of me actually liked the feeling of it, and I feel so guilty about that."

"Wow, Monica. I know what I'm about to say doesn't remotely come close to what you're talking about, but I just got a flash of my then-very-young granddaughter in a swimming pool in Florida. She found one of the jets shooting the water into the pool and she would just stand there for the longest time, crotch to jet, loving the feeling of it. I'm only bringing this up because a little kid can't help loving a feeling like that, no matter how it's happening to her. It's innocence."

"But I feel like a horrible person for liking the feeling of such a horrible thing."

I knew seeing through this was the key to Monica's freedom. She could not see her own innocence. I knew if she could it would free her from all her terror and separation from wisdom.

"Well," she said, "maybe I couldn't have helped it at three, but what about at seven, nine, ten, twelve years old?"

"What could you have done at twelve?"

"I could have told somebody."

"How come you didn't tell anybody?"

"I was scared."

"Monica, isn't that innocence? It's total innocence!"

"Well, I should have."

"You're saying that now, Monica, but you didn't have the thinking then that said you could do it. That's what total innocence is. Truly see this! You didn't have the thinking to support telling anyone because you were scared. Total innocence. Total innocence! You could only do then what your thinking allowed you to do then. Total innocence!"

Something struck Monica then, as if she realized this was the true source of her continued trauma and terror. Suddenly her face changed. Release. She looked different. Suddenly, total freedom. Her ticket out of terror. Back to leading a normal life.

This is what happens when a "reality" we're stuck with is truly seen for the illusion it is.

Please understand, it was not an illusion that all the sexual abuse happened to her. That was true, real and horrific. The illusion was Monica thinking she wasn't innocent, that she should feel guilty because some parts of it felt nice and because she should have told someone.

Monica couldn't see this before because she had not yet healed enough to see it. All the insights she had along the way through understanding the Three Principles had built up her strength so she now could see more, preparing her for this moment, making her now strong enough to have all this yucky, buried stuff rise to the surface and be dealt with once and for all. Its hidden grip had thrown her off balance. So painful to go through, but a sign something was knocking on her door desperately wanting to be revealed. She became strong enough to see; then she saw the illusion of what she'd created in her own mind.

Her ticket to freedom—if she wants to take it. And it's a free ticket.

* * *

If you couldn't guess by now, I'm a sucker for alternative healing practices. When I hear of a new practice, I like to try it out, experiment. A new practitioner, Kathleen Houlahan, arrived in Montpelier, Vermont, practicing something called "Body Talk." I met her through the Onion River Exchange, of which I was a founding Board member. We decided to exchange sessions.

In January, 2013 I received her Body Talk session. I lay on her table face-up while she scanned my clothed body energetically by lightly tugging on my wrist, getting signals she picked up from different parts of my body that allegedly "talked" to her. I have no idea how it works. I suspect this is very, very deep listening at the level of Universal Mind energy. I know only what transpired.

During the session she didn't speak but kind of mumbled to herself, unintelligibly. When she finished she said I had a weak heart. This was not news. Not only does heart disease run in my family but several alternative healing practitioners over the years had commented that my heart is something I should keep an eye on, and I do.

But she picked up some new news, too. She told me that when I was five years old I experienced a trauma to my heart, because something happened that scared me half to death. She said she pictured my father running after me.

I knew instantly what it was. It had nothing to do with my father chasing me.

When I was five, our family lived in a not-so-beautiful apartment in the Roxbury section of Boston on Parkview Street, just off Franklin Park—not the greatest of neighborhoods. I remember our house being a long, narrow apartment with a long hallway (at least that's the way it seemed at age five), my bedroom at the far end of the hall.

One night I woke up with a start. I saw the shadow of a man at my window! Scared me out of my wits. Writing this now I can still see that man's shadow on the wall. I get chills thinking about it. I let out a blood-curdling scream. My father came running down the hallway to me. Through my tears and fear I told him what I saw. He looked out the window. Couldn't see anybody.

My parents must have thought I was having a nightmare. I don't think they really believed a man had actually been at my window. But I knew he was real. I knew I wasn't dreaming. Obviously the man had taken off when I screamed. Regardless, I can't remember whether I stayed in bed with my parents for the rest of the night or whether one of them stayed with me, but it shook me to my bones. I'll never forget it.

Driving back after my session Dr. Michael Billig, my CRA practitioner, whom I brought up in Chapter 29, popped into my mind. In his gruff-but-sweet old Vermonter inimitable style, he had told me a few times over the years I had traumatized my heart. Whenever he picked up on that, he asked if anything had recently happened to me and, invariably, I had just had a bad fall or an accident or a near miss in a car or something like that. So this was not an unfamiliar notion.

As I thought this, still driving, out of nowhere I became emotional. I realized that at the moment my little five-year-old-self got scared out of my little wits, I had the thought that I needed to be protected. I needed to be taken care of. My little life of innocence was over. Then I realized, that's what I had sought in a relationship! That's why in my past I had been after a strong woman who could protect me and take care of me. I was so painfully shy when I was a little kid my mother took me to the Judge Baker Guidance Center because she was so worried about me. I realized her taking me there must have been soon after my little trauma. So for the rest of my life, from my mother to my early relationships, including my marriage, I sought a really strong woman who could protect me and take care of me. Wow! I felt it!

Then I realized something else: It didn't sit well with me to be protected and taken care of like that. Part of me didn't like it one bit! So I rebelled. As a young adult I rebelled when I took off hitchhiking around the country by myself, which my mother completely opposed. I rebelled when I married a woman who wasn't Jewish—both my parents opposed that one, but only my mother shared her disapproval with me (until Judy converted, on her own, then she was thrilled). Then I rebelled when I moved way up to Vermont without having a job, bought some land and built a house, which my mother also opposed. Rebel me.

As an adult, to escape the strong, overpowering, protective woman I was married to, I didn't know how to handle it so I sought out other women to feel totally appreciated and accepted for who I am, where I could just feel totally myself. (I already wrote about that.) A rebel again, only a lot less healthy.

I realize now as I write this that being a rebel was actually my way of not facing up to these powerful women—out of fear. Tricked by thought-seduction once again.

All that from a trauma at five years old, which had traumatized my heart! The dominoes of life.

Seeing this was my freedom from its hold on me, and I didn't even know the grip it had.

40. FOOD AND WEIGHT

I'm not sure why, but most of my clients these days come from overseas. Elizabeth from the U.K. sent an email saying she loved Somebody Should Have Told Us! *and wanted to know of my availability for counseling. Though I usually don't do this, for some reason I felt compelled to turn on my voice recorder, with her permission. I had never talked with Elizabeth, and when we began the session I had no idea we would end up talking about weight and food.*

E: …I feel like I've just wasted ten years of money and heartache on traditional counseling when I needn't have.

JP: Let's say you hadn't done all that work with them of going back into your past and unraveling it, do you think you'd be doing just as well now?

E: Um, well, I think if I hadn't ever come across your book I would not be doing as well, but if I hadn't gone through all that counseling I'd probably be doing as well. [*laughs*]

JP: You said your parents planted some beliefs in your mind that did not make you feel good. Give me an example of one of the things they said about you that you believed.

E: Well, my mum—who I'm actually about to spend a weekend with so this is very lovely timing—she has a very bad temper and is quite a negative person and a real perfectionist. I kind of grew up an A+ student and did every sport and did everything. And then my parents divorced when I was in high school and it pushed her off the edge. I moved out of our home. My mum said I left her when she needed me. I just needed to get my head straight, get out of that environment. But now she thinks I don't support her.

JP: Do you carry guilt about that?

E: Yeah. Well, I did. I'm really nervous about getting together with her this weekend because it will be a test of my newfound way of looking at things. But, yeah. She just wrote me an e-mail that said under the surface, "You're not thinking of me," and I read it and got upset. Then it was like, "Wait a second. I'm making myself upset. It's not her."

JP: I have an interesting question for you. "What does her guilt-tripping have to do with you?"

E [*getting emotional*]: The thing that just rang into my head then was that I'm not good enough, and I don't know what that relates to.

JP: And what does that have to do with you?

E: It's what I've believed for as long as I can remember.

JP: Didn't you pick up that idea from her?

E: Yeah.

JP: So if that came from her, what does that have to do with you?

E: [*pauses*] Nothing.

JP: See, that's the thing. Innocently you picked that up from her and took it on, but if you were to keep carrying that through your life right now, would it do you any good?

E: No.

JP: And the big question is, "Is it true? Is it true that you're not good enough?"

E: Everyone's good enough. I know it.

JP: I'm almost hearing a "but" there. You could come up with reasons why you're not good enough—

E: I think I could come up with reasons but then if we actually tested them I don't think they would hold water.

JP: Okay, then let's come up with a reason. Let's test it.

E: [*laughs*]. Um [*becoming emotional again*], well, because I'm overweight. That's a big one, okay? [*crying now*] But as I say that, I know in my head that's ridiculous and that your weight is not you—

JP: What is it about the overweight thing? Are you saying to yourself, "I'm not good enough because I can't get a handle on this?" Or—

E: Yes! Because all through high school when I was in my perfect phase I was very slim and hugely controlling with my food, bordering on anorexia. And then when I dropped the ball in my life I also dropped the ball eating-wise, and I've kind of been having an eating disorder for five or six years. I think I've begun to turn the corner on it and I'm feeling really good about it, but I guess it comes down to feeling like I should be able to control it, and why can't I?

JP: Do you think you were healthier with near-anorexia and being skinny, or being heavier than you want to be?

E: Um—

JP: I mean, neither is particularly healthy, but it's funny that you would equate overweight and not having control over it to not being good enough, while you weren't equating near-anorexia as not being good enough because you say you had more control then.

E: If I think back even when I could just control it, or now, it's like, why can't I just be normal about it?

JP: Well, what if your thought that you're "not normal" is the only thing keeping you from experiencing that you're normal?

E: [*long pause*] Yuh.

JP: In other words, but for thinking, "I'm not normal," you would automatically be normal.

E: Yup. Yup. I think I attribute weight to the reason for other things, like if a male isn't interested in me despite the myriad of other reasons it could be, I go, "If I wasn't overweight this wouldn't have happened." And sometimes I worry that the reason I can't lose weight—I've already lost quite a bit of weight over the last five years—is because I think, "What is there to hide behind after that?"

JP: That's a great insight. Well, do you need to be hiding behind anything? That's the question.

E: [*pause*] I know.

JP: Hiding behind something for what reason?

E: To stay small.

JP: I hear you saying, "Because then I'd have to take the responsibility?"

E: [*chuckles*] I think so, yup.

JP: So as long as you stay heavier than you think you should be, you don't have to take the responsibility.

E: Yeah. Yeah. I think I think that. I think the thought of being okay is actually scarier—even though that's the thing I want more than anything.

JP: What scares you about the fact of being okay?

E: I don't know [*pauses*], like, pressure or something.

JP: Pressure for what?

E: [*pauses*] Being perfect or something? I don't know.

JP: Elizabeth, what makes you think you need to be any particular way?

E: My impressions of what is acceptable in society.

JP: Well, why not just *be*?

E: [*big sigh—nervous giggle*] Um.

JP: That one stopped you in your tracks.

E: [*laughs*] I think I know this isn't me at my best, so I feel like I'm selling myself short, which is so ironic because I'm the one selling myself short [*laughs*]

JP: Okay, so here's how it works: You come up with a thought about what you should be like at your best, then you have a thought that compares where you are to what you think you should be like at your best, then you get bummed out by the difference and feel the effects of it. But the whole thing was your creation in the first place. You made it all up!

E: [*laughs*] So true! Oh my gosh! So true. [*sigh*] Yeah. So true.

JP: So the question is, do you need to create this whole thing for yourself? I mean, does it really serve any purpose for you other than keeping you in a low state?

E: No, absolutely not.

JP: Now don't get me wrong, it's a habit, so you're going to continue to have thoughts like that. But your power comes from deciding whether to take those thoughts seriously. See, up to this point it only appeared to be getting you what you want. But does it really get you what you want? No! What it really gets you is a low state. Do you want to continue to believe in those thoughts knowing what it gets you is a low state?

E: No. No. And I do know the times in my life I've been able to be comfortable with myself is when I'm not thinking about it. But I can hear my mum talking in my head: "You've got to be really strict about it. Really vigilant."

JP: Right now you've kind of had a lid on being the best you could be because you've come up with reasons why you can't be. [*laughs*]

E: Yeah, that's so true!

JP: Well, what if that lid were taken off?

E: Yeah, I'll say to myself, "I'll be able to be really confident about meeting someone once I lose weight." [*laughs*] Even as I say it out loud I know it doesn't make sense.

JP: Well, it made sense within the illusion of protecting yourself. But that's all it is: an illusion. Would you be interested in having me go back for a moment and talk about the Three Principles in this regard?

E: Yeah.

JP: [*I explained how the Three Principles work together, pretty much as I've explained it numerous times in this book. I ended with the following:*] So automatically we are already our best, except we put this cloud of thinking over us. [pause] And then, if we beat ourselves up for thinking that way, we put another cloud on top of that.

E: Yeah. [*laughs*] I know that cloud pretty well.

JP: Yeah, you've been mucking around in the cloud for a while now—

E: [*laughs*]

JP: —when, really, you want to realize that the cloud is an illusion, and when it is really seen for the illusion it is, it goes *poof*. And what's left is that state of pure consciousness, which is who you *really* are. Simplicity itself! You can only get in your own way! And you're not alone. Everybody, including me, does this to ourselves.

E: I know you addressed this in one of your books, but why doesn't everybody know this?

JP: It is really difficult for people to see the inside-out world compared to the outside-in world, which most of the world functions by—at least they think they function by it. It's been too much of a leap for the field of psychology, for example, to embrace it because it flies in the face of everything they learned and teach. What sets the Three Principles apart is that what is being called "reality" is really an illusion of people's own creation—and that is the only thing going on. And to realize, within our pure consciousness we are already what we're looking for, and only our thinking can make it look as if we're not.

E: I think that's the solution to everything, isn't it? This is a weird example but I've struggled my whole life to keep my room tidy. Like, I turn around and it's a mess again, and I'll be, like, "Oh my God." And it's only been in the last two months where I'm caring for myself a bit more, and now it's like, yuck, and I almost enjoy keeping it clean. I can't believe the change in me. I've read plenty of books on how to keep your room tidy, but because it wasn't coming from the right space—I don't know what I'm trying to say, really—

JP: Yeah, you were reading the book from the same level of consciousness that kept your room messy. What we need, which you apparently experienced, is a shift in consciousness, where a clean room takes on a completely new meaning. Those books are asking you to change a behavior from the same level of thinking, and that's pretty impossible. A fundamental shift is needed, where what a clean room means to you is completely different, and you feel it.

E: Yeah.

JP: So just to play with this for a moment to illustrate what I mean, if you were to reflect on what your thought about your room shifted to, what is it now?

E: Um, I really enjoy having a tidy room—

JP: What makes you enjoy it?

E: Um, because I really love a nice environment. I like to see a beautiful environment when I come home.

JP: Oh I get it: You don't want to mess with a beautiful environment.

E: [*laughs*] Yes, I think so.

JP: That's a different thought than you had before.

E: Yeah.

JP: What was your thought before?

E: I can't do this. This is too hard!

JP: Yeah. Now you can see what will happen to your room if you're motivated by that kind of thinking. But if you're motivated by, "I don't want to do anything that messes with the beautiful environment," that's a thought at a higher level of consciousness, and everything just falls into place from there.

E: Right. I think now it's like I deserve to live in a nice environment. It used to be I couldn't get up in the morning, so I'd get up ten minutes before I needed to go to work, chuck some clothes on and run out the door. Now I like to have an hour to do my hair nicely and put on makeup and stuff—so I care about myself. I didn't care about myself then.

JP: Now, what do you think this discussion has to do with weight?

E. Hmmm.

JP: Suppose you saw your body along the same lines now as you see your room.

E: [*long pause*] Hmmm. Yeah. I think with my body now I'm where I used to be with my room—actually that's unfair because I think I'm slowly changing and I'm finding exercise is less effort, but I still haven't quite gotten there—looking at caring for my body like I do with my room now. I still see it as deprivation if I can't have something to eat.

JP: So even though your mind has switched about your room, it hasn't totally switched about your body.

E: No.

JP: But it could, right? Like, what would make you not see your body the same way as you see your room now?

E: Yeah, I know. I think I've been very divorced from my body for a long time, and I'm now taking a lot of interest in it. I'm reading a lot about body image and things like that to familiarize myself with my body a bit more, which sounds strange because I've been living in my body for 29 years, but I don't think we are very connected [*laughs*]. What's changing is I'm not making rules about what I can and can't eat. I'm going more with how I will feel.

JP: It's been interesting for me lately because high blood pressure runs in my family. I would wake up in the middle of the night with headaches, feeling bloaty and with a lot of mucus, and a healer told me I needed to change to a gluten-free diet and stop eating dairy, including ice cream, which is my favorite food in the world. My first thought was, I can't do that. I didn't want to do it. But I wanted much less to take blood-pressure medication, which both my parents had to take for the rest of their lives. So I decided it was important enough to me to try what he said. Wow, my headaches went away instantly, my bloaty and mucousy feeling went away pretty quickly, and I felt healthier. That felt so much better than eating anything I wanted whenever I wanted it, so I changed pretty effortlessly. I'm not a fanatic; I'm probably 85% gluten-free. I used to have a big bowl of ice cream every night, where now most of the time I have a smoothie instead, which doesn't taste quite as good but still tastes good. But I feel such a difference in my body. Why wouldn't I want to keep doing that? My consciousness shifted about gluten and ice cream because my thinking shifted about gluten and ice cream.

E: Yeah. Yeah. Yeah. Like now when I'm getting ready in the morning I wonder, how did I ever not take the time to do this before? Because I love it. If you told me six months ago that I would have done that, I would have said you were crazy. But I have periods where I'm thinking that way, and then I have periods where the lens goes on and I'm thinking in a different way, and I need to recognize when I'm thinking in those good moments and try to—

JP: Well, let me interrupt you before you go there. That's okay, but I think it's different than that. I think it's more a question of really asking yourself what's most important to you, and answering that question honestly. Really feel your answer.

E: [*pauses*] Being healthy.

JP: If that's really true, then what you put into your body and how much you move your body around begins to be seen within the context of what's really important to you: being healthy.

E: Yeah.

JP: So it's not about where you started to go when I interrupted you—putting effort in, going out of your way to recognize, going out of your way to change your thinking. See what I mean? It's more a question of opening yourself up to a change of heart, a change of thought about *importance* or what really matters to you. It's just reflecting on, "What really is important to me here? How do I want to be in relation to food intake and weight vs. my health and how I'll feel?" And then things fall into place on their own.

E: How does that fit with, like, habit?

JP: Well, I had a habit of eating a big bowl of ice cream every night.

E: Yeah, okay.

JP: Like I said, at the time I didn't know it was even possible for me not to have ice cream every night because I loved it so much. And if I was going to keep thinking at that level of consciousness I was not going to change. As much as I said to myself, "I shouldn't have this much ice cream," it still wouldn't change because I was still a slave to it from that same level of consciousness.

E: That's what I need to know. I don't know how to get to that level of consciousness.

JP: Well, you can't force yourself to a new level of consciousness. It takes reflection. It's allowing wisdom to speak. Like for me it became much more important to not take blood-pressure medication than to eat ice cream, bread and cereal the way I was eating them. Gluten-free bread is just not the same as regular bread!

E: Pizza!

JP: I love pizza! And gluten-free pizza just doesn't cut it. It's getting a little better these days, but it's still not the same. But I don't deny myself totally. Every once in a while I'll say to myself, "I deserve this, and I'm willing to suffer the consequences." So I might get a headache or put on a few pounds, then I'll remember what's most important again, and it's not pizza and ice cream. You can't force yourself to be at a higher level of consciousness. When we reflect on what we really want for our whole being we see what's really important. How do we want to be in life? Let me ask you this, "Is it really true that there is something you have to hide behind?"

E: [*sighs, pauses*] No. I think I just can't imagine not having that. I don't know.

JP: I couldn't imagine not having ice cream either.

E: [*big laugh*]

JP: I mean, really, it was impossible for me to imagine.

E: Okay, I think it's just been so long since I've been thin, I can't even imagine—

JP: Who says you have to be thin? You just want to feel healthy.

E: Yeah. Okay. Yeah. Yup. Sometimes I have really strong insights, but other times they just creep up on me gradually and all of a sudden I realize what's happened.

JP: Yes, that's very much what happens to most people. I mean, you're the only one who's putting a time pressure on this about when you need to be perfect by.

E: [*laughs*] That's so true! That's so true! I've spent so much time in my life either on a diet or berating myself for not being on a diet—that's pretty much how my whole thing has been. Even when I was eating not very well I was still berating myself for it, so I've never had a moment in time except for these last few months when I'm just relaxed about it all. I don't want to lose that relaxed feeling, but I think from what we've spoken about today it's not about not losing that relaxed feeling it's about really knowing what's important and what you want for yourself and it kind of just follows from that, instead of, "I can't do this."

JP: Right. I mean, the reason diets are so hard is because we're doing them from that lower level of consciousness. So of course it's going to be tough to give up some food. Of course it's going to be easy to say, "This is too hard, I give up," because that's all a low level of consciousness talking. The fact is, you're still going to have thoughts like, "I want this pizza right now!" But that's just the habit. What if another thought or a question got planted in there: "Is it better for me to indulge right now, or is it better for me to go with thoughts of where I want to be for my health." See what the answer is and go with whatever it says. If you make a mistake you'll know it in the next day or two, and then you might make a different decision.

E: That seems so simple. I've always some way known it could be simple. I've read some books that say, if you've always had trouble with weight and eating, you always will. But I do believe that once you're in the right mind frame it overcomes that. That's what I read in *Modello*, like with Thelma who was an alcoholic and then wasn't anymore without any traditional treatment—at some level that felt right.

JP: It's always about new insight. It's never about anything else. So you will get thoughts of food—that's natural—but what you do with them now is up to you. The thoughts themselves can't hurt you unless you give them power.

E: Yeah, I think that's where I've been going wrong. If I think that way I'm on myself immediately with, "You shouldn't be thinking that! You're trying to lose weight!" And it doesn't matter if I've had the thought; it's just seeing it for what it is. Yeah. Okay. That is very useful!

JP: Great! Maybe it's best to just let this set with you and see what happens. If you want to have another session, I'm here, but that's totally up to you.

E: Yeah, I really appreciate it. It's been so helpful. A lot of food for thought.

JP: It's interesting that you call it that.

[*both laugh*]

41. FOOD AND WEIGHT REVISITED, AND MORE

Of all the people I've met who have been exposed to the Three Principles Mette Louise Holland from Denmark has caught on a combined fastest and deepest. When I first met the beautiful Mette Louise in Denmark on my "European Tour" she was heavier than she wanted to be and concerned about it. She then attended my Extended Professional Training (EPT) in Spain. The next time I saw her—a year later when she reappeared as a "veteran" at the EPT, her body had almost completely transformed. It looked as if she dropped fifteen or so pounds. How did she do that? I saw a blog Mette Louise had written about her experience, and I felt compelled to ask her permission to reprint it. She happily agreed and adapted it for this book:

We're in love and it shows—
The Three Principles and how we appear physically

Jack asked me to share something about the physical changes I experienced after I came across the understanding of the Principles, which I will be happy to give a shot.

In 2012 my husband had started to read about something he called *The Three Principles* and in the beginning of 2013 I reached the curiousity threshold and asked if he would explain it to me. He said something very short about how our thinking creates our feelings and our whole experience. Intellectually, I didn't understand it at all, but I instantly knew this was truer than anything else I (thought I) knew about our human psychology. As I'm a psychologist and a psychotherapist with something like twelve years of education behind me I never expected that to happen—I thought I knew a lot! But what he pointed to resonated with me so deeply there was no going back. It wasn't a choice. I had seen something I couldn't possibly forget, even if it took a while for my intellect to catch up with what something deeper inside of me had instantly heard and recognized so clearly.

I've been deepening my understanding of the Principles behind the human experience every single day since and continue to do so. What a joy and depth this has added to my life! Soon after I learned about the Principles I found incredible peace inside—my system deeply recognised there was absolutely no point in worrying, judging or planning myself out of the present anymore. I bubbled with joy and couldn't help giggling all the time. Somehow I just knew and felt how totally free I was. And how funny it suddenly seemed to me to try to make up a story that I wasn't, which I had innocently done in so many ways before. Indeed, I was waking up to a whole new dimension in life.

After about four months I thought to myself: "Well, this Three Principles thing may be fantastic and really feels good, but it's not fixed my way of eating yet." (After all, being a woman, what is inner peace and joy compared to a slim figure?) I have spent my whole life planning what to eat next and have never forsaken a chance to empty a candybag. "Hmm," I thought, "though I don't see exactly how, it somehow has to be my thinking of food that causes my preoccupation with it."

Then I had this tiny, tiny insight, *so* tiny I didn't even think of it as an insight: "In fact, when I don't think of the sweets in our locker, in that moment it won't be part of my experience—it won't be there, so it won't be a problem." What I saw right there was that our experience is made moment by moment and comes from whatever thinking is on our minds in that one moment only—no more, no less. So in all the moments I didn't think about sweets and cakes and whether to eat them or not, they simply were not part of my experience; they wouldn't exist for me at all in all these moments. Somehow this thought left me with a huge feeling of relief.

Then I forgot about it and went on doing something else. But the next day I found out that little insight-like thought had reshaped my whole pattern of thinking about food. Most of my thinking of food had simply disappeared, just like that! Even if my colleagues bought a package of biscuits and put it right in front of me, I didn't really want to eat one—which had never happened before in my whole life! Before, I used to eat sweets even if I had lost my sense of taste to a cold. Now I couldn't hold the thought of it for a second; it just slipped away like water between fingers. I was—and am still—completely amazed! I thought my preference for sugary and fatty food lay somewhere deep inside me, even in my biology (as it may actually do, but hey, biology can't make me think). I was sure I would never get rid of my sweet tooth; all I could dream of was to improve my coping with it. And now it was gone? First, I considered it magical.

Next, I realised that wanting to manage my preoccupation with food equaled thinking of food, which made it a very present part of my experience. Suddenly it didn't make sense at all that I had been so afraid of stopping my thinking of food because I had believed if I didn't think of it I couldn't control it. But now, with a little *Three Principles* perspective on it I could see I had gotten that all wrong.

I still like sweets and good food. But with less on my mind I am now able to hear my body when it tells me, "No thanks, I've had enough." Before, my thinking outshouted my wise body's voice.

I suppose it can be hard for someone not familiar with this understanding to grasp the effortlessness of it. I didn't do *anything*! We are so used to think in terms of *doing*—we think we need to do more if we're not where we want to be. But as soon as this doing arises from our personal thinking we are going backwards. Things seem harder. Problems become more real. Because the change I experienced came to me via an insight; there was absolutely no doing involved. And, by insight, I mean fresh, new thinking from the intelligence behind life, rather than from my small personal intelligence trying to figure out a solution to a problem that came from that same source of thinking in the first place.

Before I met the Principles it would never have occurred to me that to find a solution to a problem I needed to think less about it. It wouldn't have made sense to me. Now I see it differently, as I've seen there is definitely more to our minds than our intellect. We are so much more, and all we have to do to access that source of wisdom is step a little aside from our personal thinking and leave some space for something new.

From that perspective losing weight was suddenly very easy. I just tended to eat a little less than I did before. For ten years I had dreamt about losing ten pounds but found it completely unrealistic, so I was just crossing my fingers for six. Then, out of the blue, almost without noticing, suddenly I weighed fifteen pounds less than before, just like that.

I have had other insights on health issues too. Among others, I saw how when I eat something I might as well enjoy it, since it wouldn't make sense to hold on to non-joyful thinking like beating myself up or making myself feel guilty. How could I ever benefit from making myself feel bad? And the funny thing was that when I started to really enjoy eating sweets, I didn't need the second serving. Before when I ate the first bowl of chocolate my mind was not on that but filled with thinking what to eat next. And yes, I had heard about mindful eating but I thought it sounded really boring—more doing, more effort! After my insight my mind tended to be in a naturally relaxed state more of the time without any doing involved. My head became lighter with less on my mind, so my body followed and became lighter too.

I also had an insight about exercise. Before, I had always been this kind of person who starts running and then I'm not getting it done. Then it starts up again, and then it subsides—and so on. So I had the thinking about running that, "It's really tough to get started and to maintain a routine about it." But one day I saw how it wasn't the running that was the problem—it was my thinking about it, the planning. The idea that "when (if!) I reach this and this goal, I'll be happy" (and therefore if not, poor me, happiness will slip away once again!). All my ideas about "at least three times a week, thus and thus far, blablabla." The second thoughts when it was raining or I was tired and wanted to skip, and the futile feeling this thinking left me with—"it doesn't matter how much I try, I end up here every time; I'm just not one of these persons who succeeds with regular exercising"—all this crap thinking was what was so exhausting about running. I mean, running in itself is just putting on your shoes and go. After that realisation I've had absolutely no problems with running. I love it. It's easy. I just do it. And if I don't, no big deal, I'll just do it later, which is effortless since I'm now not exhausting myself with thinking that I didn't go in the first place. Without my previous way of over-thinking I suddenly find myself enjoying the simple act of moving my body, enjoying this incredible pleasure of having a body—it's a masterpiece! Blood is pumping around, sweat releases on the top of my skin, muscles move and do their thing. I'm truly grateful for this physical, sensual experience of having a body.

The more I see the huge potential for new, more helpful thinking that resides right behind my limited personal ideas, the less I hold on to the latter, which again makes more space in my mind for the first. I easier get inspired to do something new. Like, one day, I just felt like buying a juicer and making fresh juice every day to get me and my family more healthy and energized through the winter. It wasn't a "should" thought. It was a curious and light feeling of inspiration—I just really wanted to. And it turned out to be a fantastic idea. I never would have thought fresh juice tasted so good!

I also tend to prefer healthier food in general. Before I thought more heavy and fatty food was the real deal. Now, with less on my mind, I just feel like eating lighter. Maybe, now when thinking about it, my preferences mirror my lighter state of mind?

So what is it that happens to people physically when they come across the Principles? I think we stand less in our own way with our thinking and therefore blossom more. We become a better version of ourselves, and keep becoming so, as it is not a fixed thing. We're walking potential and are constantly unfolding and expressing our essence in the present moment. And as we are love and wisdom at our core, how could this not be a beautiful experience? So much of my time I feel light, joyful and loving. I'm in love with life as it unfolds in the present moment. And as our bodies mirror what is going on in our minds this state of mind is visible. To me, people with this understanding tend to look younger and happier than they did before they came across this understanding. We're in love and it shows.

Amen!

Mette Louise Holland is a psychotherapist in Denmark.

I want readers to know that when someone read what Mette Louise wrote she sent this to me:

"I got jealous and totally lost my good feeling reading this. She sounds so bloody perfect I wanted to be sick! It's now two days later as I write this, and I'm more aware what's going on. This caused lots of thinking. Her report doesn't sound like anything I experience. My mind is still racing in comparison with her description. My mind is filling up with lots of thinking still, though I often had the clarity she talks about, but only for relatively short periods of time. The only thing that changed for me, is, I know what's going on. So it's not as threatening and I'm functioning better. I wish I had more insights. I have been getting better all the time, but nowhere near perfect. So my thought was, am I doing something wrong? Through menopausal changes I have put on 13 kilos, that's 26 pounds, and I don't seem to be able to do anything about it. Lots of thinking, I'd say! Pretty real, must be seduced."

This is a beautiful thing to see! First, it's so easy to fall into this trap, no matter how much we understand the Three Principles. What Mette Louise wrote here is in the outside world to those reading it. What she wrote cannot possibly make someone feel sick. It can only be one's own thinking from within. Furthermore, Mette Louise is just reporting what happened to her, and other people have found it uplifting. I printed it here because, as in Chapter 36 with Rob's depression, one new insight completely changed Mette Louise's relationship with food, then other insights followed. This possibility exists for everyone—even the person who wrote the above. What Mette Louise wrote simply shows a new possibility along the vertical continuum of levels of consciousness. The point is not that one should have the same insight about food and weight. The point is that through our own thinking right now we have a certain relationship with food and our bodies—whatever that is—and we think that's real and we're stuck with it. Yet, it can change, and that can happen at any moment. That could be uplifting, in and of itself, and the simple fact of "other possibilities" could also be uplifting. We're never stuck with what we think about food, exercise or our bodies. It's not reality—even though we get seduced by consciousness into believing it is. Our new insight, if we have one, won't come out the same as Mette Louise's; it will be our own. But even a tiny shift means a new level of seeing, and feelings and behaviors follow what we see. And we can be open to it. That is our power.

42. REALIZING REALITY

At the last minute I found myself invited to Oslo, Norway to speak about the Modello experience for the May 2016 One Solution Conference. Meanwhile, I'd had an email exchange with a woman from Oslo who had read *Somebody Should Have Told Us!*, which really affected her, and she wanted to meet me. She asked whether I had time to give a coaching session to her brother, Arne. I asked Arne if he would mind if Richard (from Chapter 2) observed the session, as I had traveled to Oslo with him for the Conference after visiting his island in Sweden.

Arne arrived in a tiny electric car. He insisted on treating both of us to breakfast at a fancy hotel—way above and beyond the call of duty. We settled at a table in the far corner of the room to talk and eat. Arne said he doesn't usually read books, but his sister talked him into reading mine because she thought it would help him, and it did. But he needed to ask me something important about himself.

While he usually does fine, he said, periodically he experiences "times of debilitating downs," with serious emotional turmoil.

"When do you experience these most?"

"When I feel pressure," said Arne. "Sometimes the pressure gets so intense I lose all hope. I've had thoughts of ending it all—not that I would actually go through with it, but those thoughts come very powerfully. In those states I feel almost bipolar."

"If we peered into your head at those times, what would we see?"

"It looks like this: How can I make more sales in my job as a salesman? How can I keep my relationship healthy? How can I find enough time to be with my kids and be the best parent I can be for them? By the way, I can easily relate to what your book said about thought and consciousness, but I can't relate to Universal Mind because I don't believe in God. I really don't want to hear anything about it."

"You believe in science, then, right?"

"Right."

"Well, what about the fact of energy behind life?"

"I can relate to that."

"So all things have energy behind them. Einstein said that. That's what we're talking about when we talk about Universal Mind. And there's some kind of life force in us or we wouldn't even be walking around. You don't have to be a believer in anything."

"Okay, I get that."

"Okay, so back to your own mind. What does your mind look like when it's doing fine?

"I feel a lot of energy in this state. It's the way I feel right now. I don't have any thoughts like I described earlier. Or if I do I'm able to let them go. Whereas in the other state I want to let them go but I can't. And it's very troubling that I can't. Like your book said, I don't believe answers lie in the past—I know what you're talking about—I don't blame my past. So I never go there."

"Yeah, you think answers lie in the future. That's as much not true as the non-truth of answers lying in the past."

This caught Arne up short.

I continued. "In fact, what if that is your only problem?"

"What?"

"Thinking thoughts of future, like, 'How do I?' 'How do I do this?' 'How do I do that?' You say you know the answers don't lie in the past, but you think they lie in the future."

That got to Arne a bit. "Huh. Wow, you're right. I think I do. I never realized that before. I can see where it would be very hopeful if I recognized that."

"Well, you said you're in a good state the majority of the time, so your mind already works that way."

"That's true, but what I'm concerned about is when I'm in the bad state. How do I see my way clear of it? In that state I can't stop myself."

"Did you notice you again just said, 'How do I?' Notice how much of a habit it is for you to go there."

Arne became sheepish. "Ooh, I did, didn't I?"

"Yes, you did. But it's great to see that. Besides, it's not a question of doing, Arne. It's a question of seeing. Seeing it new, from a new level of consciousness."

"I know your book says not to trust that kind of thinking when you have it, but I can't help it."

Whoa! What did he just say? He couldn't help trusting his thinking because he saw that thinking as reality? Now it was my turn to be stopped in my tracks.

Suddenly I had a huge insight. "Trust" comes after the fact of seeing "reality!" Like, if you see a reality that looks and feels absolutely real, how can you not trust what is absolutely real to you? You can't! You're stuck with it. How do you not believe it? Because you're seeing reality, *you can't not believe it*! Since it really is reality to you, you have no choice. You have to believe it, trust it and follow it, because it's what you see and feel! For the first time I saw that if you're seeing "reality" and someone like me comes along and says, "Well, you don't have to believe it, you don't have to trust it, you don't have to follow it," it will be awfully frustrating because you have no choice, or so it seems. You're stuck with the reality you see and feel. This was huge! I saw the error of my ways. I had said this to so many people! Instead, the answer is *calling that reality into question*.

I told Arne of my insight.

"What do you mean by calling your reality into question?"

"I mean, first, if nothing has changed about the circumstances of your life but sometimes you're up about them and sometimes you're down, which one is real? How can they both be real?"

"Oh."

"Secondly, when you get thoughts like, 'How can I do this?' it would be helpful to ask yourself another question: "Is it true?" "Is it really true that if I think these future thoughts it really will help me in any possible way?" You've been thinking there are answers in these future thoughts—How do I do this? How do I do that?—as if it's going to get you someplace. Well, does it get you anywhere?"

"No, it really doesn't."

"So when you get one of those thoughts now, you're at one of those forks in the road I wrote about in my book—"

"What do you mean by a fork in the road?"

Arne could not relate, so I drew it out on the table with my finger.

"When you get one of those 'How do I do this?' thoughts, it places you at the junction of the fork. You can go one way or the other way, take one path or another. So one path—the low road—is to lose yourself in the reality of those thoughts. The other path—the high road—is to realize, 'It does me no good to go there; it can't.' Instead, seeing them for what they are: just habits of thought about the future that jump into my head and would not exist but for my own thinking. And what would be left? The energized feeling you described when you're not in that state. You said you feel a lot of energy in the other state. The only reason you do not feel the energy in your down state is because with that kind of thinking you put a damper on that energy."

"Wow, that's really manageable. I feel so much more hopeful."

"Great! One other thing. Let's assume for a moment that going up and down like you do *is* caused by some chemical imbalance or something, which some psychotherapists have told you, that you might be bipolar. Well, if true, that kind of thinking comes directly with the chemical imbalance. The chemical imbalance and the thinking go hand in hand. There's no separating the two. Like, you can't have the chemical imbalance without the thinking, you see?"

"Yes."

"So if it is a chemical imbalance, when you feel that way it's just the chemical imbalance acting up—it is still not reality! That's the only thing going on. We fall for it because Consciousness is doing its job perfectly, seducing us into believing the reality of it."

"Yes, I see that. Now I can see the light at the end of the tunnel."

"You think you got a lot out of this? I think I got more out of it than you did. I should pay you for this session!"

Arne laughed.

Seriously though, my realization made me much more careful about how I approach Three Principles coaching and counseling, now that I see "believing, trusting and following" come *after the fact* of seeing reality, which means the truth of that reality itself first needs to be called into question—to question whether the reality we see is a lie, to know its very existence cannot be anything but our own creation.

So important! And when we don't believe it, we are left with peace.

43. CAN PEOPLE REALLY CHANGE OUTSIDE TRADITIONAL PSYCHOLOGY? DOROTHY'S STORY

On February 5, 2016 I received an email through my website from someone I didn't know. It read: "Hi Jack, I would love to do the extended professional training with you. Your book 'Somebody Should Have Told Us' had a huge impact on my life. My relationship with my husband-to-be (we recently got engaged) has been transformed. Our relationship is flowering... the same with my sister and my parents. I am a fulfillment coach and my practice has also changed. I love seeing people transforming when they see the truth of this understanding. I would love to deepen my understanding with you being my teacher. Would love to hear back from you! Thank you. Love, Dorota"

Dorothy Martin (a.k.a. Dorota Juszkiewicz) originally hails from Poland but now lives in the U.K. I finally "met" her the following April while co-facilitating a training on Deep Listening with Jeanne Catherine at Divine Play in Charlottesville, Virginia, as she beamed into the training via Skype. And she was beaming! Instantly she impressed me. She spoke of the deep love she felt that her life had turned around completely as a result of reading my book. One month later Dorothy attended a training retreat in Spain titled "Cultivating the Art of Working with People One on One through the Three Principles," which I co-led with Gabriela Maldonado-Montano. After that training I felt compelled to interview her. This, in her own words, is her story.

I think of 2014 as both the worst and the best year of my life. It all started in early January when my relationship with my boyfriend started to fall apart. We were caught in a vicious cycle of arguments and it seemed the only thing we could do to stop it was to separate. Eventually, we decided to split up. On Friday 14th February 2014—yes,

Valentine's Day—my boyfriend moved out.

As I sat on the sofa that night, my empty flat echoed my thoughts. "*What is going on? What is wrong with me? What is wrong with him? Why can't I have a happy relationship?*" I'd had several relationships and they always ended like this, in seemingly unresolvable, horrible arguments. This was yet another painful break-up.

I also started reflecting on my recent job promotion and it was so obvious to me that it was not what I expected or wanted to do any more. *"Other people have interesting, fulfilling careers...but not me. Why? Why? What is wrong with me?"*

I felt brokenhearted, deeply sad and confused. I was putting so much effort – good effort – into making my life work and it never worked out the way I wanted it to. I felt painfully unfulfilled and exhausted. I didn't know what to do. I had given it everything and miserably failed.

At first I tried to stay positive. I tried everything to pull myself up and be happy. But the heaviness I was experiencing seemed to be heavier than anything I had experienced before. I had to pedal so hard to stay on the surface of the metaphorical ocean of my life but still I couldn't keep up.

I started losing all my energy and couldn't find anything to replenish it. I was spiraling down into the deepest darkness. I started drowning.

I experienced complete burnout: overwhelming exhaustion, cripplingly low mood, complete lack of appetite, no motivation. Nothing mattered. I couldn't even think of exercising. I couldn't meditate. I just couldn't do anything to help myself. I lived like a ghost. The only thing I could to do was to sleep, because being awake seemed like a nightmare.

This went on for a long 10 months. I had felt low before but never as low as during those 10 months. I've never admitted this in public before but at the end of November I started having suicidal thoughts. I started imagining what the world would look like without me. I was terrified because I believed there was something fundamentally wrong with me. I really felt that, this time, my life was over.

And then I found your book. Well, actually, I found your book through Michael Neill's book, *Inside-Out Revolution.* I read Michael's book that August but missed the whole point of it. In the book he says that we don't need to do anything to be well and happy, as that is our essential nature. He says that we don't even need to meditate!

When I read that I was shocked. I thought: "*He is wrong! What is he saying? That's irresponsible. I must email Michael to ask him to correct his message!*" I completely disagreed with him because I wholeheartedly believed and taught in my job that we need to have a self-care routine to achieve health and wellbeing. For me, it was essential to eat healthy food, exercise and meditate regularly and it seemed without it wellbeing was not possible.

Looking back now, life played trick on me. I fell into complete exhaustion. All the doing—the self-care routine I believed in so strongly—fell apart. (As I write this I now completely understand what Michael meant when he wrote that there's no need to do anything to maintain our innate wellbeing.)

And then, in December, I found your book listed as a resource in the back of Michael Neill's book. I couldn't get out of bed so I downloaded the e-book. As I scanned through the chapters my attention switched back on. I was surprised that I could concentrate again; I hadn't been able to concentrate on anything for a long time. I started reading and devoured your book in less than two days.

The penny dropped when I got to Chapter 8 (In Low Levels of Consciousness It Is Unwise to Believe, Trust and Follow Our Thinking), where you explain step by step how we create our experiences. The diagrams you include were such an eye-opener.

I sat in bed feeling completely mesmerised. I was reading that the way in which we experience external circumstances depends not on the actual circumstances as such but on the thoughts we are having about them.

I learnt that we are experiencing everything in life through thought in every single moment. And the question hit me: "*Is this what has been happening to me? Does it mean that my burnout, my exhaustion, my depression, result from thoughts about my life but not my life itself?*"

I remember getting up, walking quickly around the room and thinking: "*I can't believe that nobody told me this before!*" I remember laughing to myself for the first time in months!

And then I had a beautiful experience. I can only try to put it into words… Suddenly, I saw a continuous stream of thoughts flowing through my mind like clouds scudding across the sky. I saw my heavy thoughts—all the dark shadows they cast over me. But I was just watching. I remained unaffected. I saw that thought is just like breath—that thought animates our experience of life like breath animates our bodies. At the same time my attention shifted and suddenly I saw beyond the clouds. I saw a deeper perspective… I saw the sky and the sun…I saw the light…

And in parallel to all this I saw myself drowning, deep down in the darkness of the metaphorical ocean of my life—but it was now so clear that there was nothing wrong me. I was holding heavy bricks but realised it was not me but those bricks that were dragging me down. Those bricks were, in fact, my heavy thoughts about the situations and people in my life.

When I realised this, a miracle happened. The palms of my hands opened and those bricks floated away. Once released, those bricks became balloons—full of air and nothing else. I saw them disappearing into the ocean-sky. Then I looked up and saw light. Without me doing anything, the buoyancy of the ocean pulled me up. I knew I was slowly returning to the surface.

The first thing I noticed was an opening in my heart. Suddenly I felt a *yes* emerging from deep within my body. A YES TO LIFE. I will never forget this feeling of yes. Even now, as I write, tears fill my eyes.

In the days that followed, my appetite started to return. I had more energy. I wanted to buy some nice food. I wanted to text people with whom I hadn't talked for a long time. Somehow the stories and ideas I believed about them didn't matter anymore – I just wanted to see their faces. I immediately sent texts to my ex-boyfriend and sister. I wanted to go out and buy a new dress…

Since then everything has slowly started to fall into place. It feels as if life itself is the driving force and not me…

My heaviness didn't disappear immediately—it was a gentle and gradual process. I still experienced exhaustion, low mood or frustration from time to time but somehow my experience was different.

This time I could see my experience for what it was. I knew where my feelings were coming from and that getting attached to my low-consciousness thinking was not wise. I just let it pass. I didn't take it seriously and knew I didn't have to act on it.

I have learned that all my 'difficult' feelings fizzle out and my balance, calmness, positive outlook and healthy mood naturally return without me having to do anything.

I have learned to completely trust the buoyancy of life. It is there for all of us.

I spent Christmas 2014 with my sister, then started seeing my ex-boyfriend again. In March 2015 we moved in together. Everything started to unfold in the most beautiful ways. We bought a house together in November 2015 and got engaged in December 2015. We got married in August 2016 and our relationship continues to amaze me. We don't argue any more. There is lightness and at the same time a much deeper loving connection between us.

In March 2016 I left my job and started my own business. I am passionate about helping people find deep fulfillment and love in their professional and private lives. I also work with organisations to create healthy and happy workplaces where our human nature is understood and embraced. I have also started working on my first book—something I never thought I would do! I feel deeply fulfilled and excited about everything that life brings.

I often think about my life as 'before and after 2014.' The year 2014 was the long dark night of my soul and at the same time the most beautiful breakthrough or awakening into a new way of being and living. Perhaps I saw a glimpse of a bigger picture and understood more deeply who I really am.

Just thinking about it and sharing my story makes me feel even more grateful. I still catch myself thinking: "*Oh my God, my life is so amazing... how has all this happened?*" I've been so exhausted, because I was always trying so hard to make my life work. And suddenly I have this experience where I stop driving the car of my life and find that life itself is driving! My life has become effortless and everything is just happening of its own accord.

This simple and yet profound understanding of our human nature has changed me and changed my life. I simply fell in love with life. I can't pinpoint a day when it all happened, but my heart just cracked open with love. I love people, and I love life! And I want other people to know what I know. I want them to have beautiful lives too. I want people to live with less pain and more ease, with more love and joy, and with deeper understanding of life and who they really are.

That's why my coaching invitation reads: 'Fall in Love With Life'. That's what happened to me. This is not just a catchy phrase—it is our most natural way of being. And with deepest grace, it is possible for all of us to fall in love with life.

Dorothy Martin is a Fulfillment Coach in the United Kingdom.

44. EVENTS AND MAKING MEANING

I really felt for Grace. Her daughter, Cassie, in her early 20s had become a heroin addict. Not long ago she had moved back in with Grace, who tried everything in her power to convince Cassie to stop using, to no avail.

I suggested she try to get her daughter to the Gulf Breeze Recovery Center in Gulf Breeze, Florida, which as of this writing to my knowledge is the only residential drug treatment facility to operate solely via Three Principles understanding.

Cassie did not want to go. She'd had bad experiences with a couple of other residential treatment facilities. Then she'd been taken advantage of sexually by a health practitioner. After that Cassie hit rock bottom. One morning when Cassie was hurting badly, Grace talked with her. Cassie knew she had to do something to change her life or else she might soon not have a life. She finally consented. Despite having spent so much of her financial resources on the other treatment facilities, Grace brought her to Gulf Breeze and quickly felt tremendous relief. The Gulf Breeze staff made them both feel right at home.

After she left Cassie there, however, Grace went into depression. Although her daughter appeared to be doing well at Gulf Breeze, Cassie told her she had hooked up there with a new boyfriend, a graduate of the program. Grace feared it was far too soon and would distract from her recovery.

But none of that is why I am writing this chapter. Early in our conversation Grace said something that made me sit up and take notice. She said, "The Three Principles has helped me so much to be aware of my story instead of being so caught in it, but I can't really seem to free myself from it."

Automatic puzzlement. Grace is now aware of her story but can't free herself from it?

Out of my puzzlement something occurred to me. I realized being free does not come from being aware of our story; it comes from being aware of our *creation* of our story.

Grace asked me what I meant.

I said, "I mean the fear you feel would not even exist but for your own creation of it. Realizing your own creation of it is what would free you—knowing you would be totally fine if you weren't using your creative power of Thought to come up with fear about it. Really it's only fear of a future you can't possibly know. Otherwise, it's just events that happen out in the world. We put meaning onto those events with our creative power of Thought. For example, the fact that Cassie got addicted to heroin is an event. The fact that you brought her to the Gulf Breeze Recovery Center is an event. The fact that she hooked up with a boyfriend down there is an event. Then you take your creative power of Thought, this incredible gift, and make up something like fear about the event—or whatever else we can make up about what the event means to us. They are only events happening out in the world until we make meaning of them for ourselves, and very often the meaning we make is fear about the future. The meaning is our own creation."

Grace heard the difference, and she felt it.

Note: As of this writing Cassie has moved back home with her mother and appears to be doing well, after a few bumps.

45. SALLY'S STORY:
TALES OF AN ALCOHOLIC—OR NOT

Sally, from the U.K., is an amazing human being. I am so impressed with her and proud of her. I'll let her tell her story in her own words:

For the past 37 years I have been addicted to alcohol.

It began when I was 17 and met my first boyfriend. He was ten years older than me. Going to the pub every night was all he wanted to do. We would go to the pub seven nights a week and I discovered if I had five halves of lager I would start to feel happier and more confident. This became a habit. At the weekend I would wake with a terrible hangover. I soon realised if I had five halves at lunchtime (hair of the dog) my hangover would go. This highlights for me now how quickly I got entrapped in the addiction cycle of thinking and the illusion that alcohol fixed the feeling and gave me confidence. This pattern continued for about 10 years, but what I hadn't realised was that the alcohol also turned me into a jealous, angry monster. I was very emotional and put it down to hormones but it was the alcohol making me paranoid. I caused so many unnecessary arguments.

After 10 years I met my second boyfriend and my drinking stepped up. I worked full time as a senior science technician during the day and in the evening worked in a pub. This was perfect for me, as I could see my new boyfriend and help myself to free drinks for both of us whilst being paid! After work we would go to a nightclub and consume more and more alcohol. I was drunk seven nights a week. At this time drinking was fulfilling my wishes, I was happy and full of confidence.

Eventually my true drunken personality started to rear its ugly head again. My hangovers became more extreme. This brought the time of my first drink in the day at weekends to 12:00 noon, precisely. If I couldn't get a drink by this time I became very anxious and angry. If I was going out for the evening I was often drunk before I even got out the door. I ruined so many events with unacceptable behaviour, embarrassing friends and family, not realising at the time. By the morning I forgot what I'd done…

My work started to be affected. I had to take days off sick with anxiety, depression and the hangover from hell. In 2000 I took voluntary redundancy after 16 years at my college job...

Fast-forward through performance plummeting and jobs lost because of alcohol. Shame. Isolation. Getting progressively worse. Drunk driving. Attempts to get control of drinking by going into treatment. Detoxing. Failing. Joining AA. But each time the same thing happened.

Eventually the craving to have a drink became overwhelming, and I thought if I just had a few drinks in the evening I could control it. The first drink really hit the spot and I promised myself I would only have a few drinks every evening. One glass of wine soon lead to a bottle and before long I was back to square one, drinking all day, time off work, with a massive deterioration in my mental and physical health. I was absolutely devastated. How could I have let myself get back to this mere existence?...

I was vomiting every morning, not eating and not looking after my personal care. I felt so alone and desperate. I just wanted to die. I even had several attempts at taking my own life with overdoses of paracetamol and other pain killing drugs on top of the alcohol. This pattern continued for six years in and out of different treatment centres, desperate to find a solution to my addiction. I was a gibbering wreck. I was seeing shadows and imagining people, even talking to people that weren't there. I felt like I was going mad. I thought my life was over.

I had been living with my mum for 8 months who was receiving treatment for breast cancer and suffering with dementia. I was desperately lonely and spend my days doing housework and cooking and caring for Mom. My day started at 6:00 every morning when I would awake with a start, filled with anxiety and shaking from head to foot with withdrawal symptoms. I would stagger downstairs into the garage where I sat on a little stool in the corner trying to get some alcohol down me to stop the shakes. This process would take about 2 hours of drinking gin, vomiting, drinking, vomiting, eventually the shaking would pass and I would feel ready to face the day.

Then one night in December 2014 I went to bed as normal at 8:00 p.m. and began to sweat like never before in my life. I spent most of the night changing bed clothes as everything was wet through. I began to shiver so I started my drinking regime to try and relieve the symptoms. This time I could not keep the alcohol down. I could not function at all and was so frightened I eventually called an ambulance. The paramedic arrived and after some quick tests rushed me to Warwick Hospital, with lights flashing and sirens going. The paramedic told me I was on the brink of death. I had no idea I was dying. I found out later that I had acidosis and hypothermia and all my organs were shutting down.

Unfortunately my dice with death wasn't enough to curb my drinking so on discharge from the hospital I moved back in with my Mum and the nightmare began again. I found any task like cooking or cleaning overwhelming and I just couldn't cope. I would drop things, knock things over, burn myself. I just wanted to hide myself under the duvet all day and cry but my mother's demands would not allow this. I would crawl into my bed every evening so grateful I got through another day alive.

I was so scared. The noise in my head was driving me mad. I thought, I can't do this anymore. I'm going to die or end up in a mental hospital. I felt so desperate I cried out to the shadows I was seeing "Please help Me!" I had an overwhelming feeling of wanting to survive and get some sort of life back. It couldn't be any worse than this. I realised I had to make a choice once and for all to do something about it. After frantically searching on the Internet I found a treatment centre in Southampton that would take me and my dog Tilly; she was all I had so I wouldn't consider going without her. On December 18, 2014 I was admitted.

As expected it was very tough. I had lost the ability to walk properly. My nervous system was shot. I needed two weeks of detox, which was pretty horrendous. Gradually after a few weeks I started to feel a little more human. The staff at the centre treated me with some dignity, which was not what I was used to in treatment. After 35 days I was discharged, deemed fit and able but with the warning, if you don't commit fully to AA you will drink again! This thought filled me with utter despair. I left the centre in January 2015 with absolutely no aspirations. I had no job, money, family didn't want to know me. I thought I was unemployable due to my history and criminal record for drunk driving and couldn't envisage ever having another relationship. So I threw myself into AA, as I believed this would be the only way to manage my addiction. I got a sponsor and was gradually working through the 12 Steps. I threw myself into it by doing service but was struggling to accept.

Then in April 2015 I was introduced to Jacqueline Hollows from Beyond Recovery. She became my life coach, and I started seeing her on a weekly basis. She was unlike any other counsellor I had previously seen for my addiction. She just listened and guided, pointing me in the right direction. She didn't try to fix me. I learnt that if I reflected on my life and addiction I had insights about solutions for myself. I always came out of her sessions feeling empowered and hopeful for the days ahead. I realised I was achieving things without a drink that would previously have fazed me. I was amazed. I didn't realise Jacqueline was introducing me to the Three Principles.

I gradually started to realise that I didn't have to believe everything my mind was saying to me. Every time I had a thought about alcohol I pushed it out of my mind and focused on other thoughts. At first I found it hard to clear my mind of unwanted thoughts. Every time I thought of alcohol I focused on what my life would be like again if I had just one more drink. Slowly but surely I found I could go for hours without one thought of drink. When I was actively drinking, every minute I thought obsessively about drinking. I noticed I was achieving things sober that I didn't believe possible, and I wasn't anxious. I realised that by not worrying about upcoming events they didn't faze me when they arose. After a while the thought of a drink repulsed me; I would physically gag if I saw someone with a glass of red wine (my preferred tipple). My life was becoming a joy to live. I wasn't fearing anything because I knew with confidence I'd be okay if I just lived life as it happened.

I was then invited on a short training course in Birmingham with Jack Pransky. I attended with trepidation, as I assumed everyone else attending had a deep understanding of the Three Principles. Jack explained in simple terms how the Three Principles were working within us all the time and how our thinking determined every feeling we had, all our experiences in life. It was like I'd been hit by a sledge hammer! I had the insight that I had ruined nearly every life experience I had ever had by my thinking. I either dreaded something, feared something, wanted more, expected more of myself or others—always seeking for something. I had never lived in the now and just appreciated what I had. Mind you, I never had peace of mind. It became clear I could never achieve it by always wanting, expecting, predicting, regretting or self-loathing. Could it really be that simple? It had all come from my thinking!

We were then put into pairs by Jack to do a deep listening exercise. Automatically I was filled with fear that I wouldn't be able to complete the exercise properly. I had always doubted myself, saying, "I can't do it." I had previously studied counselling and had done a year's course at college, which I had found difficult because I felt I couldn't concentrate on what a client was sharing and never seemed to be able to resolve their issues for them. While they were sharing their stories with me hoping I could help them, I'd be panicking, thinking, What did she say? How do I answer that? I don't know what to say.

Jack told us just to listen; there was no need to reply, no feedback to give, nothing to fix. I said to my deep listening partner, Eileen, "I'm rubbish at this. I have never been able to concentrate." Eileen started telling me her story, and I found myself captivated. I didn't feel distracted at all and didn't even notice what was going on around me in the room, even though there were a lot of other people in the room doing the same exercise. I just listened and observed. My mind was clear, as I wasn't trying to think of things to say about fixing her. I just heard every word and in my silence she gradually came to her own resolution. I was stunned. I hadn't even said anything. This was a huge insight for me, as I had always thought I couldn't concentrate on anything. This is because my mind was always full of noise about something else. If I just listened, my mind became quiet. I had the huge insight that all the years I have been studying I had put a barrier up against learning by believing I couldn't concentrate or learn.

The weekend was life-changing for me as I saw the limitations I had been putting on myself and how my beliefs had just been illusions of my thinking. Energised and inspired by what I had just experienced, I announced as I left the room after the course had finished that, you never know, I might be flying to Spain in October for Jack's Extended

Professional Training. This seemed a very daunting task. I was determined to beat my fears so I could get a deeper understanding of the Three Principles.

After I left the training in Birmingham I felt like I was in a bubble, looking out into the world from a different place. I just wanted to be silent, so I didn't want to speak to anyone or even watch television, which is a miracle for me. I just sat in silence all the way home and went to bed still feeling in shock from the weekend events. I actually felt numb for a few days. Could my life and beliefs all have been an illusion of my thinking?

In May 2015 Jacqueline invited me to the Tikun Three Principles Conference in London. I was totally immersed for the whole three days. I listened to such inspirational speakers and heard some wonderful stories of how the Three Principles had helped people in such adversity. I felt something in the room so powerful and exciting; part of something life-changing for the world.

The last part of the conference was a video by Syd Banks. He spoke about addiction. I had never seen anything by Syd before but had heard an awful lot about him. I watched in amusement and disbelief! What did this man know about addiction? Addiction was an illusion of my thinking?! He had no idea what he was talking about. I had been addicted to alcohol for 30 years because I was born with a disease of alcoholism. OMG what a shock I was going to have!

On leaving the conference high as a kite from the feeling, I turned to my friend and said, "I'm going to be on that stage next year sharing my story of addiction!" Be careful what you wish for!

I had no idea what lay ahead for me, but I had a new confidence and feeling things were going to work out. I was so excited when I booked myself on Jack's EPT course. I loved the way Jack had delivered his program in March. He was so passionate about sharing his knowledge. I felt at peace whenever he spoke. Such a tranquil, humble man. I wanted some of what he had! But going was a huge step for me. My stomach did a somersault and I thought, "Are you mad?" Initially my friend, Jacqueline was going to come with me, which gave me some comfort. When she told me she couldn't go due to other commitments I suddenly felt fearful. I was terrified of flying, especially alone. Also, I would not know anyone else on the course and it was in

Spain! "What if everyone on the course drinks a lot? I can't possibly consider going now. I am only six months sober." I was terrified of relapsing. I emailed Jack and said I would have to cancel and that I was going on a retreat in England instead. This seemed a much safer option.

Jack saw through my fear and contacted me to discuss my decision. Within minutes of Jack's wisdom and reassurance I felt calm and assured that it would be a brilliant opportunity for me and that I would be okay. I just had this feeling that whatever happened I would be safe and get through it with ease. Jack had my back!

On the day of my departure to Spain I felt excited about my trip. I didn't predict anything. When I boarded the plane I actually felt quite calm and focused on my fellow passengers and surroundings. I had purposely booked an aisle seat so I didn't have to look out of the window. I settled in my seat and focused on the in-flight magazine. I then realised I had the whole row to myself so I could choose which seat to sit in. After take-off I decided to be brave and move to the window seat and look out at the scenery below. I didn't even think of my fear of heights; I focused on the beautiful sights passing by, including the awesome cloud formations. On landing it suddenly dawned on me that I had just completed my first sober flight and had overcome my fear of heights. On reflection about this journey I questioned why I was the only person on the plane with a row to myself enabling me to change seats. Spooky! Universal Mind in action. I also realised by not thinking about having a fear I didn't have one!

On the second day of the training I started to feel very insecure and anxious. Why? I found it difficult to be in a hotel with a bar with people drinking alcohol around me. I felt like isolating to deal with my feelings of dis-ease. I just wanted to run away, which had been my saviour throughout my life. Fight or flight. I then did a deep listening exercise with Susanne. She told me to reflect on my feelings of dis-ease. I suddenly had this overwhelming feeling of calm and the realisation that it didn't matter where I was in the world, I was safe. My wisdom told me I didn't need alcohol to feel okay, the uncertainty would pass, and so it did.

I had an incredible three days in Spain during my Extended Professional Training with Jack and my fellow students. I have made some lifelong friends and have a much better, deeper understanding of how the Three Principles work within us all of the time. I had many insights about my life and my alcohol addiction.

One massive insight I had whilst sharing with Sheela was about how as a young child of about six I had suddenly become very anxious. I was always feeling sick and waking my parents up in the middle of the night, crying and panicking, feeling very scared and lonely, and I stood in the dark crying. My mum would always get very angry and tell me to get back to bed. I longed for a hug and reassurance but that never came. Apparently I was put on tranquilizers at age six! My mum always told me she thought the reason for my anxiety and illness was because my infant school teacher didn't like me and had been cruel to me; which I always believed as I knew no better. I continued to tell Sheela about a dreadful event that happened previous to this. When I was five mum and dad were having a party at home. As usual, all the adults were drunk. I vividly remember watching them acting very oddly in my young opinion. Suddenly my mum who was very drunk loudly announced to everyone that she had never wanted me. Pointing at me she said, "I tried to abort her with a hot bath and a bottle of gin." I remember everyone laughing and looking at me. I felt so upset and ashamed. Apparently, after that I proceeded to go around the room drinking from the adult's glasses and got drunk. I was just five years of age! As I shared this with Sheela an awful feeling came over me. I almost fainted and felt physically sick. It suddenly occurred to me it was shortly after this event that I had started to become very anxious and a sickly child. It haunted me. I was speechless. I realised this is when my insecurities and anxieties had started. Oh my God, I had been disillusioned for 49 years and blamed an innocent infant school teacher.

I had another realisation in Spain about my drinking addiction. Every morning after about five units of alcohol I would begin to calm down and stop vomiting, then the cycle of thinking would begin. "How long will the alcohol last? Am I steady enough to get to the shop to buy some more? How much shall I buy? Have I got enough money? Will the shop assistant sell it to me? Will anyone see me?" AAGHHHH, it was endless; 100% of my thinking was consumed with alcohol and how much I needed just to exist. Eventually I would make my way to the shop to get my supplies for the day. I would feel extremely anxious, physically shaking from head to foot. I couldn't even hold the money in my hand. Then every day, without fail, as soon as I had paid the money and had the bottle in my hand, the shaking would miraculously stop. This now hit me like a brick wall. The fear and anxiety is brought about by my thinking!! I was so consumed by my thinking about getting the drink it would actually cause me to shake. I always wondered why I stopped shaking when the bottle was still sealed. WOW, what an insight!

On the last day of our training the group had to do a presentation to an audience who knew nothing about the Three Principles. Jack gave us all specific areas to cover. I was concerned that I would not know what to say or would say something inappropriate. Jack told us to prepare but not rehearse a presentation, as he wanted us to speak from the heart and only share what we really knew to be true. I listened in awe to my fellow students and felt so proud of them and happy to know them. They set a huge precedent for my presentation. I just told my story of addiction and transformation as it came to me. It just seemed to flow. I finished by saying, “My name is Sally and I am not an alcoholic.”

I received a standing ovation, which took me by surprise. I found it rather embarrassing. My fellow students swamped me with praise. The most emotional comment I received was from Jack when he said I had stolen the show. This was praise indeed from The Master! The main feeling I had was of astonishment that without any real preparation I was able to speak fluently about my story of transformation. I felt privileged to have come so far in my recovery due to my understanding of the Three Principles. The audience certainly seem to appreciate what we all had shared, and there was a great feeling of relief and achievement when we’d finished. I felt honoured to have been a part of it.

We had a final farewell session where we all stood in a circle together singing, “That’s What Friends Are For.” I felt a huge sense of love and the oneness everyone had been talking about. It was an amazing feeling. I felt very emotional and didn’t want it to end. I felt very privileged to have met all of these wonderful friends and share our love and experiences together. I can’t wait to see some of them again in Spain for more of Jacks wisdom!

I left Spain feeling elated and felt I had a much deeper understanding of the Three Principles. It had explained so much for me.

I came home with a new perspective about my life and addiction.

I have now stopped attending AA (although I think it is a wonderful organisation). The only time I seemed to think about alcohol was during or after a meeting! With what I have learned about the Three Principles I was going against what I knew to be true.

Since completing my EPT with Jack I have been doing some volunteer work with Jacqueline for Beyond Recovery. I have been into a prison on many occasions and shared my story with the men. We also delivered the 3-day intensive program in a local treatment centre, which is my passion. This was a brilliant experience for me and the clients gained a lot from the program.

In May of this year [2016] I was asked to share my story of transformation at the Tikun conference. I was on the panel from Beyond Recovery with Jacqueline, Anna Debenham and a former prison inmate called Michael. Michael had completed the Three Principles training course whilst in prison and he was so inspired and grateful he wanted to share his story as a thank you to Jacqueline for transforming his life. I was so touched by his story and felt proud to be part of his new life. Although speaking in front of hundreds of attendees about my remarkable transformation from addiction was daunting, once on stage with microphone in hand my fears fell away. I don't actually know what I said, but I received a standing ovation so something I said must have been powerful.

I find it truly amazing that after just 12 months of learning about the Three Principles, my life has been totally transformed! Previous to this I had had 16 years of traditional counselling for my addiction and had never managed to see through the fog and come to any resolution.

The last conclusion of my story is that a wonderful man called Sydney Banks really knew what he was talking about! I laugh to myself thinking back to when I watched Syd's video on the illusion of addiction and how I'd ranted under my breath that the man knew nothing about what I'd been through with my addiction—after all, I had been born with a disease! I can honestly say now what I know to be true, that my addiction was just a very, very long illusion of my thinking. OMG. Thank you, Syd, dear man, for saving my life.

Yes, my name is Sally and I am not an alcoholic!

46. THE FINAL SEDUCTION
(Saga, Part III)

Through this saga we've been asking, how could someone who allegedly understands the Three Principles and helps other people see them as much as Jack Pransky still get so caught in 'reality' himself that all understanding goes out the window? But that's exactly the point! As soon as I see "reality"—precisely because it looks and feels so unmistakably real—I completely lose sight of who created that reality in the first place. Me! I fall for "reality" like everyone else, because of its overwhelmingly seductive nature, manufactured by thought and brought to life through consciousness—the ultimate trickster and illusionist of the universe. Like everyone else, I miss seeing it because once I think it up, then believe it, I'm at the mercy of consciousness employing all my senses in collusion with it, conspiring, obscuring what really Is. I am stuck and remain so until *the very moment I see my own creation of illusion Itself, or until I realize the spiritual essence behind it all. I am no different from anyone else.*

So, my story is the story of us all. We all get caught in the world of form by being seduced by consciousness. At times we have all been so caught in fear we have not acted with wisdom. At times we have all been lost in anger, caught in worry, frustration—all because some thought-form, made "real" by consciousness, has been so compelling. The same story for all, some only more or less extreme. With our own creative power we have allowed some thought-form to take us away from peace, from love, from wisdom—or at least we believe the illusion of separateness. When we do, we can get lost in a nightmare, as I did. Yet, when such thinking departs, has there not been a moment, a time, even sometimes in the depths of despair, when we have not found our way out? It may have taken a while but at some point, did we not find our way out? And if anyone reading this has not yet found the way out, know it will come eventually, because our innate health/spiritual essence/wisdom is always at work within, always trying to find its way out. We need only listen deeply. Yes, my story is all our stories—only the details differ—and the way out for me is the way out for all—not the details, but the meaning...

I decided to spare readers most of the details of the next few months of my saga. It can be summed up by many, many ups and downs, similar ground covered. I suffered greatly, off and on. I'll give only highlights.

As I returned from my trip I hoped Amy and I could spend one more beautiful week together while I packed up to leave. She had said it was okay if I stayed with her unless I felt uncomfortable. I flew home late at night, filled with nice feelings. Admittedly with trepidation I tiptoed into her bedroom trying not to wake her. Unfortunately, I did.

Amy wanted nothing to do with having one last wonderful week together. Thus began a chain of events that once again gave me an excuse to allow my thinking to make me forget everything I knew. To cut a long story short, I got suspicious and acted without wisdom; Amy reacted justifiably and told me she needed to break it off formally, right now, for her own sanity; I plunged further into despair and bitterness. Reflecting in bed later that night I realized the error of my ways. I didn't blame her. I wanted to apologize to her tomorrow morning.

First thing the next morning Amy poked her head into the guest room where I stayed and told me she felt a horrible pain in her leg and needed to go to the hospital. Despite my offer she wouldn't let me drive her. As she drove off I worried. What if it was a blood clot caused by her hip surgery? This could be serious. What if she died? Suddenly any lingering resentment, bitterness and despair flew out the window into new creation. Again I felt supreme love for Amy, grateful for her very existence and for my time with her. My, how fast thoughts and "reality" can change!

Turned out she was okay, thank God. I apologized to her profusely for my unwise actions, which she appreciated enough not to throw me out of her house. I finished packing up all my stuff and loaded my rental truck—hurt my back in the process. Amy apologized in return. She said she never meant to hurt me. We ended up in the hot tub together, coming full circle (this time not nearly as much fun as the first). Finally, after one of the most difficult weeks of my life, we said our final good-bye. And I drove off down the highway of tears.

But a very touching thing happened just before I left. Amy's son told me how much he appreciated me and how much he had loved me being there. He had grown up with me from age 8 to 17. He told me I had given him a perspective on life he would never forget and would always take with him. It floored me. As a teenager he hadn't shown me anything like that before. At least that felt great. Another thing that felt good: When I hit Virginia I got an email from Amy saying she would always feel bad for what I went through this last week, and she prayed we could meet on solid ground soon. She signed it, Love Always.

After my very long drive, then unloading everything into my new Florida house, then unpacking, I still had to fly back to Vermont one more time because my flight to my training retreat in Greece left from Montreal. I had bought the ticket before I knew I'd be leaving Vermont. Besides, I wanted to spend my birthday and Father's Day with my kids and granddaughter. Amy didn't feel like helping me out with my car, which I'd had to leave in her driveway while I drove the rental truck to Florida, and I had very little contact with her that week.

Until she called and asked if I'd like to have lunch with her on my birthday. I wasn't sure. I felt I'd been treated badly when she didn't want to help me out this week. But she had tossed me an olive branch during my during my drive to Florida, writing that she realized she'd been giving me mixed messages for a long time, that she'd been confused and unsure, that she would always cherish our good memories and be very grateful for what we had, but she knows her feelings changed. She knew she loved me deeply but could not explain what happened along the way. The fact is, she said, we are no longer in a relationship and need space from each other for a while—not sure how long but long enough so we can be free of this. She did not know how to handle all this but was trying to do it with care. She hoped we could look to a future where we could truly be friends. Recalling that made me say yes.

We met at a new Vietnamese restaurant in Montpelier for a final farewell lunch, which felt somewhat uncomfortable, mostly just catching up. Then we walked to the beautiful, gold-domed Vermont

Capitol building and sat on the wide stone steps. I tried to bring up things I still didn't understand but was met with abruptness. I got quiet.

"How did we let ourselves get like this?" I asked softly. "How did this happen?"

Amy softened. She said she didn't know why she fell out of love with me.

There, she said it! Out loud. No longer in love with me. Once I heard that, I simply resigned myself. No point trying anymore.

A very nice conversation ensued. I asked why she thought she needed to hurt me at the end for her to feel protected? She said she didn't really know at the time; it was all she could see. She never wanted to hurt me, but that is always the risk in a powerful relationship.

"This, right here, right now, is the way we need to be with each other," I said.

It felt so good between us at that moment. I said we should stop now and end on this note. Amy and I parted. No more tears.

I felt called to get one more reading from Jean-Jacques, gave it to myself as a birthday present. A huge amount had happened since last we'd seen him. After about twenty minutes he said something that stopped my mind dead in its tracks.

"Amy was never really committed to you," he said.

What? I couldn't grasp its full meaning. It shook me to my roots. The rest of the session seemed a blur, skipped right by me.

He blew my mind again when he said I was giving, giving, giving and toward the end she was mostly taking and she felt guilty about it. She couldn't handle that anymore, he said, and that was one of the reasons she had to get away from this relationship because it didn't feel right to her. You are giving everything, he said, this could not have lasted like this. Because of that, toward the end our relationship had become toxic, he said. Both of us needed this split. Being apart from each other is the best thing that could happen for *both* of us; meaning, for me, too! Another shocker, since I had been thinking this split was the worst thing that could have happened to me.

Jean-Jacques also reminded me of something I already knew inside but in my consternation I'd forgotten. The answer lies in the spiritual, he said. Always. It doesn't lie in other relationships. The grieving that comes with this will make your heart like cotton, he said, and this is a good thing for you. He said being free from this dependency will make you an even more powerful teacher.

Oddly, I left feeling much more at ease. But it went by too quickly; I couldn't grasp it all. I looked forward to receiving the recording. The main takeaway from that session? For the first time I felt reconciled that Amy had to leave me. It now felt right and necessary—for me, too!

I flew off to Greece feeling stronger. I had a superb time in beautiful Peloponnese with Mick Tomlinson, surrounded by many wonderful people, including Richard. My training retreat went extremely well. Then a few of us visited fascinating ancient Greek ruins. I didn't even think about Amy much—a miracle.

With my work in Greece complete and some time on my hands before my upcoming trainings in Russia and Romania I hopped a large ferry for a holiday to the Greek island of Naxos. No one spoke any English. Alone in Naxos, going to the beach every day, sunbathing, reading, swimming, riding around on a rented bicycle, I felt my mind relax and decompress.

On my last night I felt a twinge of loneliness. Seemed as good a time as any to listen to the recording of my psychic reading, as I hadn't ever fully absorbed it. I listened. When I reached the part that before had thrown me off-kilter, that Amy was never really committed to me, I quickly shut off the recording. Couldn't handle it. Again I sat stunned. Too much to take! My spirits dropped like an avalanche.

In the middle of the night I awoke with the sweats, couldn't get back to sleep. My thinking began a downward spiral: Let me get this straight, Amy was never really committed to me and to our relationship?! What did that really mean? What were the implications? All along until the end, even when I felt her withdrawal she kept absolutely insisting she loved me as much as I loved her and wanted me as much as I wanted her. My God! Was I living a lie, deluding myself all these years? This thought shocked me to my core! I thought we'd had the greatest relationship in the world. Could this have been total delusion, total fabrication on my part? I felt used. Suddenly I felt dirty, sullied somehow, as if I needed to take a year-long shower or something to get all the contamination out of every pore of my body. For how many years had I been living this lie? I kept giving, giving, giving 100% of myself to this relationship, and Amy never gave us a real chance! Now I'm pissed, but not at Amy—at myself! How in the world could I have gotten suckered in like that? How could I have allowed myself to be so deluded? How can I even forgive her? Wait, Jack, see innocence! She didn't know—or did she? Did she take advantage of my 100% love and devotion? In the beginning I had gotten such total unconditional love from her way, way beyond anything I'd ever felt before, I wanted to hang onto that for dear life because it was the most beautiful feeling I'd ever had. And I rode on those fantasy coattails for nine more years? Are you kidding me?! I hung onto that delusion no matter what, getting just enough back to keep the delusional alive? Gut wrenching! I had been in fantasyland—of my own creation—while she kept insisting, convincing me nothing was wrong.

How was I supposed to live with this? This is not about Amy; it's about me! Whoa, the old/new thought came that no matter how hard I tried I apparently wasn't good enough to be loved like that and sustain it. No matter how much I gave to her and gave to us it could never be enough. Decades-old garbage thoughts, but what a crusher! Did Amy even know? No! No way could she have done this on purpose. That's not who she is. I'm usually very perceptive; I would have seen through it. So she wasn't doing it on purpose; that means she was deluding herself, which is why I was deluded. What was I supposed to do now, be glad I'm out of the delusion? I kept pushing, pushing, pushing to understand, to get back the supreme love I felt for her. I spent eight or nine years doing everything in my power to get it back, and no matter how hard I tried I couldn't. So I convinced myself I still had the greatest. And it was a lie. Then my pushing to get it back got to be too much for Amy to handle, and she had to sever it to be free. How could I even trust myself now? Down, down, down.

Alone on Naxos I needed somehow to be cleansed, purged of all this. That's what Jean-Jacques meant by it had become toxic! I felt a Tae Kwon Do kick to the gut. I felt sick to my stomach. Something about this sickened me—my own collusion. I felt like throwing up. I had a splitting headache. I felt shaken to the roots of my very existence.

What happened next is indescribable. All of a sudden, I shattered into a million pieces.

It was like the bedrock foundation of me shattered, scattering literally into a million pieces. I felt like Humpty Dumpty—all the king's horses and all the king's men couldn't put me back together again. Then I saw all these pieces of me slowly start to float away, in slow motion, the pieces of me began flying ever so slowly out into the universe, almost like from the big bang. I saw them so clearly, floating away, so slowly, so gracefully, so beautifully. In pieces I'm floating out into the universe. I no longer even know who I am.

And in that moment I knew. I KNEW absolutely. I knew none of those pieces of me mattered! The pieces were matter, and if it's matter it doesn't matter. None of the me even counted. Only one thing counted: the pure spiritual energy holding all the pieces together, keeping it All together. Divine Love. Divine Consciousness. There for me Always. Because it *IS* me, the True me, beyond me, connected to All. The essence of us All.

Only one thing could help me: this spiritual energy behind, underneath, throughout the Universe and beyond—because it never left me. That was the BIG delusion! That it had left me—when it hadn't! It never could. It's impossible. I surrender. I give up. I know nothing. I am yours—

In that moment I was cured.

Nothing I felt immediately before the shattering felt true anymore. Any negative, lingering thought of Amy and myself simply and completely disappeared—forever. I know I had switched back and forth before, but I knew this was forever. I felt nothing but pure love and gratefulness for her. Thank you, Amy for being in my life! For being you. For bringing me such happiness for so many years. For helping me grow when I needed to grow. Thank you! Thank you forever.

And I knew I would feel that for the rest of my life, underneath and behind it all, no matter how powerfully in the future I will again be seduced by consciousness.

* * *

***Postscript**: I came out of that experience completely rejuvenated. I not only had a new and lasting, healthy perspective on my relationship with Amy, I had a new, solid foothold on my own life and what is important. That flash of* seeing *brought me far along the road to freedom and full release from Amy. Still that stubborn little ego wanted to hold on.*

Unbeknownst to me I still had to go through two more big insights to complete total release.

The first came one night around New Year's—six months after my shattering—when on a lark I attended a "Lunar Manifestation" meetup group in Boca Raton. I walked into a small room packed to the gills—no chairs left—so I sat on the floor leaning against a wall sandwiched shoulder to shoulder between two participants. The woman leading the group told us to write down what we would like to manifest over the next year. I wrote that I wanted the number of people touched or have had their lives change as a result of reading my books to triple or quadruple. Then she led us through a guided meditation where in the middle I thought, "Why did I set my sights so low? I want 100 times, 1000 times more people to be touched and have their lives change as a result of my books!" Toward the end of the meditation the woman said, "Now it's time to let go of the old, because the old blocks the new from coming forth. Check in with yourself inside and find anything or any emotion you've been holding onto."

No surprise, Amy immediately popped into my mind. The leader said, "It is time to let that go."

I knew I needed to release Amy from me, but I couldn't! Instead, I felt emotion welling up in me, while sitting packed like sardines shoulder to shoulder with strangers. Although everyone in this meditation sat with eyes closed I didn't want to get all emotional in there. What was going on with me? I had been doing really well. I realized why. My ego did not want to release Amy! Whoa! It threw me for a loop. Why didn't I want to let her go? What good would it do for me to hold on? I could not come up with one good reason. I could find no good reason to keep hanging on. At that moment I knew I *had to* release her. It made no sense to be the only one left holding on. Besides, it would not be fair to Amy for me to still have an energy hook in her.

So I tried. Still couldn't! My eyes filled. I knew I had to do this; I'd be in big trouble with myself if I didn't. So I tried to will myself to do it. But jumping levels of consciousness does not lend itself to personal will. I struggled mightily. Finally, the insight came. I had to. No question. As hard as it was I finally forced myself to release her. I want to be very clear here: At first I tried to apply my will from a low level of consciousness and it didn't work. It took a new thought—new insight that it made no sense to keep hanging on—to ascend levels of consciousness enough where I could let go. I watched Amy float off into the universe. Utterly sad. But I knew it was right. Immediately I felt lighter. That act of release allowed another giant step toward almost full cure.

The second. Warning: If some readers found the first one weird, this one may especially be. About two or three months after that experience I attended another meetup group in Boca, this one run by the lovely Katy Simmone, who had become a friend. Katy calls herself an "Advanced Channeler of Light Beings." One of the light beings she channels claims to be Aristotle. Katy even wrote a book on those channelings, *Aristotle's Teachings for The New Age*, which she offers for free over the internet.[23] Anyway, in this meetup group Katy led us through a guided meditation where first she cleared our chakras, then instructed us to call in our "spiritual medical team." She said everyone has a spiritual medical team. This did not surprise me because my daughter, Jaime, told me of the existence of this team when she went through the Barbara Brennan School of Healing. Katy told us to scan our bodies and locate an organ or anything we would like healed. So I scanned. Immediately I landed on my heart. Katy said, "Ask your medical team to heal that part of you."

I prayed silently, hearing myself say, "I'd like you to heal my broken heart." Then the team allegedly did its work. We thanked them. As the session ended Katy said, "Don't expect to feel any difference right away. Your team will keep working on you and it may take two or three days before you'll feel a difference."

Exactly three days after this meetup I'm walking on the beach and out of the blue a thought hit me: "You released Amy from you, but you did not release yourself from Amy."

Whoa! Instantly I knew its truth. I knew if finally I could do this I

[23] For anyone interested: https://www.smashwords.com/books/view/575068

would feel total and complete freedom from Amy and our relationship. Again my ego would not let me do it; I could not bring myself to release myself from her! Again I felt emotion well up. Not again!

I spotted someone down the beach flying a kite. I realized the kite could only be held in place by the string being held at the other end; otherwise it would fly off freely. In that moment I knew I had to cut the final cord. I had once overheard Katy tell someone that when a relationship ends it is very important to cut the spiritual energy cord that exists between the two people in love. I knew my ego was afraid to. But without cutting that cord I likely would continue to hold myself back—not only from becoming involved in other relationships, but also from the ultimate relationship with my true Self.

On the beach walking I asked myself, "Why am I afraid to let go of this final remnant of our relationship?" By this time tears are streaming down my face. It came to me. I was afraid Amy would feel the severing, and her last connection to me would be gone forever. The question came to mind, "What would that mean for me? What am I holding onto?" Once again, I had no good answer. I thought I had cut the cord during that lunar manifestation meditation, and I may have, but it wasn't the only energy cord that needed cutting. I had missed the most important and serious one. As much progress as I had made, I realized I had not let go fully and completely. Again, from that lower level of consciousness I tried to force release of myself from her. Still I couldn't! In the worst way I did not want to cut this final cord! Why was this so hard for me? Bang! I realized why. I wanted to hold onto her forever! I realized such a "reality" would be nice if it served me in any way, but it did not. It could not possibly serve me well. New insight, courtesy of wisdom: If I didn't cut this final cord it would continue to hang around my neck like an albatross. I had no choice. Armed now with seeing the futility of holding on, from this higher level I had no choice.

Poof! I released myself from Amy. The cord severed. I felt us separate energetically—forever. A huge moment!

Relief! I'm not losing anything, I realized. I can still cherish all the great memories I want to, so long as they bring me a nice feeling. But now I am free, 100%. Forever.

I've never looked back...

I shall be released—
from my own thinking—
and what remains is the miracle of new life…

I marvel at how learning never stops. One big lesson: so long as I tried to solve my problem from my mind—my little mind—it could never happen; it would never work. I could never have "let go" from my mind as it was. I needed new seeing. I needed to submit myself to Universal Mind. So long as I tried to resolve my issue from a low level of consciousness it would be impossible. I needed to transcend it, jump to a higher level, see it new from a completely different perspective. Only then could I be free from the seduction of the lower levels. In my case, I reached the point where my little mind could no longer support its own logic; its own system of protection failed and headed off the cliff until it exploded and cleared in that instant, and in spite of myself I leaped to a far higher level where everything looked different.

I don't recommend the shattering approach—it is much too painful. A far better way would be to ask of Universal Mind to help us see what we need to see, then take our so-called problems off our minds, and fall into the quiet and listen, and wait patiently for new sight. The latter is far easier on the nerves, the mind, our entire being.

When we give ourselves up to Universal Mind, Universal Consciousness, Universal Thought, our petty thoughts of fear and ego disappear, thoughts of anger fall by the wayside, thoughts of frustration and irritation are no more. When we give ourselves over to Universal Mind we are free, and there is nothing we need to do to get there. All that is necessary is for us to not take any seductive thoughts of form as reality, to know they are not what really is. We forget about ourselves, give ourselves over to the One connected to pure consciousness within—where there is no seduction, where it has no power.

Our problems are only problems when we think they are.

When connected to the Source, we don't.

47. DEEPER KNOWING:
(Saga Revisited, with New Sight)

Originally I intended to end this book with my moment of redemption—my shattering experience and major revelation. Among other things I liked its dramatic effect. Best laid plans of mice and authors. Turned out not to be the end of the story. I see many things differently now than when I first wrote my saga, and certainly from when I initially experienced it. Astute readers already have observed how much I still saw from the outside-in. Initially when I wrote my saga I believed I had a pretty deep understanding of the Three Principles. Ironically, regarding this particular aspect of my life, I now see even more blindness than I'd initially realized. Looking back, when it came to relationships I did not have a deep understanding at all. I became far too seduced by the reality of what I felt and believed.

Upon initially reading my saga, both George Pransky and Dicken Bettinger called me on it, pointing to the places they believed I needed deeper understanding. After kicking and screaming a bit—I thought I'd finished my book and wanted it out of my hair—because I greatly respect their understanding of the Three Principles, I listened. I heard. I also listened to two close friends, whom I also respect greatly for their deep connection with the spiritual world; i.e., to Universal Mind, or what they call Source or Spirit. As a result of all these conversations new insights arose within me. I had to reexamine parts of my saga from what seems to me now a higher level of consciousness. What I thought I had finished, I hadn't.

Readers may remember when I first introduced my saga I said it represented my blind spot. By the time I wrote the saga I had already realized my creation of illusion that I needed other women around me to experience happiness. I didn't realize my blind spot's tentacles extended far deeper.

Whenever we "need" anything outside ourselves to be happy—such as eating junk food, needing a sports car, playing golf, needing alcohol or other drugs, needing sex, insisting that one's partner be a certain way, needing a woman or man to fill us up—we turn in the wrong direction. The truth can never be found in the outside world; truth resides in the opposite direction. Becoming lost in ego/fear-based thinking creates the illusion that something is wrong and needs to be changed or fixed. As a result we suffer. We become so expert at looking outside ourselves for happiness we truly believe and feel that happiness really can be found out there, when happiness, joy, peace and love reside below the noise of our thinking. When not lost in thought we are at peace. What we seek—in fact, what we truly are—resides within.

While seeing the illusion of my initial blind spot, I had no idea a far deeper, more insidious blind spot lurked below the surface, trapping me still. So let's look back, with new perspective.

SUFFERING

From the moment I heard Amy say, "I think I need space," my mind retreated into fear, which caused me to suffer. The suffering became greater and more intense as it became increasingly clear my relationship with "the love of my life" had really come to an end. It intensified the more I felt she turned her back on me, hurt me. After our beautiful ten-year relationship I suffered on and off for about a year and a half, despite how much I believed I knew about the Three Principles.

People may ask legitimately, "If Jack Pransky supposedly knows so much about Three Principles, why did it not help him during the year and a half he suffered?" It would not be a great leap, then, for some readers to conclude that Three Principles understanding is inadequate to relieve suffering, or that it takes far too long. Such conclusions would be dead wrong.

First, the Three Principles show us the reason suffering occurs in the first place. We get a thought of how bad things are, we compare it to thoughts of what we would like to be happening instead, we have thoughts about what this discrepancy means for our lives; we might further impose judgmental thinking that because we know the

Principles we should know better. Consciousness picks up all this heavy thinking and gives us a deep feeling of suffering. Suffering can only exist as a result of such thinking.

Second, sometimes when people learn the Principles they conclude we will no longer suffer because we understand where suffering really comes from. Too simplistic! It is human to use our thinking from time to time in ways that make us suffer. The question is, how long do we want to stay in that state? Three Principles understanding says suffering will lessen to the extent we truly realize that 1) we are making it up with our own thinking, and 2) we are able to fall away from thought into the formless. In my case, I knew I was caught in personal thinking but I could not fall away from it precisely because *I saw it as reality*. When Amy left me, my fearful thoughts that I could not be happy without her felt utterly real, which led to despair, which led to suffering. I missed seeing the fact of my own creation of illusion, and I missed seeing the possibility that I could fall out of my personal thinking and rest in the formless. This is not the fault of the Three Principles; it is not that Three Principles understanding is not enough. The problem lay with *my own seeing*, my own grounding with regard to this particular, issue—being blind to seeing the Principles in action in my life in those moments. We often believe once we realize how the Three Principles create our experience of life we are home free for the rest of our lives—and we are, except when we do not recognize the Principles in action in any moment. When I didn't, I suffered. I did not suffer because Amy left me; I suffered because I was caught in the illusion of my own despair-thinking.

Third, the Three Principles show us the way out of suffering—if we are able to see it. A huge difference exists between the situations and circumstances life throws at us and the meaning for our lives we give to those situations. As soon as we truly know our suffering has nothing to do with anything happening out there—even if we lose the love of our lives; even if a loved one dies—and realize our suffering *would not exist* without our own creation of the meaning we give it, we become free from that suffering, or at least it takes the edge off. I'm not saying we won't encounter very difficult things in life—we will—but what we make of them for our lives is up to us. Even better, when we realize all suffering ends when thought drops away and we fall back into the quiet into our pure consciousness connected to the Oneness of all things, and we see this is only another experience of life and all is love, we do not suffer. [More on this later.]

In sum, in my year and a half of suffering the culprit was my limited seeing at the time. Because I fell for the seduction, I could not see the Three Principles in action, and my own grounding slid off-base.

But here's something interesting. Out of my personal suffering I had a major revelation when my personal thinking shattered and I realized the only thing that mattered was the formless energy behind all life. So, was my year and a half of suffering worth it? Speaking personally, for a revelation of that magnitude I would gladly endure all that suffering because as a result of this major insight I came out the other side stronger and more solid, and it will help guide me for the rest of my life. But would I have reached the same realization had I not gone through that suffering, then shattering experience? Impossible to know. Maybe it would have happened over time; I'll never know. But what could be a huger shift than at first to believe my suffering was caused by Amy leaving me, then to see my suffering caused by my illusory separation from the formless. After being ruled by ego and fear, once I shattered I glimpsed the power and beauty of formless Universal Mind in all its grace and glory. I would not have traded it for anything. Thank you, Amy; I am very grateful to you for helping me see.

Further, through conversations with my two very deep, spiritual friends, who during our conversation tapped into Universal, spiritual intelligence, I came to understand something even deeper about suffering. Here is how I heard it:

The process of getting lost is also the process of getting found. The formless energy behind all life does not think it a failure if one gets lost—even if lost in the desert for the rest of one's life. No judgment. Problems, difficulties, pain and suffering afford people the opportunity to see what is going on and to awaken. Most of us do have not have the good fortune to be awakened as did Syd Banks, or with as much power. Just because people learn about Mind, Consciousness and Thought does not mean they will awaken—if they don't truly *see* it. However, the more one looks toward spiritual intelligence and surrenders to it, the more opportunity one has to be lifted out of pain and suffering.

Within the realm of spiritual intelligence everything is right; we can never make a bad choice. All is the perfect unfolding. Your situation could have unfolded perfectly in many different directions. Also, when people say one should be achieving a good outcome, or that a good outcome is supposed to look like this or be that, value judgment is attached—for example, saying a good outcome looks like there is no suffering, or looks like staying married, or looks like there is no burden and if you only had a deep enough understanding you wouldn't be burdened. But a perfect unfolding is just that. Everything just *is*, and we have the free will to think about it in any way we want; then we get to live with whatever feeling that brings.

MY BLIND "NEED"

Ten years before suffering over Amy leaving me, I experienced a different kind of suffering when I agonized over whether to have an illicit relationship with the woman about whom I'd heard clearly, "She's the one." After setting that aside for about two years, once I went on that first hike with Amy an extraordinary feeling overcame me. The more we got together the more powerfully I felt it. Unbeknownst to me I had become blinded by the brilliant light I felt from Amy and the powerful love I felt for her. Best feeling I'd ever had. I wanted to feel it for the rest of my life. I didn't realize at the time but I saw Amy as my soulmate who would complete me as a person. In her I saw my opportunity to have the happiness and love I longed for and deserved.

So blind to this was I, in fact, I didn't even want to comprehend the negative fall-out that would result—leaving a wife of thirty-plus years devastated, my children alienated, being party to a painful break-up of Amy's family. All that greatly disturbed me, but apparently not enough to supersede the powerful vision of what I selfishly believed was the best thing I could do for myself for the rest of my life. After all, how often does such an opportunity present itself in life? How could I possibly turn it down? I believed in us and what we could create together and threw a blanket over how bad I felt about the harm we caused. Amy continued to feel haunted by it.

In retrospect, I was blind to the fact that the light and love I felt for Amy were simply thoughts, too. I wanted her to be a certain way for me, and so long as I thought it, she was. I wanted to hold onto it forever, even after Amy backed off in her mind. Still worked for me. Such is the blinding power of Thought combined with Consciousness. It worked for me until she actually left me—then I had different powerful thoughts of what that now meant for my life; hence, despair and suffering. Consciousness brings thought to life so perfectly that a powerful thought disguised by the senses can appear to be an independent reality that we truly perceive, making it completely understandable how blind spots are so much a part of the human condition.

Even before Amy, looking through my blind spot lens (which I didn't know I was looking through), I believed I could only be filled by finding other women who could give me something I felt I didn't get in my marriage. All a fallacy! "Needs" are self-created by thought believed, and as I have said repeatedly, can never be filled by anything "out there." I had felt a hole inside, a "need" I filled by feeling close to other women with whom I believed I could truly be myself. But "truly be myself" was itself a creation of my own thinking that consciousness made me believe as truth. Who said I needed to be filled by other women? Me! I made that up. Out of that "reality" I then created thoughts, out of those thoughts I had compelling feelings, out of my compelling feelings I behaved accordingly—all creations of me, by me and for me. A hole inside me that needed filling? Impossible! No such thing! My own creation of delusion! Inside I am filled completely with spiritual energy, filled with the essence of mySelf, perfect and whole. That I needed to fill myself up with anything is a complete fallacy. Everyone is perfect inside! Me. You. Everyone we know. Everyone we don't know.

DECISION ABOUT LEAVING MY MARRIAGE

Approximately fifteen months later when Judy announced she wanted me back, I again found myself agonizing—this time over whether I should return to my marriage. Thought kicked in again.

Although I did not have such a bad marriage, in comparison to the way I felt with Amy my relationship with Judy looked controlling and difficult. I saw how hard it was to relax and enjoy myself in her presence. It almost appeared as if I had woken up to the reality of my marriage. Making my present marriage work seemed a bridge too far. I saw this in a clear and accurate way—or so I believed. But I agonized because another thought barraged me: staying in my marriage was the "right" thing to do.

I agonized until I heard Gabriela say, "wait for clarity." I took that to heart. I thought, "of course," and my agonizing stopped as I got quiet and waited for an answer. It took a couple of months to hear clarity. I knew this decision had nothing to do with Amy; at that point I had no idea whether she and I could make it together over time. My tug-of-war pulled between returning to my life with Judy or being alone. Clarity suddenly came in the form of a strong and certain knowing from deep within. It declared unequivocally that I needed to choose peace of mind over going back to Judy. I truly believed I heard wisdom speak.

Some will take issue with this in a couple of ways. Did I really hear wisdom, or did I hear something masquerading as wisdom but wasn't? I will revisit this issue in a bit.

Before going there, even in my initial writing about it for this book I didn't see something extremely important. As stated above I equated peace of mind with being apart from Judy, believing she was not easy for me to live with. But Judy is the outside world! Peace of mind cannot come from external circumstances. Though I see this very clearly with my clients and trainees and in most of my own life I now see, humbly, that when it comes to my own personal love relationships I regularly miss this and look to the other person for whether or not I am happy or at peace. I believe it. I feel it. It's so real to me. I get lost. Something tells me I am not alone.

Some highly regarded Three Principles practitioners, such as George Pransky, even say we could be in a relationship with anyone and live in a state of peace and happiness. Why do they make such a radical claim? Because everyone at their essence is beautiful and lovable, and any two people thrown together who see and appreciate the beauty and goodness in the other would have a good relationship, no matter what their habits or personality characteristics. While I can understand this perspective I, personally, would not go so far to say that we could be in a love relationship with anyone and be happy or joyful. I'm not talking about a couple having different values, because values are just thought and for the most part are not deal-breakers. For instance, it is quite possible for a couple to agree to disagree on certain issues, even if they can't come to a meeting of the minds. I get that. Where I have difficulty comprehending how it could work is in situations where the couple is diametrically opposed, such as one partner wanting monogamy and the other wanting polyamory. Or (this may be an extreme example) for a woman with a reasonably high level of consciousness to be happy in a relationship with, say, Charles Manson, no matter how much she saw his essence. (Of course, a few women were happy with Charlie, to the point of even murdering for him, but my guess is they weren't exactly functioning at a high level). Or if one partner is abusive to the other. I am sure it's possible for the victim or survivor of abuse to see her partner as lost and with compassion, but still not want to be with him—although Linda Pransky told me of a client who didn't mind occasional abuse but said if he ever had an affair she'd be out of there in a shot. Everyone has a different opinion about what's not right and what's acceptable. I do think it's safe to say that what often appears on the surface to be a deal-breaker may not be. Even if I can't personally see it, the point of these well-regarded Three Principles practitioners is well taken.

I had a very interesting discussion with George Pransky around this:

JP: What is wrong with me seeing that a certain relationship had outlived its usefulness, which allowed me to then be with someone who helped me be on a much higher plane?

GP: Because you're assuming that "outlived its usefulness" is a quality in the relationship, rather than a level of consciousness in Jack Pransky.

JP: No, I'm seeing it is a level of consciousness in me.

GP: If you saw it as a level of consciousness in Jack Pransky, you would be saying, "What is the problem with me that I cannot see the goodness in the beauty in Judy? What is my problem? I need to raise my consciousness because I cannot see the beauty and the goodness in her. I am so blinded by her behavior it eclipses her beauty and goodness. I can't see the sun through the clouds." If you said that, you would move in the direction of higher consciousness, rather than finding someone else who looks appealing at your present level.

JP: Okay, I get what you're saying. Yet, when I did find someone else, it was so much easier and more beautiful.

GP: But that was you, Jack. You changed your thinking. If you had been that way with Judy it would have been the same way. You were hopeful, you saw the beauty in Amy, you saw the innocence in her, you saw other beautiful qualities in her, you were open to them, you enjoyed them. Of course you're going to enjoy her and enjoy life. Your thinking was oriented to her.

JP: This feels like my cutting edge.

GP: Maybe this will help, Jack. At any given level of consciousness a person can find better choices. When they go up to a higher level, everything changes—their mate is more beautiful, their life gets easier, their life gets better. Now in George Pransky's opinion, I'm affected by the fact that at your level of consciousness, internal well-being was not easy to come by. You are not easily satisfied. [JP: Certainly true when it comes to relationships.] You see this as, "I found a possibility that was way better than what I had." And I would say, "Jack got carried away in an idea he had, and he lost his 'easily satisfied with life.' He's no different from a drunk who feels better when he goes into a bar and gets intoxicated." I'm overstating it, but Amy was a very good coping mechanism. He wasn't happy, and when he was with her, he was. So instead of going to the bar every night, Amy was his coping mechanism. If he was more easily satisfied, he wouldn't have needed a coping mechanism.

What George said interested me. So, could I have found peace of mind and happiness had I gone back to Judy? Yes, I could have—*if* my own then-limited thinking had allowed it. My peace and happiness could not come from Judy, nor could it come from Amy, nor could it come from being alone; it could only come from within me, no matter what my circumstances or with whomever I have a relationship. Why didn't I go back to Judy, then? Because I didn't see the possibility. All I saw then was it would be much easier for me to live in peace without being with a woman around whom I often believed I had to walk on eggshells whenever she got upset or so she wouldn't get upset. I thought it would be easier to find peace of mind without that. But, as George said, the problem was within me, not Judy! I walked on eggshells because of my own thinking. I could have turned more toward the beauty and goodness in Judy than to what I believed were problems. I didn't realize I innocently saw an exception to the fact that we can't look to outside things for our peace of mind, happiness or unhappiness, when there are no exceptions. Our own thinking is always the reason we are not happy. This is a beautiful thing to see, because although it is quite humbling and we don't want the responsibility—I certainly didn't—it is very freeing. If I saw Judy's essence strongly and felt compassion for what made her not exactly exude peace, I might have had a different experience in that relationship.

Recognizing this is my first line of defense—something akin to the relationship an American football quarterback has to his offensive line. If a quarterback doesn't have a good offensive line he is going to be rushed, blitzed and sacked by the other team's defensive line before he can get off a pass. Life keeps throwing things at us that try to rush and tackle us. Our own offensive line—what protects us—is realizing our own thinking is the culprit. So long as we look to the outside world to escape from unhappiness we are vulnerable to the ravages of the rushers and tacklers. I am still in the process of learning this lesson for myself in relationships. As I said, it is my cutting edge of understanding. Everyone has a cutting edge.

TOXIC RELATIONSHIP?

Toward the end of our relationship I felt Amy distancing herself from me and felt myself giving a lot more to our relationship than she did. At first I chalked it up to a passing phase. I still wanted her; it felt so good to be in her presence that I overlooked it. Therefore, I was still happy with our relationship. Once she told me she needed space I started to look at back at the imbalance and it started to bother me. Then the psychic told me we ended up in a toxic relationship. His reason? Because I was doing most of the giving, she was doing most of the taking and she felt bad about that; therefore, our relationship had become unhealthy and could not have continued like that. Hence, toxic, or so the psychic labeled it.

Back to my conversation with George:

JP: But she did change toward me! She admitted she gave me mixed messages for a whole year. She realized she stopped giving the way she used to.

GP: If I'm sitting here thinking there is a sniper out there, and my palms are sweating and my heartbeat is going up, it makes no difference whether a sniper is really there or not. It's still me freaking out. So when at first you're thoughtlessly giving without thinking of getting anything back, it's wonderful, and then you switch to, "Wait a minute. What's the deal here? She stopped giving." That switch in you is what changed your feelings. And it would have changed your feelings whether she was giving you less or not. The fact that she was giving you less doesn't mean anything in the Principles' world.

Hmm. Could George really be right? I hate to admit it, but now I think so. It's a pretty radical notion, so please bear with me. Here is how I see it now.

First, what comes through the senses and the feelings they bring can be all-powerful! We get swept away. For example, in the first chapter of this book I talked about the tsunami scene in the movie, *The Impossible*. Because of the superb special effects in that movie I felt caught in the middle of that tsunami. My senses of sight and sound were so engaged my heart started to pound in awe and terror. But it was only a movie! I was perfectly safe sitting in that theater. The special effects captured me, so I felt otherwise. Humans are equipped with even greater special effects than the best special effects movie. We truly believe what the senses make us feel. But what the senses make us feel can *only* be what our thoughts tell the senses, through consciousness, to make us feel. That's how we get seduced. We create the script. We direct. We act. We are the audience. So if I have the thought, "I am happy in this relationship," even if at the end Amy was not, I still was happy because I felt it through my senses. If I thought she was beautiful, she was. If I thought she was wonderful to be around, she was. Nothing can take that away from me—except my own thinking. That's how powerful the Three Principles are.

I now see that with Amy I was the happiest I'd ever been—because I thought I was! My thinking made it so. I wanted it to be the greatest relationship; therefore it was. Even in the last year when I felt Amy's feelings for me wane somewhat and felt I gave more than I got in return, I ignored it. If toward the end of our relationship it had become toxic I had been oblivious to it; therefore, to me, it wasn't.

In the middle of my total despair on Naxos I remember having the wildest thought. "Let me get this straight: With my own thinking I had tricked myself into being happy with Amy, even if allegedly it was no longer a healthy relationship? I truly was happy! Is that bad?" I almost laughed. At the time it felt like the most bizarre thought I ever had. I had no answer.

Now I do. So was I in a great relationship or not? As I said, I thoroughly loved this relationship. I loved her so much! I thoroughly enjoyed being around her and with her. I felt so grateful for it and her. It was the best thing that ever happened to me. So even though Amy had begun to withdraw some, by me remaining happy in it, even if I was only kidding myself, it worked for me! Since we all create our own reality via the Three Principles, if I was very happy in it, did that not mean I still was in a great relationship even if Amy fell out of happiness with me or with us?

Does this mean it only takes one person in a couple to think it is a great relationship; then it is? Can one person a great relationship make? Can a great relationship exist unilaterally? Hmm. Now I believe the answer is yes! It's true. For that person, it really is as great as he or she thinks it is. Why? Because of the power of Thought comes through Consciousness and our senses, and we *feel* it.

So, while from a low level of consciousness it looked like, "I thought we had a good thing going, but we didn't. I was the giver; she was the taker. It was toxic," from a higher level it looks like, "What am

I talking about? Those with the best nine years of my life. I loved everything about her. I loved her company. I saw the beauty in her. What a wonderful person she was! I overlooked that she had insecurities and doubts."

Given that's what I felt, I gave all of myself to her happily—until I questioned it. To be giving in a relationship is a wonderful thing, so long as it is aligned with wisdom. If it is, the giving will feel right. We don't want to give for the purpose of getting something in return; it is something we sincerely want to do for our loved one. No problem exists with giving, unless we think "sacrifice," and if we do we get an unhealthy feeling.

WISDOM

Which brings me back to whether I heard wisdom tell me it was time for my relationship with Judy to end. Did I truly feel guided by wisdom to leave that relationship and start a new life, or was I kidding myself? Some would say I was kidding myself, but I know what I heard, loud and clear. What I heard was no typical, everyday thinking. This internal voice came from another realm. It took at least a couple of months to hear it. Once I heard it, it was unmistakable and unshakable. Before the moment I heard it, clarity eluded me. Wisdom sounds like nothing else and is never something to be confused or taken lightly. With wisdom we don't hear second thoughts.

This raises deeper questions about the nature of wisdom itself. As George implied in our conversation, he sees wisdom as something that always raises our consciousness. He would also say we can make better choices within the same level of consciousness but that is not wisdom. He sees my choosing peace of mind over Judy as such a decision. I understand what he means, as I can see where it could be a convenient excuse for anyone to rely on what they believe is wisdom but really isn't; in so doing they could potentially close themselves off to deeper wisdom about the very nature of life. This is worth considering and being cautious about. However, I have a broader definition of wisdom.

I define wisdom as the intelligence behind life, drawing from Universal Mind itself. It is from this intelligence, of which each of us is a tiny part, that we are able to hear wise thoughts when our head clears. When we hear it, we know it. It doesn't come from us; it comes through us. So it can be seen almost as a direct feed from the intelligence behind life that appears as new thought coming "out of the blue." It does not come from analytical processing, or from our typical thinking. Wisdom comes to us in the form of insight, "a-ha!," intuition. I see wisdom coming to us on a spectrum of levels, from the ordinary—a wise idea about whether it is in my long-term best interests to go see a doctor—to the sublime—an epiphany about the illusory nature of life. Wisdom feels different than our typical thinking. It feels right, certain, sure, unshakable. Wisdom at its higher levels, such as wisdom about the nature of life, will be a constant and stand the test of time. Wisdom in the vernacular is sometimes referred to as common sense, seeing the obvious, intuition, higher consciousness.

Many spiritual masters say we are here in this life in human form for the growth and development of our souls. Might we get involved in certain relationships to have the opportunity for our souls to experience growth and development? What if my relationship with Judy had run its course spiritually? What if wisdom truly was speaking to me about this? There is no way of truly knowing, of course, except what I feel in my heart from deep inside. If true, I can see where wisdom could tell me, "It is time to move on." But when listening, we have to be very, very careful. We have to know beyond a shadow of a doubt it truly is a knowing and not something that just feels like a better decision in the moment. In my case, I heard clearly that it no longer served my long-term best interests to go back to that relationship. Is it a coincidence that when I was with Amy I felt a skyrocketing in the growth and development of my soul? What if my relationship with Amy existed for the purpose of renewing my spiritual growth? I certainly grew more, spiritually, in my ten years with her than at any other time in my life (other than my experience with Syd Banks and its aftermath). While this possibly could have also happened with Judy, it could not have happened at the level of consciousness I had back then; it may have been possible after my later jump in my level of consciousness. This is still something I, personally, need to see more about. In any case, wisdom is found in the quiet, in silence from within. All wisdom comes from the silence, when the mind clears.

Which brings me back to what I gleaned from the wonderful conversation I had with my spiritual friends as they deeply connected with spiritual energy and spoke out of an almost trance-like silence:

Spiritual energy is All that exists. Once spiritual energy comes into form it is very easy for us to forget it is all One. We use our free will to either see the form and separation, or to fall back into the formless. Like Syd said, a bad feeling signals us to know we're moving away from our built-in well-being. Recognizing this, at any moment we have the opportunity to fall out of our personal thinking back into the formless—fall back into that which does not change. We have the capacity to sense and to know *that which does not change*. We use our free will to either fall into it or continue to make choices out of our form-based thinking.

If we allow attention to be directed within, we will be guided. This is where wisdom resides. If we look outside and stay attached to what already has form, we get lost. It does not matter if you know where this guidance comes from—whether from spirits or angels or Universal Mind or our higher self or simply from our own wisdom—because it amounts to the same thing. The guidance comes from what has not yet taken form. This Knowing exists within all of us, because it is the only Truth. Fall back into the quiet, into the thing that doesn't change, and new thinking arises via new insights. And it always comes with a good feeling. It's a feeling of wide-open spaciousness, through no effort.

The more we surrender to the formless the more we see there is only the formless living in form. The self, which is not even really real, falls away, and what is left is only the Divine expressing itself through form. The more we fall into it, the more it lives us. Then we have its life. It's like falling back into the quiet and letting life unfold from this place where we have no idea what is going to take form. The formless takes form through us—we are only a vessel through which the formless lives its life. If we look to the form or to the outside world to try to make our lives be what we want them to be, it often leads to a fearful, striving, efforting, anxious, clutching feeling, in contrast to falling back and allowing, learning how to surrender.

So it is very important to fall back into the quiet and ask wisdom to guide us, in living our entire lives, with the work we're doing, where we're living, how we are with our children, spouse or partner, what to do when we're up against a problem—with everything. Fall back into the quiet and listen for a Knowing.

Spiritual energy wants whatever is arising. The message from spiritual energy is, I want you to become a window through which I shine. I want you to fall back into Me and love everything that arises. Thus, we turn into love, the opposite of ego. The ego is tricky because it has an agenda and it wants to get somewhere, and it is certain that "somewhere" looks a particular way. But that is not love. No matter what we encounter—even extremely difficult things—it is saying "yes" to everything that arises in life: The death of my child, yes. My own anger, yes. Your imperfections, yes. Losing your love relationship, yes. We become aligned with that energy. Whether or not there is a Divine plan is of no consequence. What matters is how to be *love* toward what is imperfect and flawed. Everything in life is an opportunity to see this. It doesn't matter what happens to us—it is just another experience; what matters is it's an opportunity to see it through love. Everything is a reflection of what is happening *now*. Everything that arises is an opportunity to see, no matter what form has arisen. Spiritual energy is never gone; there can never be an absence of the formless. So if we fall back into the formless we will Know, and there will be solace there. There will be comfort. There will be peace.

No matter what unfolds, our thinking is reflected back to us. Your whole experience of shattering, for example, is about your personal, egoic thinking shattering. But there is no particular way things have to unfold. We stand at the crossroads before a thousand different paths. And they all take us to the same place, because everything takes us back to what is within. The particulars will look different, but it will be the same in the essential and important way. There is no one particular path.

Beware of those who judge whether one experience is better than another, or what the good path is supposed to look like. There is a subtle, judging mind that very easily happens with the ego. For example, what the enlightened Three Principles person needs to be or look like. That is unwise. Because love doesn't care. This larger place doesn't judge. No matter what path each of us walks, no matter what level of consciousness we're on, nothing is ever wrong. We are all on the path, even if lost. There is no lost. There is no arrival. We are already there, even when it truly seems like we are not.

The process is more important than the arrival. The process is becoming love, aligning oneself with love, no matter what form we are in. The more aligned we are with love—in the choices we make, with the thinking that seems true to us—this is what makes the thinking mind shift. But it's not true that we have to get to better thinking. Falling away from the ego is loving what is present as is, and that naturally evolves into different kind of thinking. People want to create "this is how it is," "this is what you need to believe." That is not helpful. Everyone has the capacity to fall into the quiet and know what they need for themselves. If we want to know why something happened and its meaning, we can ask of spiritual energy or Universal Mind, and just listen. The Source/Spirit wants more of that than for people to understand something external that they don't have to listen for themselves. It becomes an excuse not to look.

About three-quarters of the way through our conversation I (Jack) got a flash of insight. I saw that the quiet, which is the process, is also the end. *The process is the end.* The process *is* the outcome. The means and the end are inseparable. The process of reaching a quiet mind happens through a quiet mind. There is no *trying* to get to a quiet mind—the very act of trying busies the mind. There is no *how to do* a quiet mind; there is only a Knowing that when our mind quiets or clears it is the only place from which wisdom arises, the silence from which happiness and satisfaction arise, the silence from which true love is found.

The conversation continued: The silence is our pathway, via our own spiritual essence connected to the intelligent energy of All things, both form and formless. Once the insight comes, however, it is important not to rest in the insight. The insight itself is form. We are after the feeling of falling back into the quiet, resting in that place, looking in that direction. The quiet is the direction. The looking and the quiet are one.

Sometimes we look and can't find the quiet. But the quiet is always there! Sometimes when things look horrific, like Jesus on the cross, we can't remember the feeling—"Why hast Thou forsaken me?" We can't find the feeling. But when we look and can't find the quiet, it means the looking has been sabotaged by personal thinking, or ego and fear, so it is not really *looking*; it only seems like looking. Because the real looking must be in the quiet. This is why it is not wise to resist what is. We can rest in the feeling, relax into it, kind of like a Yoga pose when we relax into a stretch. It is unwise to try to use thinking to change thought. We want to relax out of thought, into being, just allow. This takes so much surrender to trust that somehow it's okay, that nothing is wrong. Nothing needs to be fixed. We don't have to try to shift or to change it. Like a storm, it passes. The quiet is within, but we get lost. Getting lost is following thought in dis-alignment with spiritual energy.

And on that note, I have the feeling this is all that needs to be said here. I still have much to learn. The process in never-ending. The learning continues. But I have come so far. Thank you from the bottom of my heart for joining me here…

THE END, AND A NEW, NEW BEGINNING

OTHER BOOKS BY JACK PRANSKY

Somebody Should Have Told Us!

Paradigm Shift: A History of the Three Principles

Modello: A Story of Hope for the Inner City and Beyond

Parenting from the Heart

Prevention from the Inside-Out

What is a Thought? (A Thought is a Lot), co-authored with Amy Kahofer - a children's picture book

What is Wisdom (and Where Do I Find It)?, co-authored with Amy Kahofer - a children's picture book

Healthy Thinking/Feeling/Doing from the Inside-Out, co-authored with Lori Carpenos - a prevention curriculum for middle school students

Prevention: The Critical Need [Note: Not a Three Principles book]

CPSIA information can be obtained
at www.ICGtesting.com
Printed in the USA
BVOW04s1319300517
485506BV00001BA/34/P